Shakespeare's Political Imagination

RELATED TITLES

Shakespeare: *Actors and Audiences*
Edited by Fiona Banks
978-1-3501-6453-6

Staging Britain's Past: *Pre-Roman Britain in Early Modern Drama*
Kim Gilchrist
978-1-3501-6334-8

Early Modern Actors and Shakespeare's Theatre:
Thinking with the Body
Evelyn Tribble
978-1-4725-7602-6

Shakespeare and the Politics of Nostalgia: *Negotiating*
the Memory of Elizabeth I on the Jacobean Stage
Yuichi Tsukada
978-1-3501-7507-5

Shakespeare's Political Imagination

The Historicism of Setting

Philip Goldfarb Styrt

THE ARDEN SHAKESPEARE
LONDON • NEW YORK • OXFORD • NEW DELHI • SYDNEY

THE ARDEN SHAKESPEARE
Bloomsbury Publishing Plc
50 Bedford Square, London, WC1B 3DP, UK
1385 Broadway, New York, NY 10018, USA
29 Earlsfort Terrace, Dublin 2, Ireland

BLOOMSBURY, THE ARDEN SHAKESPEARE and the Arden Shakespeare
logo are trademarks of Bloomsbury Publishing Plc

First published in Great Britain 2022
This paperback edition published in 2023

Copyright © Philip Goldfarb Styrt, 2022

Philip Goldfarb Styrt has asserted his right under the Copyright,
Designs and Patents Act, 1988, to be identified as the author of this work.

For legal purposes the Acknowledgements on p. vi constitute
an extension of this copyright page.

Cover design by Charlotte Daniels
Cover image: Europe as a Queen, Woodcut from Sebastian Munster's
Cosmographia, 1588 (© Granger / Bridgeman Images)

All rights reserved. No part of this publication may be reproduced or
transmitted in any form or by any means, electronic or mechanical,
including photocopying, recording, or any information storage or
retrieval system, without prior permission in writing from the publishers.

Bloomsbury Publishing Plc does not have any control over, or responsibility
for, any third-party websites referred to or in this book. All internet addresses
given in this book were correct at the time of going to press. The author and
publisher regret any inconvenience caused if addresses have changed or sites
have ceased to exist, but can accept no responsibility for any such changes.

A catalogue record for this book is available from the British Library.

Library of Congress Cataloging-in-Publication Data
Names: Goldfarb Styrt, Philip, author.
Title: Shakespeare's political imagination: the historicism of
setting / Philip Goldfarb Styrt.
Description: London; New York: The Arden Shakespeare, 2022. |
Includes bibliographical references and index.
Identifiers: LCCN 2021030365 (print) | LCCN 2021030366 (ebook) |
ISBN 9781350173972 (hardback) | ISBN 9781350174009 (ebook) |
ISBN 9781350173996 (epub)
Subjects: LCSH: Shakespeare, William, 1564-1616–Political and social views. |
Shakespeare, William, 1564-1616–Settings. | Historicism in literature. |
Social structure in literature.
Classification: LCC PR3017.G65 2022 (print) |
LCC PR3017 (ebook) | DDC 822.3/3–dc23
LC record available at https://lccn.loc.gov/2021030365
LC ebook record available at https://lccn.loc.gov/2021030366

ISBN: HB: 978-1-3501-7397-2
PB: 978-1-3502-7787-8
ePDF: 978-1-3501-7400-9
eBook: 978-1-3501-7399-6

Typeset by Integra Software Services Pvt. Ltd.

To find out more about our authors and books visit www.bloomsbury.com
and sign up for our newsletters.

CONTENTS

Acknowledgements vi

1 Introduction 1

Part One   The British past: Medieval England and Scotland

2 *King John*, the Magna Carta and the medieval English monarchy 17
3 *Macbeth*, thanes and medieval Scottish feudalism 49

Part Two   The European past: Ancient Rome

4 *Julius Caesar*, factions and the end of the Roman republic 77
5 *Coriolanus* and the tribunes in the early Roman republic 101

Part Three   Contemporary Europe: The Venetian republic

6 *The Merchant of Venice* and the weak dukes of Venice 127
7 *Othello*, soft power and the search for truth 147
8 Conclusion: *Measure for Measure*, topicality and performance 161

Notes 178
Works cited 206
Index 222

ACKNOWLEDGEMENTS

This book would not have been possible without the support of a great many people, too many to mention them all here. My wife, Katie Styrt, has been immensely supportive throughout, as have my parents, Richard and Marjorie Goldfarb. Richard Strier and Joshua Scodel were invaluable for their help in conceiving and nurturing this project from the very beginning through various stages of my work at the University of Chicago, as were the members of the University of Chicago Renaissance Workshop, notably Lisa Scott, Greg Baum, Tim Harrison and the late David Bevington. My thanks as well to Caryn O'Connell both for her insights at the workshop and for the index. I am also grateful to Elizabeth E. Tavares for some very helpful thoughts later in the process. Portions of the project research were funded at the University of Chicago by the Nicholson Center for British Studies, the Tillotson travel award from the Department of English and the Hanna Holborn Gray Fellowship. Chapter 5 was conceived of while working as dramaturg for a production of *Coriolanus* directed by Evan Garrett. A version of Chapter 4 first appeared in *Shakespeare Quarterly* Volume 66, Issue 3, Fall 2015, pages 286–307.

1

Introduction

My interest in Shakespeare's settings began with an observation and a pair of questions. The observation is this: none of Shakespeare's plays are set in his own time and place. Many are not set in either. The vast majority of the characters are long-dead, live in other countries, or both, and the action is likewise distant from Shakespearean England in both space and time. Of course Shakespeare's plays had local meaning to his contemporaries, but the fact remains that the plays are explicit that they do not take place in the England of Shakespeare and his audience. The questions are these: what did these distant settings mean, and why might they matter?

In this book, I answer these questions by arguing that the settings are important because of how they showcase Shakespeare's political imagination, which was sparked by ideas circulating in the period about how the political cultures of the settings differed from that of his own England. I suggest that Shakespeare presented his audience with settings that were recognizably identifiable as belonging to the time and place in which the plays claim to be set and that the plays draw heavily on these political differences. As a result, I argue that exploring the ideas circulating in the period about the political structure at play within each setting gives us insight into both Shakespeare's artistry and the meanings of the plays themselves.

Reading the plays in this way allows us to address issues that have long confounded critics, such as why the Duke does not stop Shylock in the trial scene of *Merchant of Venice* or why Magna Carta is absent from *King John*. It also provides a different perspective on modern critical debates, like the question of whether Shakespeare could have set *Measure for Measure* in Vienna, or whether that setting must be a later emendation by Thomas Middleton. It also gives us new insight into how Shakespeare modified his narrative sources to respond to contemporary thoughts about the political structures present in his settings.

This approach requires us to engage with what I call the historicism of setting: the idea that Shakespeare and his audience were actively aware that other times and places differed from their own, and that those differences mattered to interpreting action set in that location. As a result, the details of the setting are highly significant, and we should not rush too quickly to general philosophical or theoretical considerations about the politics of the setting or to topical or exemplary readings of the plays. At the same time, we must admit the possibility of competing historicism*s*: differing accounts of the same other cultures. Thus, at times Shakespeare drew on sources that disagreed, or on multiple sources with overlapping but distinct visions of the politics within a given setting. However, I do wish to suggest that the plays themselves are more closely aligned with certain ideas about their settings, and that those particular ideas circulated widely in the period. An awareness of these ideas illuminates elements already present in each text, allowing us to better understand the plays on their own terms. As such, I argue that the meanings we can access through the historicism of setting are vitally relevant both for understanding the text and for contemporary interpretation in whatever context: personal reading, scholarly interpretation, performance and so on.

Because my primary purpose is to demonstrate the value of this kind of reading for understanding Shakespeare, I have organized this book into three main sections, each focusing on a particular type of setting. In order to explain this, it might help to clarify what I mean by setting. I mean neither the physical geography of the plays (what rivers, mountains, churches or houses they depict) nor a particular theatrical *set* but the societies and cultures that the plays purport to represent. Therefore, my focus is on how the political and social orders of the plays function rather than on the physical space in which they take place. When I write, for example, of Shakespeare's plays set in Venice, I am not asking you to think of about a specific arrangement of canals and bridges on the edge of the Adriatic but of a particular city-state at a particular time with a particular society and political system in place. As mentioned above, this is what I mean by Shakespeare's political imagination: his ability to conjure up a political society different from his own. We can look at this element in each of Shakespeare's plays, since each play is set someplace other than Shakespeare's England.

In this regard, we can think of the settings of Shakespeare's plays as being distributed along two axes: time and place, and particularly (Shakespearean) contemporary/past and British/(continental) European.[1] By 'British' here I mean set in the nations united in 1603 under James I, who preferred the style 'King of Great Britain'. While I do not mean to suggest that Shakespeare personally supported James's unification project, it is, I think, relevant that Shakespeare's works set in the non-English British nations all appear to have been written after James's ascension to the English crown and touch on the relationship between England and the other nations.[2] These axes then define four categories: contemporary British, past British, past European and contemporary European. I have already suggested that none of Shakespeare's plays fall into the first category. Therefore, the three sections of this book each treat two exemplary plays from the other three categories: *King John* and *Macbeth*, set in medieval England and Scotland, respectively, for the British past; *Julius Caesar* and *Coriolanus*, set in different eras of ancient Rome, for the European past; and the two Venetian plays, *Merchant of Venice* and *Othello*, for Shakespeare's contemporary Europe. I also treat a third contemporary European play, *Measure for Measure*, in the conclusion, which directly addresses the questions of how the historicism of setting can still account for issues of topicality and performance both in Shakespeare's time and our own.

I have chosen this particular group of plays not just as exemplars of the various kinds of settings Shakespeare used but also to cover a wide range of political arrangements and approaches to the use of historical material. We will encounter two different kinds of republics in *Coriolanus* and the Venetian plays, two different monarchies in *Macbeth* and *King John*, an archdukedom within an empire in *Measure for Measure*, and a Roman state somewhere in between monarchy and republicanism in *Julius Caesar*. In addition, the plays in each section illuminate a particular aspect of Shakespeare's dramatic method for constructing setting out of the available sources. The two medieval plays demonstrate how Shakespeare worked with settings where there were major competing accounts in his own time about how politics and society functioned. Thus, *King John* and *Macbeth* show Shakespeare navigating between those accounts, choosing to side with one particular strain of historicist thought in the period over another. This also has the benefit of distinguishing the historicism of setting from the search for Shakespeare's narrative sources, as for these plays his primary narrative source, Holinshed's *Chronicles*, depicts the other competing version of the political structure. On the other hand, the two Roman plays show how Shakespeare worked within a more coherent sense of a particular political structure, since contemporary sources show a broadly consistent set of assumptions about the cultural and political expectations of the political cultures depicted in each play. The Romes of *Julius Caesar* and *Coriolanus* are distinct, but each responds to a single dominant narrative about its Rome circulating in the period. Finally, the two Venetian plays demonstrate Shakespeare's use of common materials to produce differing outcomes within a setting depending on the necessities of the plot. This shows that setting was not a straitjacket for Shakespeare but a tool: that he was capable of emphasizing different elements of the same setting for differing effects. This set of plays, then, allows us to see Shakespeare engaging with ideas about the politics of his settings that circulated in the period in three different ways, depending on the nature of the ideas and the needs of the theatre.

In exploring Shakespeare's political imagination, I argue that we must understand the plays' own politics: not the politics *derived from* the plays, the lessons they teach about engagement with public life and power relations in the world outside the theatre, but the politics *within* the plays, how the characters engage with the political realities of their own worlds. In particular, I suggest that Shakespeare's political imagination works through the political structure of these settings: how individual characters within the plays might reasonably expect politics in their own world to operate. I define politics broadly here because the plays dramatize public action and speech in such a way that even where the scene is locally private – as between the Macbeths, or among the conspirators in *Julius Caesar* – or even solitary – as with Coriolanus debating with himself over how to treat the plebeians – they are always invested in a larger public, political world. While the political structures of the plays are frequently quite specific, the implications of those political structures within the plays' respective worlds are broad. Shakespeare clearly imagines how individuals respond to their own historical circumstances, and he portrays those historical circumstances in political terms. While there has been much work over the years on politics in Shakespeare, critics far too often flatten out issues of idiosyncratic political structure by moving to transhistorical or theoretical models of politics on the one hand and topical application of the plays' politics to Shakespearean England on the other. Thus when the historian Peter Lake talks about *How Shakespeare Put Politics on the Stage* in his book of the same name, and brings up the 'political imagination ... of the period', he is referring to the depiction of 'current [i.e. early modern English] circumstances and concerns', rather than medieval ones, even as he works with the medieval history plays.[3] This connects to a broader habit of the new historicist and cultural materialist readings over the past forty years to read for how each play 'incorporate[s] ... aspects of its historical moment', expressed in terms of those same contemporary politics (to quote an essay by Jonathan Dollimore on *Measure for Measure* to which I will return in the conclusion).[4] On the other side, critics frequently move, as John E. Alvis observes, directly from a character's 'participation in the corporate life of a city or realm' to a general sense of how this helps in 'understanding ... human nature' and 'a view of what essentially defines human beings'.[5] At one extreme, this arrives at the argument that Shakespeare's 'interest is in the psychological rather than the institutional basis of politics', and that he therefore pays little attention to political structure at all.[6] Thus, his approach to the particular historical moments depicted in the plays becomes 'an occasion to work through ethical and political thought-experiments' and evaluate competing political theories rather than a close engagement with the politics in each setting on its own terms.[7] This frequent focus on 'abstract principles and problems' even in the presence of 'the precise rendering of concrete detail' (in the words of Robert Miola),[8] like the emphasis on topical early modern application, places our attention too often on the broader political *lessons* of the plays, rather than the local political *worlds* they represent, even in works (like Miola's) whose focus is on a particular setting (in his case, Shakespearean Rome).

The historicism of setting is intended as a counterbalance to an overreliance on these topical and transhistorical approaches, emphasizing that the local political structures of the plays are carefully drawn and highly significant. By revitalizing our awareness of these political structures, my readings correct some longstanding misapprehensions about the plays. For example, recognizing the importance of the immediate change in the political structure created by the establishment of the tribunes in *Coriolanus* allows us to push back against interpretations that read the centuries-later fall of the Roman republic into its very beginnings, while careful attention to the Duke's position in Venice allows us to think beyond the commercial readings of the courtroom scene that have dominated recent interpretations of *Merchant*, including those of thoughtful historicist critics like Graham Holderness and Julia Lupton.

Thus, the historicism of setting emphasizes Shakespeare's active historical and political imagination and the way he presented political cultures to his audience that were rooted in contemporary ideas about the political structures at play in the settings. As such, I am deeply concerned with the various understandings available in early modern English culture about each setting, and how each play draws on those understandings. In this sense, what I am examining is similar to what András Kiséry has recently identified in the political references in *Hamlet*: a 'textual universe' beyond what are traditionally considered sources, to which the various political references connect in order to 'situate' and 'illuminate' the behaviour of the characters.[9] While I am less interested than Kiséry is in the profession of politics in Shakespearean England itself, I share his conviction that the kind of detailed, contextual political thinking going on in the period is highly relevant to the plays. This thinking is likewise similar to the kind of 'circumstantial', legalistic thought that Lorna Hutson has recently identified in Shakespeare (which I will engage with in more detail in the chapter on *Macbeth*), though with more attention to broader implications of setting rather than specific contingencies of plot.[10]

Shakespeare's plays are part of a continuum of early modern English understanding about politics as practiced in other times and places, and participate in a larger set of conversations about their settings going on in the period. My purpose throughout is to demonstrate the kind of assumptions and conceptions of these times, places and political structures that might have been available to Shakespeare and his contemporaries in writing and experiencing the plays. These elements are present in Shakespeare's plays already, but modern readers may not attend to them without the outside reference provided by the other texts. Thus, I am in sympathy with Dennis Austin Britton and Melissa Walter's recent collection on *Rethinking Shakespeare Source Study* and their insight that 'sources' can include a wide range of texts that bear on how the universe of a given play might be conceived.[11]

While the historicism of setting focuses on the plays' relation to this broader textual universe, rather than on a study of Shakespearean audiences and their reactions, it is worth noting the ways in which Shakespeare's potential audience was particularly primed to respond to these kinds of political elements within the settings before we turn to the individual plays themselves. In referring here to a potential audience, I draw on the burgeoning field of early modern repertory studies, which deals with how early modern playing companies and playwrights conceived of, performed for and wrote for the market their audiences comprised. Elizabeth E. Tavares has argued that, in order to cultivate that market, the playing companies curated their repertories so that playgoers could have some idea of what they might encounter on a given day, and in turn 'playgoers referenced a horizon of expectations' created by their own interests and their previous playgoing experience.[12] I suggest that these expectations would have included expectations about the setting itself, including the political and historical elements I examine in this book. The plays operate within this 'historical matrix' made out of contemporary historicisms, and their meaning emerges through those imaginatively shared historical and cultural understandings.[13] As Mark Hutchings has suggested in his study of Turks in early modern English drama, references to distant times and places 'called up a certain knowledge underwritten by a shared cultural memory' so that the audience could make use of that knowledge in understanding the play.[14] Of course, in repertory studies the focus is typically on how companies used this cultural memory to produce and market the plays, while my emphasis is on interpretation of the texts, but we share this common interest in how the plays engage with the ideas circulating more generally in the period among their potential audience.

Early modern playwrights and their audiences paid close attention to the kinds of politically and historically related materials that I examine here. As Cyndia Susan Clegg has suggested, Shakespeare and his audiences were 'immersed in a textual culture' even when they themselves were not necessarily great readers, in terms of either quantity or proficiency, and playwrights drew on that culture to craft their work.¹⁵ Specifically, Lucy Munro has recently traced the approach of the minor playwright Robert Daborne as reflected in his letters to the impresario Philip Henslowe, a process that begins with Daborne asking Henslowe to provide him with books that then lead into the creation of the play.¹⁶ Daborne was of course not Shakespeare. But both Munro and Sarah Wall-Randell have traced the possibility that this kind of consultation with printed texts about the settings of plays was typical in the period, including the strong likelihood that the playing companies had libraries of books for playwrights to use – though of course such libraries are now lost to us.¹⁷ This suggests that there were active connections between the world of print and the world of the theatre. If so, the ideas found in printed texts in the period would be reflected in the plays derived from them, as I suggest they are in Shakespeare.

Similarly, recent research on both theatrical and reading audiences in Shakespeare's time suggests that readers and audiences in the period were particularly attuned to interpreting historical and foreign material with political and social lessons in mind, especially in ways related to political structure.¹⁸ Several critics have proposed that this kind of detailed engagement would have been even more typical of Shakespeare's imagined *reading* audiences, whose reading and re-reading of the play would reveal complexities of the text beyond those most easily followed live in performance.¹⁹ But whether in performance or reading, we have evidence from contemporaries that at least some of the audience was highly aware of the political and geographical differences at work in the plays: contemporary critics of Shakespeare frequently focused on his treatment of other times and other places, while readers' marginalia seems to have often been preoccupied with the political wisdom of major characters.²⁰ At the same time, as Annabel Patterson has observed, the political thought expressed in the theatre at the time was not abstract, ahistorical or transhistorical work, but carefully constructed in ways connected to both time and place.²¹ This suggests that Shakespeare was writing for a potential audience that was attentive to the possibilities inherent in the historicism of setting: that cared about political, historical and geographical difference and came to the theatre or the playbook with those concerns in mind. In making use of historicized political structures, then, Shakespeare was 'responsive and responsible to the desires of [his] playgoing publics', who cared about such things.²²

This attention to political, historical and geographical difference was continually re-emphasized within the early modern theatre. Those plays in the period that are set in other times and places, not just Shakespeare's, frequently insist on that time and place even when the characters act more like early modern Englishmen and -women, suggesting that the distant settings were something they expected the audience to be aware of. The theatre produced this expectation not just through the text but through its physical conditions as well. Matthew Steggle has recently explored the use of title- and scene-boards for early modern drama, suggesting that the frequent use of these to passively indicate both the play's title and the location of the action would have made 'the geographical location literally legible'.[23] As Sir Philip Sidney famously complained, plays would have '*Asia* of the one side, and *Affricke* of the other' of the stage; and when they did not do so by scene-boards, they would do so by having the actor 'begin with telling where he is'.[24] Sidney objected to this, but his very objection is evidence that the question of where the action was taking place was considered important enough to keep the audience aware of it. And of course for historical plays like those analysed in the first two sections of this book, any reminder of the historicity of the title characters would also have reminded the audience of the time period as well.
  While we do not typically use scene- and title-boards in modern theatre, modern audiences for Shakespeare plays are also made aware of setting through cultural knowledge of the plays, printed programs, costumes, sets and other techniques. While Shakespeare's plays are often *re*-set by modern companies, depending on a given production's approach, this awareness of place and time is nevertheless a major element in the experience of modern Shakespeare as well. I will treat the question of how contemporary theatrical practice might intersect with the interpretations suggested by the historicism of setting at more length in connection with the case study of *Measure for Measure*. In general, however, I suggest that these interpretations deserve attention when approaching modern production but are by no means dispositive. Instead, they are simply one more piece of information about how the play constructs meaning that performers and production staff might use to convey their own particular interpretation of the play.
  Just as modern production re-settings help audiences appreciate the play onstage, so too the early modern signifiers of setting

were part of how Renaissance theatres engaged and affected their audiences. As David McInnis, among others, has proposed, the active mental participation of the audience was a key element in conjuring up the seeming reality of the settings.[25] This means that the playwrights engaging with their potential paying audience were working to produce a collective sense of where and when the action was taking place, so that their audience could play its part. I suggest this is the reason for the use of both verbal and physical markers of place. By reminding contemporary audiences of the play's setting, these kinds of signifiers would have activated the meanings that I suggest we can now unlock through the historicism of setting.

The plays were of course subject to other influences than just the market, or the expectations of a potential audience. Censorship was real in early modern England, and both playwrights and companies occasionally fell afoul of the law for what they wrote and performed, especially those who came too close to controversial contemporary issues.[26] But while it is well-established that some early modern plays were set in other places and times to avoid censorship, it is still valuable to examine what the plays might gain by where they were set instead. After all, there is still a difference between setting a play in Venice and Vienna, even if London were not an option, so it is worthwhile to discover what those settings contributed. In addition, Shakespeare himself was unusual in how consistently he avoided contemporary English settings. Most of his major contemporaries set at least some of their works in their own England.[27] Shakespeare did not. Thus, while it is true that censorship may have played a role in Shakespeare's avoidance of his contemporary England as a setting, it cannot be the whole story. Shakespeare's plays undoubtedly had local, topical application to their own time and place, wherever they were set. I will address those applications head on where they seem most relevant, especially in the courtroom scene of *Merchant of Venice* and in the matter of the succession in *King John*, and the conclusion about *Measure for Measure* engages with this issue explicitly in more detail. But I argue that whatever topical application the plays would have had would, in turn, have been affected by the choice of setting itself, and thus my focus is on how those settings contribute to the meaning of the play, rather than on how they might be used to evade censorship.

In the chapters that follow, I will demonstrate that the historicism of setting can produce readings of Shakespeare that are coherent, interesting and original. In the process, I will also show that the readings produced by the historicism of setting are strongly present in the plays. That is, I argue that our understanding of the plays would be incomplete without considering the possibilities inherent in the setting.

In the first chapter I examine *King John*, arguing that Shakespeare's version of the story stakes out a position within an ongoing debate in early modern England about the historical significance of Magna Carta, siding with legal scholars who attributed Magna Carta to John's son Henry III over chroniclers like Holinshed who traced it back to John's own reign. In doing so, I suggest, Shakespeare's play depicts John as a king whose struggles against the traditional constraints on his power were used to justify a new statutory regime under his son, thus inaugurating the historical process that would lead to the government of Shakespeare's own time. Placing John before Magna Carta, rather than having him issue it, allows the play to reject John's efforts to reign independently of his nobility while at the same time sympathizing with his political plight and depicting his death as a moment of triumph rather than defeat. This interpretation in turn re-centres the play on the character of John himself, rather than the Bastard, who has tended to dominate more recent analysis of the play.

The second chapter treats another medieval British monarchy, the early feudal world of *Macbeth*. Focusing on the play's often-neglected last speech in which Malcolm creates earls in Scotland, it shows how Shakespeare drew on the burgeoning early modern historiography of feudalism to create a Scotland transitioning between two types of feudal law. The change from thanes to earls serves as a solution to problems within the play ranging from internal dissension to an over reliance on the king, and particularly on his choice of whom to trust. This transition within feudalism provides hope that Malcolm's reign will end the cycle of violence and dispel the horrors that have visited Scotland during the play while at the same time dispelling the chronicle tradition's concerns about the new titles' impact on Scottish masculinity, giving a more optimistic outlook on the end of the play than most recent scholarship has produced.

From medieval Britain, I then turn to ancient Rome. The divided politics of *Julius Caesar*, I argue, reflect a common understanding among the early modern English that this period was characterized by continual factions, from Marius and Sulla to Caesar and his assassins. I argue that the conspiracy to assassinate Caesar relies upon the factional pre-history of the play, as does the formation of the triumvirate after Caesar's death. The language of friendship and love that pervades the play only emphasizes these factional lines. Characters who call each other 'friends' are political allies, while those who are 'lovers' are tied by bonds of affection. Politics in the play is therefore factional, not individual. Failing to understand this factional structure is a fatal mistake for both Caesar and Brutus; by contrast, Antony succeeds because he understands this factional world and capitalizes on it.

The fourth chapter goes back in time, though forward in Shakespeare's career, to the early Roman republic in *Coriolanus*. The first scene of the play features a major structural change in the Roman state: the establishment of the office of the tribunes as a response to a plebeian riot. The chapter examines the early modern English understanding of this transition, showing that Coriolanus's troubles arise not only from a personal clash with the new tribunes but also from an unwillingness to adapt to the new structure the tribunes represent. When the tribunes drive him out of Rome, he finds himself equally unable to adapt to the world outside. By focusing on the changing political structure, this reading reveals Coriolanus as a man tragically displaced in time from the only world in which he can properly belong: the Rome before the introduction of the tribunes. Differentiating the people's interest from the tribunes', as many critics have failed to do, and focusing on their relationship with Coriolanus reveal the play not as a tragedy of Rome looking forward several centuries to a post-Republican fall, as some have argued, but as a deeply personal tragedy focused on Caius Martius Coriolanus's own individual struggle.

If the Roman republic in *Coriolanus* is in a state of flux, the Venetian one of *The Merchant of Venice* and *Othello* is much more stable. In the chapters that consider these plays, I show that Shakespeare draws on a view current in early modern England that emphasized the highly formal organization of the Venetian state, with particular focus on the role of its duke. In this view, the duke of Venice had a peculiarly restricted form of power, one that gave him space for persuasion and consensus-building but left him almost no individual authority. I argue that Shakespeare uses this model of limited ducal authority to depict Venetian states in which the duke is a mediator rather than a ruler. In each play, Shakespeare added a Duke who was not present in his sources, and a critical sequence in each play centres on the other characters' reactions to the duke's role; however, he used these common elements to very different ends. In *Merchant*, Shylock's legal arguments during the trial scene and Portia's responses to him both reflect knowledge of the duke's limited power, and the details of the Venetian political structure shape the resolution of the trial over and above the commercial considerations that have been the focus of most recent criticism. By contrast, in *Othello* the duke's mediation between Othello and Brabantio models the rational enquiry that Othello tragically fails to implement in Cyprus, thus leading him towards his murder of Desdemona despite frequent opportunities to discover the truth and turn aside.

Finally, the conclusion turns to consider the relationship between the historicism of setting and two other major concerns for Shakespearean audiences: topicality and performance. By examining *Measure for Measure* and its use of Vienna against contemporary critical and theatrical practices of re-setting, I argue these two issues, which might at first seem distinct from the historicism of setting, are in fact closely related to it, and that a careful examination of the historicism of setting has major implications for them as well. At the same time, I show that the Vienna of the play connects clearly to the rising power of the Dukes of Austria in the early sixteenth century, thus countering the recent argument by Gary Taylor and others that the Viennese setting held no significance in Shakespeare's time and must be a later emendation.

My argument throughout the book is that Shakespeare shows real consideration for the particular and idiosyncratic political structures of his settings, and that the plays draw heavily on the political elements of the settings for their meaning. At the same time, I do not suggest that there is a simple one-to-one correspondence between the textual universe and the plays: Shakespeare's own political imagination is always at work. The early modern perspectives I examine were available to Shakespeare and, I argue, are significant to the plays. But there are times when Shakespeare honours them more in the breach than the observance: where what is notable is the deviation from a potential audience's expectation, rather than the conformity, or where Shakespeare makes a choice between two competing sets of expectations (as in the medieval

British plays). I believe that throughout the plays Shakespeare demonstrates an active political imagination, using the setting of each play not as backdrop against which fundamentally English or broadly universal scenes could unfold but as a setting in the fullest sense of the word: a place different from, but still comprehensible to, his own everyday world, where the action of the play could be transformed by contact with a different geographical, historical and political situation.

That transformation is in fact the point. I believe that Shakespeare was fascinated by how individual behaviour differs in different circumstances. His plays take seriously the worlds they claim to present, and experiment with precisely how action is related to its context. I argue that the plots and characters of the plays themselves consistently reinforce the meanings activated by the historicism of setting, and understanding those meanings helps us interpret the plays. Success and failure within the plays depend on the characters' relations to their political worlds, and the particular details of the setting make those relations possible. Shakespeare's political imagination manifests itself in details and particulars, in a profound interest in the ways in which specific circumstances constrain and give meaning to specific actions. The universality of his plays comes not from denying the importance of the local, particular and contextual but from embracing it. In these plays, every action is embedded in its own particular set of political and cultural circumstances, and we must therefore engage directly with the setting in order to more fully understand the meaning and explain the outcome of the action.

PART ONE

The British past: Medieval England and Scotland

2

King John, the Magna Carta and the medieval English monarchy

Let us begin with a play set in the country most familiar to Shakespeare's audience: their own. But while *King John* takes place in England, the almost four hundred years between John and Elizabeth I meant that the political structure of the England of the play differed significantly from that of Shakespeare's own time. This difference would have been highly visible to the early modern English, and it deserves consideration in our own interpretation and staging of the play.

In particular, I suggest that Shakespeare's version of the King John story stakes out a position within an ongoing debate in early modern England about the historical significance of Magna Carta, siding with legal scholars who attributed Magna Carta to John's son Henry III over chroniclers, like Holinshed, who traced it back to John's own reign. Here we can see Shakespeare's political imagination at work as the play prioritizes one strand of contemporary historical analysis over another.

Reading the play this way solves the longstanding puzzle of why Magna Carta does not appear in the play. But it also, I argue, allows us to see King John himself as a more central figure in the play than most critics assume he is. Shakespeare's play depicts John as a king whose struggles against the constraints on his power were used to justify a new statutory regime under his son, thus inaugurating the historical process that would lead to the government of

Shakespeare's own time. This depiction results from Shakespeare's choice to combine the legal tradition with a religious historiography that emphasized John's rightful defiance of the papacy. Placing John at the end of the old system rather than the beginning of the new and representing him as correct about his religious authority allow the play to reject John's efforts to reign independently of his nobility while at the same time sympathizing with his political plight and depicting his death as a moment of triumph rather than defeat. This interpretation in turn re-focuses the play on the character of John himself, rather than the Bastard, who has been at the heart of much criticism of the play.

Let us begin by examining what the sixteenth-century English knew about John's reign, and how *King John* fits into that narrative. Opinions in the period were divided between two primary accounts of John's era. One, primarily derived from chronicle histories, held that John and his predecessors had repressed the ancient common law and that the Magna Carta restored it. The other, a product of a lengthy legal tradition, considered the Magna Carta instead as the first of the formal statutes that had modified the common law, and saw John's reign as the last time when England was governed by the unmodified common law.

I believe that the second of these potential narratives is most relevant to *King John*. This represents a strain of legal-historical thought rooted in the fifteenth-century work of Sir John Fortescue, whose treatises on law and government in England were read consistently down through the eighteenth century. Fortescue believed that the English constitution and common law were of great antiquity, providing the basic form of the English state. He claimed that this form was unique among the nations: neither 'politic' in the manner of a republic like Venice, nor fully 'regal' in the manner of an absolute monarchy like France, but 'politique and regall' together.[1] While 'politic' realms were concerned with the consent of the people (or the aristocracy at least) to the laws, and 'regal' realms looked only to the will of the king, the distinctive feature of the 'regal and politic realm' of England was counsel.[2] As Alan Cromartie has observed, in Fortescue we find the foundational indication in English constitutional thought that kings 'had an *obligation* to take counsel'.[3] This requirement was how the political structure could be simultaneously absolutely regal and constitutionally politic: the king made the decisions, but the people (or at least the aristocracy) had the right to help guide those decisions along. I suggest that this element of obligatory counsel is critical to properly understanding *King John*.

This belief in the obligation of the monarch to take counsel became widespread among practitioners of the common law as the sixteenth century progressed. Two points eventually became central to their legal theory: to borrow Cromartie's terms, that 'first, the king is subject to the laws; second, it is necessary for the king to have advisors'.[4] These basic requirements were believed to be fundamental to the common law. Statutory regulation of how law, king and counsel interacted came later.[5] The first of these statutes was the Magna Carta. The lawbooks of the sixteenth century all identify it as such; the book of the oldest statutes was sometimes referred to simply as the 'Boke of Magna Carta'.[6] This origination of statute with Magna Carta is particularly clear in the work of William Lambarde, one of the first and most influential English antiquarians, but it is also reflected more widely in the legal scholarship of the time.[7] Magna Carta was considered the first statutory addition to the common law, and served as the point from which all later accounts of statutes began.[8]

However, the need for the king to take counsel was believed to be an ancient part of the common law, linked to the pre-Roman past. We can see this in the notes of an early seventeenth-century meeting of the Society of Antiquaries, where two scholars made sense of the role of the nobility in medieval England by reference to Tacitus's description of earlier German chiefs: '*nec regibus infinita potestas de minoribus rebus principes consultant de maioribus omnes*' (and the power of kings is not infinite; about the small things the principal men consult, about the larger, everyone does).[9] Tacitus's '*principes*' were individual chieftains, but a marginal gloss on one copy of this text makes it clear that these '*principes*' were understood here to be nobles, with the quotation as a whole glossed as supporting evidence that the 'Saxons had a form of Parliamentary assemblies'.[10] The strangely hybrid nature of the quote, which is pulled from two different sections of Tacitus's *Germania*, further suggests that this parliament, the '*principes consultant*', is intended to be understood as the check on the king that results in the '*nec regibus infinita potestas*', the non-infinite power of the ruler. In both instances where it appears in these texts, the quote is followed immediately by one from Bede about King Edwin of Northumberland consulting with his friends and nobles before converting to Christianity, further suggesting an interest in the consultative nature of early English kingship.[11] Counsel was believed to have always been safeguarded under the common law, with statutory regulation of the monarch a later and more permanent innovation to protect the people, beginning with Magna Carta.

The difference between this perspective and that of the chronicles, including Holinshed, is significant. The chronicles saw Magna Carta as restoring the common law, while the legal tradition saw it as correcting that law. This difference was bound up in another crucial disagreement between the lawyers and the chroniclers: the dating of Magna Carta. The Magna Carta treated by Elizabethan authors, and collected in Tudor lawbooks, was not the Magna Carta we know today. Some chroniclers, notably including Holinshed, correctly traced the origins of Magna Carta to John's negotiations with his nobles at Runnymede in 1215, but the majority of legal commentators referred to it only as the statute of 9 Henry III (1225), believing it had come into existence or at least significance under John's son.[12] In legal circles specifically, there was general agreement that 'Henry the third granted the great charter'.[13] This legacy was surprisingly longlasting. Henry III's charter remained the most-cited version of the charter throughout the seventeenth century.[14] This implies that John's role in the promulgation of the charter was seen as less important in legal circles even after the chronicle view of its creation became widespread, well after Shakespeare's play was written.

These different dates for Magna Carta had obvious implications for the understanding of John's reign. For the chroniclers the charter issued in 1215 at Runnymede confirmed the common law because it was intended to curb John's violations of already existing law, and did not need to amend that law to do so. Among the lawyers, by contrast, John was not understood as the man who granted Magna Carta, but rather as the last king to reign entirely before the great charter became law. His reign was the last during which the common law stood unamended, and his governance was moderated by counsel but not by statutory restriction.

We can see the tension between these two readings of John's reign in the history of the work of Robert Snagg, an Elizabethan lawyer and member of parliament whose 1570 'reading' (exposition of law) at the Middle Temple was later published in 1654.[15] Snagg was an Elizabethan lawyer speaking to other Elizabethan lawyers, so his exposition of the law, which focuses on Magna Carta, is concerned only with the details of the law itself: its legal logic and its value as a statute.

What sets Snagg apart for our purposes is the prefatory matter he (and his mid-seventeenth-century publisher) later added to the legal analysis, material which attempts to situate this commonplace reading of Magna Carta not within the tradition of the legal institution at which he spoke but in relation to the chronicles. In a prefatory epistle that the published text dates to 1587–8, seventeen years after he actually delivered the reading, Snagg posits that the time between the Norman conquest and Magna Carta was a time of 'will-government in the Kings', rule by royal prerogative, and claims that Magna Carta 'allow[ed] Englishmen their English laws' and restored the common law.[16] Snagg writes that he believes this because of what he 'found in stories' (which, from the level of historical detail he brings to bear out of them, are most likely formal histories rather than folk tales) as a supplement to his knowledge of the common and statute law.[17] Because of this, Snagg's prefatory analysis reflects the chronicle perspective on John's reign, despite his legal background, since his historical knowledge was derived from the chronicles rather than from legal texts. Yet not a hint of this perspective appears in the reading proper, as delivered in 1570, which treats Magna Carta as purely statute law.[18] Whatever thoughts Snagg had about the significance of Magna Carta as a document concerned with restoring liberty, rather than an amending statute, were not a common part of the legal discourse of his time, but speculations voiced only almost two decades later in a preface that in turn remained unpublished for almost seventy years.[19]

In regards to *King John*, Andrew Zurcher has interpreted Snagg's preface, rather than the reading itself, as a representative statement of legal theory under Elizabeth, deriving from it the assumption that the Elizabethan English saw the time before Henry III as 'the only period in which Englishmen were, if only for a time, not governed by their ancient customs', being ruled by monarchical whim, and thus not by the common law.[20] He therefore expounds a reading of *King John* that emphasizes tyranny and the excesses of personal monarchy. I suggest instead that the very reticence that Snagg showed about making such claims in front of his legal colleagues at the time demonstrates that he was aware that his chronicle-based understanding conflicted with the legal tradition surrounding Magna Carta and John's reign. The 1654 publication date is suggestive, since it means that Snagg's later prefatory recontextualization of his 1570 reading remained unpublished until under Cromwell, long after Edmund Coke and others had made the chronicle interpretation of Magna Carta mainstream among legal circles as well as historical ones. Snagg's reading and its curious prefatory history can still help inform us about Elizabethan legal doctrine around Magna Carta. But what we learn is that despite his later doubts he treated Magna Carta exactly as his legal audience would have expected: as the first statute enacted under Henry III, leaving John's reign as a time ruled by unamended common law.

Although John's reign was believed to have been before the beginnings of statute law, the common law in his period was still understood to be fundamentally the same as that of the Elizabethans' own 'monarchical republic' (in Patrick Collinson's famous phrase).[21] This was a system organized around the monarch, but at the same time highly reliant upon the advice and activity of the counsellors and advisers surrounding the ruler. It relied on 'reciprocal obligations to seek counsel and to give it'.[22] These obligations did not apply equally across the political nation, a fact made plain by Sir Thomas Smith's assertion that there was a 'sort of men which doe not rule'.[23] It was only a 'right and necessity for the powerful of the realm to give counsel', a right which was 'believed to descend on them by right of their birth and office', and not as the result of any statute.[24] It was, in other words, a politic state, governed by a monarch who was obligated to involve the nobility in decision-making.

But if this state was thus 'politic', in Fortescue's sense, it was still also 'regal'. The monarch retained the right to weigh and reject the advice received from the nobility. There could be no forcibly coercive assertion of the right to give counsel, much less to have that counsel adopted; in this sense, 'a ruler's obligation to seek counsel was strictly moral', and 'counselling was a duty, not a right'.[25] Yet if it was a duty, it remained a *reciprocal* duty; a king who could not be forcibly compelled to seek advice was still morally obligated to seek it. The line between 'must' and 'should' was a matter of enforcement, not duty. The monarch was required to seek counsel, but the subject had no right to compel their sovereign to do so.

This balance was similar when it came to taking the advice once it had been sought out. Where the dictates of advice differed, the monarch could choose what advice to take. The content of that advice still mattered, however; the cry to replace false or villainous counsellors was a constant feature of early modern politics.[26] At the same time, there arose the vexed question of what was expected when those who gave advice were in rare complete agreement: was the monarch obliged in such a case to take such unanimous advice? Elizabeth's own answer was no.[27] But hers was not the only opinion, and others at the time, including her close advisor William Cecil, disagreed. As Steven Alford has documented, Cecil 'believed that the Queen's *imperium* was limited by the advice of her councillors' under certain circumstances, specifically unanimity, a view others have traced in the thought of Smith as well.[28] Cecil, Smith and others believed that the governance of the state lay at least partly in the Privy Council's hands as well as Elizabeth's, and that in order for them to exercise that governance it was necessary for the queen to 'resolutelie followe theire opynions in waightie affars'.[29] This was a perspective that countered the queen's theoretical absolute power with the practical reality of governance. It was not a general challenge to the queen's authority; it was only when the Council offered an 'agreed and corporate opinion' that they 'offered advice which they thought had to be taken'.[30] But in those cases where the queen's counsellors stood in united agreement, they believed it was her responsibility under the common law of the land to take their combined advice.

But if this was true, what of the longstanding tenet that 'counsel could not be turned into compulsion',[31] and was merely offered to the monarch for consideration? As Alford has shown, one of the keys to this complex balance between monarch and counsellors lay in the freedom of those counsellors to resign. While providing counsel was a duty, if unanimous advice was rejected the Council was prepared to stop serving or refuse to administer the policy in question.[32] While this in no way extended to rebellion or resistance of the monarch, a passive refusal to advise and serve was an appropriate response to royal intransigence. The monarch's power was unlimited with respect to counsel in theory, but limited in practice by the need to have counsellors, advisers and ministers who would serve. A sovereign who ignored the unanimous voice of counsel was acting against the precepts of the common law and thus in the wrong, even if the only punishment available was the refusal to continue to give counsel.

This practical limitation was particularly associated with earlier monarchs. As we have seen in Fortescue, the presence of politic counsel was understood to be a basic condition of the English state. Cecil and his contemporaries saw their arguments for the position of the monarch's counsellors in the state as traditional ones reflected in English history. The importance of counsel was not a matter of statute or decree, but of tradition and legacy; in other words, of the common law of the land and the royal prerogative that accompanied it. Since John reigned before the Magna Carta, the only limits on his arbitrary power would have been the common law and the pressure of a united group of counsellors.

I argue that Shakespeare chose to portray this legally derived narrative of John's reign in *King John*, rather than the version (now known to be more historically accurate) that he found in the chronicles. This context provides a comprehensive solution to a classic question about the play: why it does not include the Magna Carta.[33] By not including Magna Carta, Shakespeare aligned himself with the long-standing body of historical legal work referenced above, which was increasingly accessible to his potential audience and which harmonized easily with the political realities of his own time.[34] He was no doubt aware of the chronicle tradition that included Magna Carta in John's reign, given his use of Holinshed, but the story he chose to tell aligns more closely with the legal tradition and thus omits Magna Carta.

But understanding *King John* in this context illuminates more than a single question about an event that does not even appear onstage. It has wide implications for the meaning of the play as a whole. A *King John* that is interested in the requirements of counsel is a play that focuses upon its title character in a way that it is often criticized for failing to do.[35] It is a play that requires us to look at John with new eyes, seeing in his self-made plight a man trapped by circumstances he only partly understands, fighting myopically against a structure that overwhelms him. Such a vision also allows us to see redemption at the end of the play, as England comes together again under the future Henry III.

To fully grasp the tragedy inherent in John's misunderstandings, however, we must first turn to the other primary current of political thought about John's reign present in late Elizabethan England: the Protestant religious view that cast him as a hero of the English church against the pope. Much like the legal-constitutional perspective outlined above, this understanding of John had a long pedigree throughout the Tudor era. From the Act of Supremacy in 1534 through to Shakespeare's time, histories of John's reign frequently focused on his relationship to Rome and papal power.[36] Like those legal and constitutional arguments, this view was also soon to change under James I. Still, we must view Shakespeare's play in its own time, and not import the views that would be current a decade later, or now. In this tradition, John was lionized for his rejection of papal authority. His eventual surrender and submission to the power of the Holy See were seen as an unfortunate footnote, and focus was placed instead on his role as a precursor of Tudor claims to royal supremacy over the church.

Because of this tradition, the limits on John's religious authority were seen as different from the limits on his political authority. His political authority, as we have seen, was thought to have been restricted by the common law and to have necessitated the use of counsel. His religious authority was thought to have been much stronger but to have had a tightly limited scope. John was not a Tudor head of an independent Church of England. Still, he was seen, in this particular sixteenth-century view, as a protector of his people's religion against an outside usurper in the pope. As such, he was lauded for rejecting papal authority, not for asserting his own, so the two conceptions of his authority did not conflict. The negative religious authority protected England from the intrusions of a foreign power, the papacy, while within England John's positively asserted political authority remained subject to the limits we have already seen.

The fusion of these two viewpoints on John – the Protestant-inflected religious view and the legal-historical view – is Shakespeare's alone. It does not appear in any direct source for the play and the religious and legal texts do not refer to each other. Shakespeare melded these two common, disparate, but not inherently conflicting views of John's authority, and in the combination we find the source of John's confusion about his own position. He mistakes his power to reject the papacy for a larger power to act unilaterally, ignoring and evading the traditional requirements of advice, counsel and law.

That mistake is the root of John's great failures in the play. These include his second coronation, his treatment of Arthur and the nobles, and his submission to Pandulph. In each case, he acts on his own and either fails to heed unanimously agreed-upon counsel or does not solicit counsel at all from those who ought to be his advisers. In each case, he makes a bad choice. In no case does his method reach his stated goals, and indeed his resulting actions often worsen rather than improve the initial situation. In addition, by failing to heed the unanimous advice of his natural counsellors, he drives them away, weakening his own position in his attempts to strengthen it by unilateral action.

In demonstrating this, I will draw on the differences between Shakespeare's *King John* and an earlier play that seems likely to have been Shakespeare's primary source: *The Troublesome Raigne of King John*, an anonymous play published in 1591 that shares much of its plot with *King John* but almost none of its words.[37] *The Troublesome Raigne* is much more concerned with the religious aspects of John's reign, aspects which I believe Shakespeare subordinated to the political issues that they raise. By analysing the differences between the two, I intend to show how *King John*'s thematic emphasis is derived not from the chronicles or the other play but from the broader legal and religious traditions circulating in the period.

It has often been noted that Shakespeare's alterations to *The Troublesome Raigne* run in one major direction: removing religion from the plot.[38] *The Troublesome Raigne* attacks the Catholic church at every opportunity; Shakespeare's play does not. He removes scenes in which the Bastard ransacks a monastery and John interrogates Peter the prophet; he reduces both French and English devotion to the pope; and he alters Arthur's pleas for Hubert's mercy by removing the religious elements of their argument. As Carole Levin observes, the cumulative effect of these and other changes is to make the *King John* 'a far more political play' than *The Troublesome Raigne*, by which I take her to mean a play about national and dynastic rather than denominational politics.[39] But I must disagree with her suggestion that the political end to which the plot now points is the danger of rebellion.[40] After all, Magna Carta and Runnymede still do not appear, and Shakespeare removes from *The Troublesome Raigne* both a specific debate by Hubert and Arthur over obedience and a discussion between Lewis of France and Count Melun about the treachery of the English lords. These changes seem out of place if the play is primarily about rebellion.

If, however, the play is primarily about King John's individual reaction to the political structure in which he finds himself, as I argue it is, the changes make sense. As we have seen, the choice to avoid Magna Carta places John within a legal-historiographical tradition associated with a particular view of the political structure, and of John's place in it. Removing the debate between Hubert and Arthur about obedience takes some of our attention from the question of whether Hubert is right to obey John's order and turns it towards the question of whether John's order itself is justified. Similarly, eliminating the conversation between Lewis and Melun focuses our minds on John, England, and his nobles instead of on the French. Shakespeare reduces the role of religion and the pope in order to give us a play about secular political authority, then focuses on John's particular position as a king constrained by the political structure inherent in the common law.

These constraints are marked for us as important from the first scene of the play on. Both the challenge to John's title reported by Chatillon and the debate over how to resolve Sir Robert Faulconbridge's will point to the question of what right and authority John can claim as his own. The first part of the scene challenges his right to be 'England', as Chatillon calls him (1.1.4).[41] The second part, introducing the Faulconbridges, both reflects the anxiety about inheritance expressed in the first part and adds another layer to the problem: that although John is king, there are limits even on the king's authority.

These twin issues – the legitimacy of the king and the constraints under which even a legitimate king operates – are deeply intertwined in *King John*. This is particularly true because of a major deviation in *King John* from *The Troublesome Raigne*. Shakespeare maximizes the importance and strength of Arthur's claim to the throne, creating a John who is more than half usurper.[42] He takes a contested title and removes much of the contest; even John's mother, Eleanor, admits that he holds his title by 'strong possession much more than … right' (1.1.40). Indeed, I suggest that the issue of John's legitimacy looms over the play, from Chatillon's challenge in the first scene on. The arguments at Angiers, the whispers between Hubert and John over the captured Arthur, the French invasion and the noble revolt all hinge on the contested title.

But, I argue, the strong signs pointing towards John's potential illegitimacy do not stop him from being king. In the same moments that the French proclaim Arthur's title, they call John 'England', not only to his face but among themselves (1.1.4; 2.1.52, 56, 89, 90). Similarly, John's nobles do not question his title. They stay with him despite the French proclamation of Arthur's right, and argue against his second coronation because 'this "once again", but that your highness pleased, / Was once superfluous': that is, because he is already king (4.2.3–4). It is Arthur's death, not his life, that proves dangerous to John, and the greatest challenge to John's rule comes from a claimant even less legitimate than John himself: Lewis of France, whose claim derives only collaterally from his marriage to John's niece, Blanche. Despite his seeming illegitimacy, Shakespeare's John *is* king. It is, in many ways, his defining feature, more so than any particular tic of personality.

The one potential exception to John's functional kingship is in regard to the town of Angiers,[43] where John and Philip are forced to debate the issue of right before the sceptical spokesman for the town. Yet John leads English troops into the battle for the town, and he does ultimately defeat the French forces, satisfying the town's condition that 'one must prove greatest' (2.1.332) in order to convince the citizens to serve that greater lord. While this may not prove his right – which is, as I have suggested above, extremely shaky – it certainly does prove his ability to rule England, which is the aspect in question here.

But for John, *de facto* kingship is not quite enough. He demands to be acknowledged as king by right. In his mind, his right of kingship is embodied in his crown. He expresses this belief twice in the play: once when he asks the people of Angiers 'Doth not the crown of England prove the king?' (2.1.273), and a second time when he insists upon his second coronation. In both cases, John relies on his possession of the physical object of the crown to signal his right and authority.

In both cases, however, his belief turns out to be in error. Angiers will not open the gates until he first makes a treaty with and then militarily defeats the French, while the nobles believe his second coronation, far from assuring his right, may weaken it. The crown may symbolize kingship, but to everyone but John kingship itself is something else, and the two cannot be equated so simply.

John's error shows us that he does not know where his power comes from or how to sustain it. He believes that kingship is something tangible, something to be physically possessed. He thinks that people will obey him if he simply points out the fact of his possession. But in the view we have examined above, kingship, or at least effective kingship, is not so simple. A king is a king once crowned, but effective action (such as commanding Angiers or subduing unrest) requires proper engagement with counsel and the law. John will indeed remain king as long as he has his crown, but, as we will see, he finds it difficult to rule when he ceases to rule properly.

At the start of the play, however, John does rule well. The 'strong possession' (1.1.39, 40) he and his mother refer to in the first scene is not merely 'possession', it is 'strong', precisely because he accepts advice and does not overstep the law. In this he differs from Richard II, another Shakespearean king whose play was likely written around the same time as *King John*. Richard suffers under a belief that the majesty of the crown will provide quasi-magical assistance to his cause, and treats the law (particularly the law of inheritance) with disdain. John is like Richard in that he has an elevated view of the importance of his crown to his kingship, but unlike him in that John, at least initially, practises his kingship in a manner that still upholds the law. He is a more practical version of Richard, even if a similar self-conceit will trip him up, and (unlike Richard) he is able to ultimately correct his failings.

Since *King John* was written in the mid-1590s, a period of major tension about the English succession, we might expect that the play's treatment of a questionable succession would be topical, as indeed the similar story in *Richard II* is often taken to be. Yet because of the displacement of the issue across time, it becomes difficult to claim any direct relation between the play's succession and the situation in the 1590s. It is not as simple as drawing a straight parallel: of declaring Arthur to be a stand-in for Mary, Queen of Scots, for instance, as many critics have proposed.[44] Precisely because the play insists on the specific and complex historical circumstances surrounding Arthur and John, I suggest, it asks us to go beyond this model of using history and instead consider what more complex lessons we might draw from the situation portrayed in the play. It asks us to conceive of exemplarity in a slightly more advanced form than the one it sometimes appears in, a form that requires a different understanding of the relationship between the time depicted and the play's own time of composition.

Neither John nor Arthur directly represents any particular early modern figure in this reading. Instead, the depiction of their historical relationship to each other and the consequences that resulted combine to permit a new understanding of the succession controversy. Every attempt to change the *de facto* succession settlement in place at the start of the play results in disaster: Philip of France's forces are defeated, Arthur is captured, John's nobles desert him and Lewis's invading force is washed away. Even the town of Angiers is threatened with destruction from both sides for their insistence that the issue must be resolved. Their (temporarily) successful solution to the threat is to ignore the succession entirely. The marriage of Lewis and Blanche will not affect Arthur's right one whit, but it is 'at this match' that the town will 'give you [John] entrance' without a fight (2.1.447, 450). Only by letting the issue of succession go by, unquestioned and unanswered, can there be peace. The same might be (un)said about the succession in Shakespeare's time, and indeed Elizabeth declared as much to the many parliaments that she criticized for attempting to raise the issue.[45] This illustrates what I see as the typically Shakespearean mode of topical commentary through history: neither allegorical nor direct, but resulting from a careful consideration of past circumstances and their thoughtful applicability to contemporary situations. John is the king; any further discussion of it is not merely unhelpful but actively destructive. On the other hand, accepting John's kingship often has very good results.

We see this positive side of John's kingship throughout the first two acts, beginning in the first scene when the Faulconbridges come before him. Here Shakespeare crucially deviates from his source in treating the circumstances of the scene.[46] In *The Troublesome Raigne* the Sheriff of Northamptonshire has brought the two Faulconbridges before the king because they have 'of late committed a riot, and have appeald to your Majestie' (I.67–8).[47] Shakespeare's Faulconbridges appear to have 'come from the country to be judged by you' by their own volition as part of a civil suit about inheritance (1.1.45). Thus while *The Troublesome Raigne* touches on the inheritance question because it was the cause of the violence that in turn led to a criminal case, *King John* focuses on the inheritance as the only question in a civil suit.

The legal resolution of each scene is also different, though the practical effect on the inheritance is much the same. *The Troublesome Raigne* has Essex question the two brothers on John's behalf as witnesses, and Philip eventually is prompted by something speaking in his soul to declare himself 'King Richards Sonne' (I.279). In light of this, John decides the case and gives everything to Robert, knighting Philip afterwards (I.284–5). It seems in this case that Philip's bare declaration of misplaced paternity is enough to disinherit him. As soon as he acknowledges himself not to be Sir Robert's son, he is no longer the heir.

Shakespeare's John, by contrast, accurately cites the common law rule of inheritance against this sort of verdict: 'your brother is legitimate: / Your father's wife did after wedlock bear him' (1.1.116–17). Crucially, he also places that legal legitimacy above even the power of a king (in this case Richard I) to alter: 'your father might have kept / This calf, bred from his cow, from all the world, / In sooth he might. Then if he were my brother's, / My brother might not claim him' (1.1.123–6). Under the legal regime John correctly describes, neither the father in his will nor the king by his authority can deny Philip Faulconbridge the inheritance of old Sir Robert Faulconbridge. As long as his mother was married to Sir Robert when he was born, he is Sir Robert's heir, no matter who fathered him: 'my mother's son did get your father's heir' (1.1.128). In this John admits the existence of a power beyond his own, the power of the law: specifically a part of the common law that was in force during John's reign but had been amended by statute before the play was written.[48] It is noteworthy that Shakespeare's John makes this particular decision under the rule of the ancient common law instead of the later statutory revision current in Shakespeare's own time.

But Shakespeare's John still finds a way out of the case's difficulty, with his mother Eleanor's help. He does not press Philip Faulconbridge about his parentage because the law makes it immaterial. Instead, he and his mother offer Philip a bargain. If Philip will 'forsake [his] fortune', actively refusing his inheritance and giving it to his brother, he may become 'Sir Richard, and Plantagenet' (1.1.148, 162). Philip takes this deal and all is resolved. In this moment, John acts precisely as a proper king should, using the power of persuasion and the ability to create a new knighthood as tools to arrange a solution to a thorny issue without breaking the law.

Unlike the John of *The Troublesome Raigne*, then, Shakespeare's John has both acknowledged the power of the law over the king – Richard I could not claim Philip Faulconbridge as his son even if he wanted to, nor can John make that claim on his behalf – and found a politic way around the inconveniences of that law without violating it. Instead of being disinherited, Philip Faulconbridge is given an opportunity to proactively choose a different path. In the process, John's part is transformed from that of a passive describer of the (incorrect) law that disinherits Philip to an active participant in the bargain. His knighting of Philip is not an attempt to salvage Philip's blurting out of his status but a wise offer that defuses the situation.

This is a place where Zurcher's reliance on Snagg's preface, and thus on chronicle history, leads him astray. Operating under the assumption that John must have ruled outside of the common law, because Snagg's preface accuses him of doing so, Zurcher claims that *King John* dramatizes the same resolution of the scene as *The Troublesome Raigne*, in which 'even as the elder son, [Philip] will not inherit' because of his bastard status.[49] He then suggests that John's proposed resolution of the situation is a form of corrupt self-dealing because it results in John gaining Philip's services, arguing that it is an example of what Snagg called 'will-government'.[50] But as we have seen, in Shakespeare's play Philip would still have inherited despite his bastard status, and John's solution is not a legal decision but the equivalent of settling out of court in a way that serves not only John's interests but that of both Faulconbridges as well. When we pay careful attention to the details of the scene, rather than looking for incipient signs of arbitrariness in John, we can see in him a model of good kingship within the limits of the common law.

It is not coincidental that this moment represents John's best decision in the entire play and provides him with his greatest ally in the Bastard. All of John's successes, few as they may be, are associated with this sort of proper action: listening to his advisors, in this case his mother Eleanor; acknowledging the law; and coming to consensual rather than arbitrary decisions. Conversely, his many failures and setbacks grow from his disregard for the limits of his position.

Besides the negotiation around Sir Robert Faulconbridge's estate, John's greatest success is the resolution of the siege of Angiers. In that moment, John plays the king perfectly. He shows strength against the external threat of France, but more importantly, he listens to advice, twice in fact. He first takes the Bastard's suggestion to ally with

France and 'conjointly bend / Your sharpest deeds of malice on this town' (2.1.379–80). Then, after that threat has broken the town's defiance, he takes the Citizen's and Eleanor's advice to have Blanche and Lewis marry and so resolve the war. In each case, though both John and Philip of France act upon the advice, John is the first to agree, and the advisors are John's subjects. He tells the Bastard that 'I like it [his proposal] well' and instructs the Citizen to 'speak on, with favour; we are bent to hear' (2.1.398, 422). He proves in this scene his ability not only to hear advice but to recognize its value.

John proves capable of both listening to advice and taking the larger opportunity it provides. He offers Philip the union of Blanche and Lewis, as the Citizen suggested, but he also goes further, offering to 'heal up all' by 'creat[ing] young Arthur Duke of Britain / And Earl of Richmond' (2.1.550, 551–2). This move resembles the solution reached above to the Faulconbridge dispute, in which John sidesteps the issue by creating a compromise outside the point of contention. Unfortunately, Arthur is not there to accept the offer. Still, the impulse shows John in a good light. He takes the spirit of the Citizen's advice to end the war and not merely the letter of his suggestion to have the two young royals marry.

Of course, the glow of this success barely outlives the act. John's peace is undone by others before it can bear fruit. The papal legate, Pandulph, appears and demands that John allow Stephen Langton to be installed as archbishop of Canterbury; upon John's refusal, he declares him 'cursed and excommunicate' and orders Philip to 'on peril of a curse / Let go the hand of that arch-heretic' (3.1.173, 191–2). In *The Troublesome Raigne*, this is the immediate end of John's French alliance (I.1014). Shakespeare's version of the scene, however, has 128 lines of argument about whether Philip should let go of John's hand. In this space, we see Philip's hesitation and uncertainty play out (3.1.221, 225–52, 262), set against Pandulph's ever-increasing threats (3.1.222–3, 253–61, 263–97). Each time Philip asks for guidance and help, the legate threatens him. Philip's decision to leave John is inspired not by a holy thought, as in *The Troublesome Raigne*, but by Pandulph's move from a generalized warning to a specific threat: 'I will pronounce a curse upon his head' is followed directly by 'Thou shalt not need. England, I will fall from thee' (3.1.319, 320). The pregnant space Shakespeare opens up between John's excommunication and Philip's abandonment of the alliance allows us to see both Pandulph's and Philip's true characters: the former a bully, the latter reluctant but cowed. This development is missing from *The Troublesome Raigne*, whose characters are comparatively flat, and where the Pope's word is simply law to Philip.

Shakespeare's change also allows us to see John in his element. Having denounced the legate and his threats, he speaks only twice, briefly, between Pandulph's command and Philip's execution of it (3.1.202, 217). Otherwise he is silent, neither influencing Philip's choice nor pre-empting it. He alone of the characters onstage, saving perhaps the silent Arthur, seems beyond Pandulph's threats.[51] Indeed, while Pandulph has blustered and threatened Philip into his choice, John calmly warns Philip after the choice is made: 'France, thou shalt rue this hour within this hour' (3.1.324). The contrast between the two is striking, and John's confidence in his power is borne out. The English defeat the French, and Arthur is captured. Shakespeare makes that triumph all the greater by removing a scene in *The Troublesome Raigne* in which Eleanor is captured by the French (I.1057–88). In *King John* this moment is merely a 'fear' of John's, immediately beaten away by the Bastard's reassurance (3.2.7). John and his army triumphantly overcome the French and sail back to England in victory.

It is in these two scenes that we see Shakespeare bringing out the Protestant religious perspective on John. As mentioned above, John has the power to deny the pope's demand: 'no Italian priest / Shall tithe or toll in our dominions' (3.1.153–4). He claims to be 'under God', the 'supreme head' of the church, and rejects all papal authority (3.1.155). In the context we are considering here, this position is correct. As Smith put it, 'in warre time, and in the field the Prince hath also absolute power',[52] and John's immediate victories over the French and their papal backer seem to confirm his right to defy Pandulph and the powers behind him. In addition, his echoing of the early Tudor title of 'supreme head' of the church may be a sign that John is right to break from Rome. If we are to think along those lines, however, Elizabeth I's refusal to take that particular title herself – settling instead on 'supreme governor'[53] – may indicate the difference that was understood to exist between his time and hers.

In turn, the heady power he can wield against a foreign foe distracts John from his domestic responsibilities. He takes too seriously the idea that 'where we do reign we will alone uphold /

Without th'assistance of a mortal hand' (3.1.157–8). He finishes this statement with a flourish that makes it clear this is intended to apply to religious matters – 'So tell the pope, all reverence set apart / To him and his usurped authority' (3.1.159–60) – but the claim of plenipotentiary power is expressed universally, even if it is addressed in this particular instance to the pope. This is the key moment when John steps away from his previous acceptance of the limits on his authority. From this point forward John appears to believe his own rhetoric, and to apply it not merely to the pope and France, but to English affairs as well. This misunderstanding of the extent of his authority will lead John into a series of errors that cripple his promising reign.

The most obvious of these errors is the one we have already touched on briefly: the second coronation. In the aftermath of Arthur's capture, John decides to have himself crowned for a second time. Here Shakespeare once again alters *The Troublesome Raigne*. In the older play, we actually see the coronation itself and the decision process that led to it, and it all plays out in front of the audience before John's coronation speech (I.1480–1560).

In *King John*, however, we only see the aftermath of the second coronation. The first line of the scene is John's 'Here once again we sit, once again crown'd' (4.2.1). Yet despite the fact that the second coronation has already happened, Shakespeare still shows us the nobles arguing against it. Pembroke and Salisbury spend some thirty-two lines advising against a decision that has already happened (4.2.3–34). But, as Salisbury is forced to conclude, 'to this effect before you were new crowned / We breathed our counsel, but it pleased your highness / To overbear it' (4.2.35–7). John has already heard them, and ignored them. Given the vigour with which they still urge their disagreement, I agree with the Arden editors that Salisbury is at least somewhat 'ironic' in his pleasure when he suggests that 'we are all well pleased, / Since all, and every part of what we would / Doth make a stand at what your highness will' (4.2.37–9).[54] But while the pleasure may be ironic, the statement of power politics that follows is not.

In this moment, we see the precise conflict between absolutism and constitutionalism that occurred at the margins of Elizabethan political thought. Salisbury's statement sounds remarkably like Sir Francis Knollys lamenting in the parliament of 1572 that 'all was vain without the Queen's consent'.[55] While this is John's reign, not

Elizabeth's, the point remains, as we have seen, that the obligation to hear counsel was not the obligation to heed it. But it was not always that simple: it was also Knollys who believed that the monarch had a duty to 'resolutelie followe [her Council's] opynions in waightie affairs'.[56] John's unwillingness to listen to unanimous advice not to be crowned violates the reciprocal bonds between king and council.

The nobles remind John that he is acting against a united front; the repetition of their advice after the fact is a reminder of his reciprocal duty. John seems to recognize this, as his immediate reaction is conciliatory: 'Some reasons of this double coronation / I have possess'd you with, and think them strong', and then 'Meantime, but ask / What you would have reformed that is not well, / And well you shall perceive how willingly / I will both hear and grant you your requests' (4.2.40–1, 43–6). John is unwilling to bow before their unanimous advice, thinking his own reasons weightier than theirs, but he is quick to move from the past argument to the potential of the future. Specifically, he offers to 'reform' whatever troubles the lords, and assures them that this time he will do what they ask.

By moving this conversation to after the coronation, and taking the coronation itself offstage, Shakespeare strengthens our sympathy for the ignored lords. In *The Troublesome Raigne*, there is a disagreement about the coronation, John makes a decision and then we see him crowned. In *King John* by contrast, we do not see him crowned or the earlier discussion. The first change removes any chance that the audience will be affected by the coronation ceremony itself and thus decide that John was right about its effect. Instead the coronation has already happened, but nothing has changed; John is the same John he has always been. This underscores the ineffectiveness of the coronation and works against John's argument. The second change simultaneously increases the appearance of John's high-handedness and emphasizes the depth of the lords' convictions on this point. Although we are told that this advice was given before the coronation, we only see it afterwards. From the audience's perspective, then, John did not actually hear this advice before, since they did not hear it with him. The fact that the nobles continue to argue is thus evidence that they strongly oppose the coronation and feel the need to make their voices heard. This argument places our focus squarely on how the decision was made and whether it ought to have been made differently.

John's error here is neither being wrong nor failing to heed his lords' advice as a general matter. It is specifically ignoring the unanimous advice of all his lords to the detriment of the realm. Even Elizabeth at times bowed to such combined pressure, although we have seen that she did not share the somewhat constitutionalist view from which this requirement derived.[57] John acts unilaterally. There can be no doubt that he has ignored the nobles' advice or that that advice was given for the good of the realm, because the lords explain their reasoning. The second coronation is 'troublesome / Being urged at a time unseasonable' and it 'startles and frights consideration, / Makes sound opinion sick and truth suspected' (4.2.19–20, 25–6). The people were 'ne'er stained with revolt' before but, according to the nobles' counsel, this second coronation will make them uncertain and unsure (4.2.6). This is the sort of advice and information John is supposed to get from his lords, and precisely the kind of counsel he is supposed to listen to when they provide it with one voice. Instead he puts them off with unclear reasons and does what he wants regardless. This is extreme high-handedness, precisely what we might expect from a man who believed he ruled 'without th'assistance of a mortal hand'.

It might seem that John's high-handedness itself cannot be the problem. After all, John technically consulted with his lords. But here John is faced with that unusual quality of unanimity on a point of great import to the realm, precisely the kind of counsel he was expected not merely to seek but to take. It seems as if even he is partially aware of this, as he immediately offers to take their counsel in another way, attempting to deflect the error he has made. But that offer brings in the issue of Arthur, and with it an even worse betrayal of the reciprocal bonds of trust, advice and consent between John and his nobles.

As part of examining that betrayal, however, we must first examine John's treatment of Arthur himself and its relation to the political issues at play. We have already seen how Arthur's status as a claimant to the crown affects our perception of John's position. But John does not simply deal with Arthur in the abstract, but in the flesh as well. After the battle between Philip and John, Arthur is John's prisoner. John places him under the care of Hubert but takes a moment to whisper some words into Hubert's ear while the boy is distracted by Eleanor. With those words, he condemns Arthur to death.

Or at least, so it initially appears. Certainly the end of the exchange suggests strongly that John and Hubert have come to an agreement about Arthur's future demise (3.2.66). And John clearly does not want Arthur alive, telling Hubert 'he is a very serpent in my way' (3.2.61). But whatever agreement John and Hubert have come to here, their actual treatment of Arthur differs significantly from their whispered conversation. Instead of a quiet, unremarkable death unconnected to John, there is a formal warrant. And instead of ordering Arthur's death, that warrant commands his blinding.

The existence of a physical warrant for the blinding is a major weakness in John's new plan. The warrant is referred to four times: once when the first executioner asks about it (4.1.6); twice when Hubert gives it to Arthur and demands that he read it (4.1.33, 37); and once more, and most importantly, when Pembroke sees Hubert and tells his fellow nobles 'this is the man should do the bloody deed: / He show'd his warrant to a friend of mine' (4.2.69–70). The warrant is trouble. While it might help Hubert keep his executioners in line, it can also be revealed to those, like Arthur and Pembroke, for whom it is a sign of John's and Hubert's perfidy.

What prompts these changes, both in the detail of what is commanded and in the creation of a physical warrant? I believe they represent John's decision to explore the boundaries of his authority once again. While he practically might be able to order Arthur's death, to do so would be an almost textbook definition of tyranny, given both the laws within which he must operate and the demands of his nobility. In this he resembles Shakespeare's Macbeth, who 'could / With bare-faced power sweep him from my sight / And bid my will avouch it, yet I must not'.[58] But while John does not do that, he still exercises his power over Arthur. The order for Arthur's blinding occupies the zone between what he cannot get away with and what he might be able to, and so he does it. That it is also likely to lead to Arthur's 'accidental' death as he is blinded with hot irons is also a consideration. This explains why Hubert, though ordered to blind Arthur, will falsely report his death rather than his blinding to John (4.2.85). This represents a change from *The Troublesome Raigne*, where he begins with a report of blinding (II.1662) and only then moves on to one of death (II.1667).

Unfortunately for John, the nobles already know about his plans for Arthur. We must take seriously, I think, Pembroke's aside that he knows what Hubert is commanded to do, and 'the bloody deed' need not only refer to a murder (think of what happens to Gloucester in *King Lear*). Pembroke's foreknowledge casts in a new light, I believe, his insistence not on Arthur's good treatment but on his 'enfranchisement' and then repeatedly on his 'liberty' (4.2.52, 63, 66). The request goes beyond Pembroke's other argument for lifting Arthur's 'barbarous ignorance' and giving him 'the rich advantage of good exercise' into a specific demand that he be freed (4.2.59, 60). I believe that the imminence of harm implied by the warrant prompts this demand, and that the demand's specificity is crafted in response to John's previously mentioned promise to act on the lords' advice. By making this particular, united request at that particular moment, the nobles turn the question of Arthur's treatment from a personal and domestic issue into a larger constitutional one. In particular, they make treating Arthur properly the only way for John to redeem his previous failure to take their unanimous counsel.

Shakespeare here alters the constitutional question surrounding Arthur from what it was in *The Troublesome Raigne*. There, the question raised is one of obedience: specifically, whether Hubert can safely obey John's warrant against Arthur without damning himself. Hubert and Arthur engage in a lengthy discussion of resistance theory, the proposition that there were some commands even by a lawful sovereign which ought not to be obeyed (I.1391–1435). Shakespeare moves this conversation from a religious and political focus to a personal one: Hubert's relationship with Arthur and their love for each other. Their argument also centres on the actual blinding rather than death. Where *The Troublesome Raigne* argued that 'no commaund should stand in force to murther' (I.1393–4), Shakespeare's Hubert concedes that 'I shall not touch thine eye' (4.1.121). Shakespeare has abandoned the political implications of resistance theory and its particular focus on royally commanded murder in favour of a personal connection and an acknowledgement of what John has actually ordered.

Instead, Shakespeare locates the constitutional question at a structural level: what duty does the king have to listen to his nobles, and can he act against their advice, particularly if it is unanimous? *King John* raises this question first in terms of the coronation, and then immediately again in relation to Arthur. By putting the two moments in direct succession, Shakespeare shows us how John's constant pressure on the bounds within which he must operate eventually puts him in a situation from which he cannot escape. He has already rejected the nobles' unanimous advice once, and their second request is one that he has already ensured he cannot grant. And so he lies to them. It does not go well.

John's greatest trouble is that all these problems come together in the same moment. It is not just that (he thinks) Arthur is dead. It is not just the timing of that death, so close to the argument over the coronation. It is not even just that John lied to his counsellors by knowingly claiming to grant a request he had already made impossible, a lie that is obvious to him, the audience and even Pembroke. It is all of these things together with his consistent rejection of their unanimous advice that finally snap the ties between John and his nobility. They yielded to him about the coronation because they could not force him to take their advice; here he has promised to take it, knowingly broken that promise while pretending not to, and in doing so endangered the state by acting against Arthur's life. Rather than yield to him again, they leave him, exercising the right to no longer give counsel when it has been rejected.

The lords' departure is followed immediately by the discovery of two pieces of information which force John to realize the enormity of what he has done. First he learns of the loss of his French provinces and Lewis's invasion of England, then of the death of Eleanor. The sudden shock of these tidings speaks to the isolation that his unilateralism has brought upon him. His mother died on 'the first of April', and this news is clearly not recent (4.2.120). Yet John is only hearing of it now and, until this moment, thought that his mother was still in charge in France (4.2.117–19). He is cut off from the 'intelligence' that he vitally needs (4.2.116). His rejection of other counsel has reduced his ability to govern his kingdom properly.

Indeed, with Eleanor's death he has lost one of the few advisors he did listen to. In this moment, we not only observe the isolation that has accompanied John's turn away from counsel, but also see him become more isolated by the loss of Eleanor. This combines with the departure of his nobles to leave John almost utterly alone. In that moment, he realizes his situation, and the only way out of it. He begs 'Occasion' to 'make a league with me, till I have pleased / My discontented peers' (4.2.125, 126-7). In the wake of his mothers' death, he recognizes his need to reconcile with the nobility in order to save himself. He cannot keep England if he tries to rule alone. This realization, I believe, is the source of his claim to the

Bastard, later in the scene, that 'I have a way to win [the nobles'] loves again' (4.2.168). This line is easy to interpret as referring to Arthur still being alive, when we read it with hindsight at the end of the play or with our special knowledge as the audience that Hubert has lied about Arthur's fate. But it actually comes well before Hubert's admission to John that 'young Arthur is alive' (4.2.251). John must have something else in mind. Most likely, he has in mind some combination of the three options the play itself sets up: to give them Hubert as a sacrifice (a move he lays the groundwork for by accusing Hubert of murder at 4.2.205–48), to offer to give them command in the present crisis (as he will later do for the Bastard at 5.1.77), or to remind them more forcefully of the importance of unity in the face of invasion (as the Bastard will do in his place at 5.2.151–3). Whatever his precise plan might be, this moment shows us John reaching the awareness that he has overstepped his bounds and must do something for the nobles in order to save himself.

I do not mean to suggest here that the nobles' rebellion is justified, even in this political context. The question of the right of rebellion was and had been a contested issue in England and across Europe for centuries, dating back through the Reformation to the *Policraticus* of John of Salisbury, written during the reign of John's father Henry II, and even earlier.[59] Rather, I argue here that neither side is fully in the right or in the wrong. John is obviously wrong to have failed to take their unanimous advice. But his subversion of the requirement to take counsel justifies at most the nobles' departure, not their active rebellion. John has to appease them not because they are right to rebel, but because appeasing them consists of doing what he is already bound to do: taking counsel from them for the good of the realm. He cannot rule without them, and their decision to violate their oaths to him does not change that.

The nobles are in a similarly difficult situation. They cannot, in good conscience, treat John as if the coronation and the situation with Arthur had not happened, or else the king's duty to take their unanimous advice would cease to have any meaning. But the theories that suggested that duty in no way justified rebellion. Salisbury's summary of the situation – 'the king hath dispossessed himself of us' (4.3.23) – is precisely correct, if not in the way he means it. John's actions have violated the terms under which they advise him, and thus in a limited sense dispossessed him of them, but that does not give them any right to forcibly or directly oppose him. John may not be able to force them to serve him, but they certainly have no right to give allegiance to any other. The nobles pass beyond the warrant provided by John's actions when they join the French invaders.

On this point, the play is explicit. Even in the moment that Salisbury swears loyalty to Lewis with 'a voluntary zeal and unurged faith', he feels compelled to add that he is 'not glad that such a sore of time / Should seek a plaster by contemned revolt' (5.2.10, 12–13). Lewis takes this sorrow as natural: 'a noble temper dost thou show in this' (5.2.40). The Bastard adds his more colourful rebuke later, calling the nobles 'ingrate revolts' and 'bloody Neroes, ripping up the womb / Of your dear mother England' (5.2.151, 152–3). Finally the Count Melun, in his dying speech, tells the nobles that even the French condemn their revolt: Lewis has secretly sworn that they will 'pay[] the fine of rated treachery / Even with a treacherous fine of all your lives' (5.4.37–8). Their only hope of salvation is to 'seek out King John and fall before his feet' (5.4.13). What exactly the nobles *can* do about John's overreaching is unclear, but what is clear is that his mistreatment of them does not justify the revolt.

Besides John's direct mistreatment of the lords, Arthur's death is the main factor that causes them to abandon the king. In *King John*, Arthur's death stands for all John's abuses of authority. We have already seen the perfect mistiming of Hubert announcing Arthur's death just as the lords have identified Arthur's fate as the symbol of John's willingness to heed them. It is this significance of Arthur that leads John to say that 'hostility and civil tumult reigns / Between my conscience and my cousin's death' and causes the Bastard to tell Hubert when he later picks up the boy's dead body 'how easy dost thou take all England up!' (4.2.247–8; 4.3.142). In each case, the speaker recognizes that Arthur is both more than himself and less than what he symbolizes. He is simultaneously an embodied person – 'my cousin', or as the Bastard puts it, 'this morsel of dead royalty' (4.3.143) – and a space that can contain 'all England', across which 'hostility and civil tumult' sweep.

This dual significance of Arthur lies behind the difference in treatment between *The Troublesome Raigne* and *King John* surrounding Arthur's actual death. In both plays, Arthur is not actually killed by Hubert or any other agent of John's, but dies trying to escape his prison. In both plays, his body is discovered by the nobles who have come to his prison. But the scenes surrounding that discovery are very different. In *The Troublesome Raigne* the nobles have come on a pilgrimage to 'find the Princes grave', find the body immediately and then decide amongst themselves to send for the Dauphin to invade (II.30, 81–3). In *King John*, however, Lewis's force has already landed in England, and Salisbury's first line – 'Lords, I will meet him at Saint Edmonsbury' (4.3.11) – makes it clear that the nobles are already in contact with the French invaders. The Bastard enters, and only then do the nobles find Arthur's body by accident: 'what is he lies here?' (4.3.34). Hubert enters after this line; Shakespeare splits a single Hubert appearance in *The Troublesome Raigne* into paired but separate arrivals of the Bastard and Hubert.

Together these three changes – the timing of the French invasion and the nobles' contact with it, the finding of Arthur's body and the introduction of the Bastard – give the nobles a very different arc in the scene. While in *The Troublesome Raigne* they are swept away into rebellion by the passion of seeing Arthur's unburied carcass, in *King John* their emotional reaction is secondary. Salisbury makes their claim of being 'dispossessed' by John eleven lines before they find the body; the first discussion of their connection to Lewis comes still earlier. These nobles are already fully disaffected.

These changes are best explained in light of the political context we have explored. Arthur's death is undoubtedly important to Shakespeare's lords, but their disaffection is not as closely tied to the physical body of the prince as it is in *The Troublesome Raigne*. Rather, Arthur's death is a symptom and a symbol of a larger problem, and the appearance of his body is simply the crowning instance of issues that already exist. The Bastard's attempted intervention has a place in *King John* that it would not in *The Troublesome Raigne* because Shakespeare's nobles are not swayed by their emotions alone. Salisbury may say that 'our griefs and not our manners reason now', but those manners have been at issue throughout the play (4.3.29). There is a tight interplay here between the dual meaning of 'griefs' – emotions and grievances – and the dual meaning of 'manners'. 'Manners' refers to politeness – the 'good words' the Bastard asks for, to which Salisbury replies (4.3.28) – but it can also refer to what is customary or traditional.[60] The nobles simultaneously claim to be so overwhelmed with emotion as to be unable to be polite and to be so wronged that it voids their customary duty to counsel John and to serve him in the wars that result from his rejection of their counsel. This second meaning is unique to Shakespeare and the legal material he employs; it does not play a part in *The Troublesome Raigne*.

Another critical scene whose significance is substantially changed between the two plays is John's resignation of the crown to Pandulph. In *The Troublesome Raigne* no reason is given for this moment, except for John's personal religious submission to the papacy (II.632–3). Shakespeare similarly makes John submit personally: 'Thus have I yielded up into your hand / The circle of my glory' (5.1.1–2). But *King John* then adds an explanation for this action not found in *The Troublesome Raigne*: 'Now keep your holy word, go meet the French, / And from his Holiness use all your power / To stop their marches' (5.1.5–7). This reveals John's submission as an act of political strategy, aimed against both the French invasion and the nobles: 'Our people quarrel with obedience', and so 'This inundation of mistempered humour / Rests by you only to be qualified' (5.1.9, 12–13). This puts the scene in a national political, rather than a denominationally religious, context. John has submitted not for absolution but for safety.

Of course, it does not work. This is unsurprising, since John's initial rejection of the pope was, politically speaking, correct. Pandulph cannot call off Lewis, who is 'too wilful-opposite' to be controlled, and the English nobles likewise pay him no attention (5.2.124). This episode with Pandulph is just another of John's attempts to rule his kingdom without his nobles, and it too fails. Given the Bastard's surprise when told that John has 'made a happy peace' with Pandulph, the submission to the Pope seems to be entirely John's own idea, without his having sought any advice (5.1.63). As Smith suggested in his own analysis of this historical moment, the submission fails because it was 'neither approved of his people, nor accorded by act of parliament'.[61] Even with the papal legate on his side, John cannot rule his country without domestic help and advice. But as it turns out, he does not need to do so. As soon as Pandulph has left to try to convince the French and revolted English to lay down their arms, the Bastard enters. At this point, something happens that is important from the political perspective we have explored here: John takes counsel. The Bastard is sceptical that Pandulph will do any good, and counsels John to 'let us, my liege, to arms!' (5.1.73). John listens, and delegates his authority to the Bastard to go organize the defence: 'have thou the ordering of this present time' (5.1.77).

This line has often been taken as the first sign of John's withdrawal from the world.[62] This is true, but not in the sense that it is generally meant of John's abdication of interest in or authority over England. In the context of counsel outlined here, we can see this as the moment when John has finally come to accept that he cannot be king *alone*, that others must have a voice and a say in the management of the kingdom. The withdrawal here is John's withdrawal from the position that the king can act unilaterally against the dictates of unanimous counsel. It follows, then, that the Bastard's successes and his powerful speeches are not a rebuke of John's poor leadership but a sign that he has finally done the right thing.

This interaction between John and the Bastard is also crucial to our understanding of the nobles' rebellion, and of the Bastard's relation to it. The Bastard serves as the model for what the nobles ought to be. He and Hubert remain true to the king, but Hubert knows that Arthur is not dead by John's command; this leaves the Bastard as the only man who hears of Arthur's death, has reason to think it is John's fault and does not rebel. What's more, he hears of it from the lords themselves: 'I met Lord Bigot and Lord Salisbury, / ... going to seek the grave / Of Arthur, whom they say is killed to-night / On your suggestion' (4.2.162, 164–6). Unlike those lords, he does not turn to the French upon hearing the news; on the contrary, he continues on his way to John, and continues to serve him by giving John the counsel he requires.

That service is neither silent nor unthinking. His voice is not subservient but admonishing: 'if you be afeard to hear the worst / Then let the worst, unheard, fall on your head' (4.2.135–6). This tone snaps John out of his malaise, reminding him of his obligation to listen to counsel: 'I was amazed / Under the tide, but now I breathe again / Aloft the flood, and *can give audience / To any tongue, speak it of what it will*' (4.2.137–40, emphasis mine). When John then sends the Bastard to speak to the lords, he similarly corrects them, although to less effect: 'whate'er you think, good words I think were best' (4.3.28). Here he cuts to the heart of the trouble between the nobility and their prince: John may have failed them as king, but they are failing him as nobles. They should be correcting John, as the Bastard does, not leaving him like traitors. Even if they are justified in removing themselves from service because of John's rejection of their counsel, they cannot be justified in going over to the French. When the Bastard demands that they 'keep the peace' during the exchange of threats between the lords and Hubert (4.3.93), his words apply not only to the immediate quarrel but to the realm as a whole. He can see clearly the effect that full revolt will have on England, not only in this scene, when he predicts that 'vast confusion waits' (4.3.152), but in the next act when he castigates the 'degenerate ... ingrate revolts' (5.2.152) and when he closes the play by declaring that 'nought shall make us rue / If England to itself do rest but true' (5.7.117–18). He provides a model both for service to the king, bearing his messages and ultimately leading his armies, and for the rejection of rebellion.

The solution to the conflict between king and nobles that the Bastard embodies is one of continued service combined with honest, harsh counsel. After his rebuke of John's fear of bad news, he continues to provide precisely the intelligence John had lacked about 'the news abroad', bearing information about superstitious rumours, the nobles and the invading French (4.2.160). He then reports the progress of the war (5.1.30–6, 39–41), and when that once again dispirits John he admonishes him again (5.1.44–61). He also speaks out against the papal league (5.1.65–76). This continued service, and particularly the element of counsel, has its effect. John takes advice for the first time since Angiers, and allows the Bastard to act in the defence of the nation. In this, as much as in his explicit speeches on the topic, the Bastard presents a rebuke to the nobles' treatment of John, and provides the solution for what they should have done. The nobles' abandonment of John plunged him into despair and the kingdom into civil war. The Bastard's continued service and counsel rescue both. Now that John is willing to take advice, the people come back to him; Salisbury admits in frustration that he 'did not think the king so stor'd with friends' (5.4.1), with friends here suggesting allies.

Yet even as this happens, John falls ill and quickly dies. There is a gesture to the traditional manner of his death in the chronicles – 'the king, I fear, is poisoned by a monk' (5.6.23) – but as many critics have pointed out, John seems to be ill before that,[63] and *The Troublesome Raigne* made much more of the murder than *King John* does, portraying both the planning (II.869–929) and execution of the poisoning (II.983–1031). More important to *King John* than the manner of John's death is the timing. He dies at the moment when the kingdom is returned as closely as possible to the *status quo ante*. The French are defeated; 'the lords are all come back' (5.6.33); and even the royal army has been swept away in a flood. There are no armies left in England, and peace both internal and external has come to the land. John dies at this moment of renewal, and his last formal act is to pardon his nobles for their rebellion (5.6.35).

With John's death, the kingdom can start anew, and the symbol of this is the appearance of the (previously unmentioned) heir to the throne, Prince Henry. He arrives, appropriately, with the returning nobles, 'in their company', and it is by his 'request' that John pardons them all (5.6.34, 35). Henry's accession will re-knit the bonds that John had broken. His reign begins with precisely that sort of delegation that John had ignored: at the lords' request Salisbury, the Bastard and the 'other lords' are placed in charge of the peace negotiations, while Henry takes direct care only of his father's funeral (5.7.93). The Bastard's final patriotic declaration cited above lands much more effectively in this context. Here it is not a religious statement of Protestant identity (as Lukas Lammers has suggested[64]) but a political statement about the nature of regal and politic government. It is not only a reminder to the nobility that they should not revolt, but also to Henry that the king – 'England' – should follow the laws and customs of the land and be 'true' to them. It is a reminder both that the initiative to do so lies with the king and that not taking that initiative can be disastrous for both king and country.

Henry was believed to have been true to those customs and laws, at least in the legal tradition which we have explored. Most Elizabethans traced Magna Carta and parliament to Henry's reign, and saw that document and institution as bulwarks against the sorts of abuses John had committed. Specifically, under Henry III Magna Carta was enacted to curb the king and parliaments began to be called on a regular basis. Magna Carta may not appear in *King John*, but its spirit lives in Henry's succession. It is the spirit not of Runnymede but of 9 Henry III, the spirit of statute and not common law.

So while we celebrate Henry, we should not go too far in condemning John. John makes mistakes, but he is not a tyrant. We cannot forget that the victory is won during John's life, even if Henry and his barons are left to work out the details of the peace.

King John is not *The Troublesome Raigne*, where Lewis declares peace only because John is dead (II.1158–60). Shakespeare's John has defeated France and made peace with his nobility; just as importantly, he has finally stopped struggling against the system in which he found himself, and learned to take counsel. In this way John exceeds Richard II's example: he adapts to the world around him and is ultimately victorious. His death seals the moment of victory by making way for a new generation that promises a more consistent future of cooperation between crown and barons, but that future is not a repudiation of John. Rather, it is a result of the final success of his career: his knowledge of his limits and his acceptance of beneficial counsel.

3

Macbeth, thanes and medieval Scottish feudalism

At first glance, there is a surprising degree of similarity between the England we have just encountered in *King John* and the Scotland of *Macbeth*. In brief, a medieval monarchy suffers from discord and rebellion. A foreign invasion threatens to topple the king, while some of the local nobles flock to the invaders' banner. The king employs a charismatic collateral member of the royal family to organize the national defence, and waits away from the battlefield to hear who won. The troubles facing Scotland under Duncan sound very similar to those facing England under John, merely substituting Norway for France (1.2.50–2), Macdonald and the Thane of Cawdor for Pembroke, Essex and their fellows (1.2.9–12, 53–4), and Macbeth for the Bastard (1.2.16). But while these troubles constitute much of the plot of *King John*, they are merely the prologue to *Macbeth*.

I am hardly the first to observe Scotland's crisis at the start of *Macbeth*. A wide variety of critics have noted the many troubles facing Duncan's kingdom at the start of the play.[1] But less attention has been paid to the solution to those problems (as well as to the other ills Scotland suffers during *Macbeth*): Malcolm's final speech, in which he transforms Scotland's thanes into earls. Most critics pass over this speech entirely.[2] Those who engage with it typically do so in one of three ways: considering it as the first stage of a repetition of the same troubles that plagued Scotland at the beginning of the play; treating it as a tyrannical consolidation of royal power; or, following Shakespeare's sources in the chronicles, seeing it as an Anglicization of Scotland that threatens the Scottish national character. This has led to a general trend in recent new historicist criticism of treating Malcolm's ascension at the end of the play as dangerous for Scotland.[3]

I believe that all of these approaches miss the point. Malcolm's reforms represent a change in the political structure of Scotland that promises an internal Scottish solution to the troubles that have plagued the country under kings both good (Duncan) and bad (Macbeth). I will show that this positive view of Malcolm's reforms derives from Shakespeare's attention to what his contemporaries knew about the political structure in medieval Scotland, in particular the role of the thanes. In *Macbeth*, Malcolm's transformation of thanes into earls represents a major step in the development of feudalism in Scotland. This change in political structure is intimately connected to other major themes of the play: the contentious language of masculinity in the play serves as a counterpoint to the nation's political maturation, while Macbeth's oft-noted psychological isolation is a manifestation of his political isolation within the old system. In each case, Shakespeare makes changes to his chronicle sources that bind these themes to the political arc of the play, ensuring that Malcolm's reforms can serve as a solution to all of Scotland's problems. This cuts against the critical tradition, most notably expressed by Lorna Hutson, which suggests the ending of the play is cyclical or otherwise pessimistic in nature, and helps to differentiate the historicism of setting from Hutson's 'circumstantial' form of reading.[4] As in *King John*, here in *Macbeth* we see Shakespeare making a choice between accounts current at the time, this time by engaging with the emerging Renaissance historiography of feudalism against the older chronicle histories. As a result, the reforms instituted by Shakespeare's Malcolm empower the nobility, stabilize the state, unite his father's proper conception of manliness with a political structure in which it can flourish and protect the king from becoming isolated.

In order to understand how Malcolm's reforms can do all this, we must first understand how Shakespeare and his potential audience might have understood the transformation from thanes to earls that lies at the heart of the reforms (5.9.28–30). This requires establishing what those terms might have meant in early modern England, especially 'thane', a title – and indeed a word – unique to *Macbeth* within the Shakespeare canon.[5] While there are no thanes in Shakespeare's other plays, there are many in *Macbeth*; the characters of Rosse (1.2.45), Cawdor (1.2.54), Glamis (1.3.48) and

Fife (4.1.71) are all explicitly called 'thane', and Lenox, Menteth, Cathness and Angus are likewise historical Scottish thanes.[6] Significantly, there is a distinct lack of other titles in the play until the end besides 'king' and 'Prince of Cumberland' (1.4.39), the title Malcolm receives from Duncan as his heir. *Macbeth* gives us a world in which the thanes and the royal house together seem to constitute the entirety of the nobility.

Although thane, unlike earl, marquess or duke, was not a title in active use in Shakespeare's time, there were three overlapping yet distinct meanings of the term in circulation during the sixteenth and early seventeenth centuries: a purely English one, a joint English and Scottish one, and a purely Scottish one. I suggest that, while all three of these meanings likely contributed how Shakespeare would have expected his audience to receive the play, the third is the most relevant for our understanding of *Macbeth*.

In the purely English context, thanes were lower nobility under the Saxons and the early Normans. The antiquarian William Lambarde found in the 'Saxon lawes' the rank of 'thein'.[7] They ranked above churls and underthanes but below earls, though social mobility was possible. Richard Hakluyt cited this definition of thane in his *Principal Navigations*, as did the slightly later John Selden in his *Titles of Honor* and Arthur Hopton in his *Concordancy of Years*.[8] These thanes were medieval figures, but Anglo-Saxon ones, not Scottish. This would make them strange in *Macbeth*, where the office of thane seems intended not as a connection to England but as a method of providing Scottish local colour alongside the many Scottish placenames.

However, Selden cites a second meaning of thane in use among the Scots as well as the Saxons: 'steward',[9] one who administers something under another's authority. His source for this is George Buchanan, the famous Scottish humanist, republican theorist and tutor to James VI (later James I) whose *History of Scotland* may well have influenced *Macbeth*.[10] This meaning of 'thane' also found its way into both John Skene's Scottish legal dictionary, *De Verborum Significatione*, and John Cowell's English one, *The Interpreter*, and was used by Sir George Buck in dedicating an eclogue to King James in 1605.[11] Similarly, William Camden's influential *Britannia* described the office of thane as 'King's Minister'.[12] In this definition, thanes were not nobility themselves but agents or ministers who acted under specific delegated authority.

The third definition of thane in use in early modern England was the most common, and the most distinctively Scottish. It referred to the baronial office of early Scotland, the holders of which administered justice and law in their territory in service of the king. This is the sense of the thane that we find in Sir Thomas Craig's *Jus Feudale*, among others. Craig is of particular interest because he represented the first wave of British scholarship on the newly emerging concept of feudalism in the early modern period. As Susan Reynolds and others have demonstrated, feudalism was not an originally medieval concept, but one originating among the 'academic lawyers and historians in the sixteenth century'.[13] In fact, Reynolds traces belief in feudalism in Britain to exactly the time of *Macbeth*'s composition, as 'before the end of the sixteenth century, the Scottish lawyers Thomas Smith and Thomas Craig had taken up the subject, and in the seventeenth Henry Spelman brought it to England'.[14] Spelman's work is actually predated in England by that of Selden and especially Lambarde explored above, though Craig was the first of them to explicitly work out a theory of feudalism as a whole ('Thomas Smith' seems to be an error[15]). Selden's work first reached print in 1610; Lambarde's, on which Selden built, was published under Elizabeth.[16]

It is somewhat unclear exactly when Craig's work was written and when it began to circulate. John Turner and others have claimed that Craig's *Jus Feudale* was published (in Latin) in 1603, only a few years before *Macbeth* was probably written.[17] More recent scholarship has cast doubt on that specific date, suggesting that Craig may have begun writing as early as 1590 and made a major revision around 1605–6, but did not actually authorize print publication before his death in 1608.[18] However, as Leslie Dodd, Craig's most recent editor, notes, while the *Jus Feudale* may not have been printed in Craig's lifetime, 'it quickly circulated among lawyers and aspirants in manuscript form' and became a widespread and well-known reference work before ever seeing print.[19] Indeed, recent scholarship on Scottish manuscript culture suggests that in the period manuscript was an alternative to print, not a lesser mode of publication.[20] It is thus possible that references to its 'publication' in 1603 (as for example in the British Library Stowe MS 385, an abridged version of the *Jus Feudale*) are to manuscript publication.[21] We do know that there was substantial cross-border movement of manuscripts, that such contact seems to have increased over time (especially after the Stuart succession) and that 'subject matter' was the primary driver of such circulation.[22] This would have put Craig's manuscript in high demand, given the immediate need after 1603 for Englishmen to learn about the Scottish legal and political traditions familiar to their new king. Even before its print publication, Craig's work was influential in Scotland, highly identified with that country and circulating widely enough to have drawn substantial notice, including an English audience (as in the Stowe manuscript).

Craig was very interested in thanes. Craig's thanes are feudal, or rather proto-feudal, barons. When Craig turns from general descriptions of feudalism to Scotland, he comments that barons are much more common in Scotland than in the Lombard sources from which feudal theory originally derived.[23] However, as he observes, the barons 'were called thanes, and their baronies thanedoms' (in the original Latin, '*thaindomes*') (332, 333). But these Scottish thane-barons were not exactly the same as barons in other nations, where the term was used broadly. In Scotland, it was a technical term for nobles given the right to judge capital cases and who were also frequently, but not always, granted the right to hold markets on their land and to build castles to defend that land (331). Thanage, then, was a limited form of feudalism, providing the thane with the right of jurisdiction but not necessarily conferring all other rights that could be held over land. This contrasts sharply in Craig's view with a fully realized feudal system (the metaphor he uses is a boy becoming a man) in which a newly enfeoffed vassal is granted 'the whole rights, liberties, and privileges' of the property unlike the more restricted rights allocated to thanes.[24] The Scottish thanes, in Craig's description, do not technically represent a rank below earls, because there were no earls at the time, but they do represent a more adolescent feudal station than earls. Thus *Macbeth*, where as I will argue we see the transition into the adult form of feudalism, presents a distinctively medieval set of political structures.

Although no other authors in the period were quite as precise as Craig was in their definitions of thanes as feudal barons, many others also identified a thane as something more than either a member of the gentry or a steward, often relating them to earls. These include claims that thanes were the same as earls,[25] references to the title of thane later evolving into that of earl (including one in Holinshed),[26] and Selden's observations that 'the *Baron* and *Thane* were often and most vsually confounded' and that a thane was 'equall with the sonne of an Earle' in rank and authority – though notably, this was only true 'after they had Earles'.[27] Before then, he notes, Scottish nobles were 'all vnder the name of *Thanes*'.[28] Skene's dictionary likewise identifies 'Thanus' as a 'name of dignitie' which 'appearis to be equall with the Sonne of ane Earle'.[29] The published *Acts and Constitutions of the Realm of Scotland*, issued in 1566, differentiated between earls and thanes, requiring greater fines for earls breaking the law as a sign of their higher rank in society.[30] Given the clear importance Shakespeare's characters place on the title of thane, as well as Malcolm's conversion of thanes into earls, the 'thanes' found in *Macbeth* seem to correspond to this Scottish noble usage: a lesser state beneath and preceding earls.

At the same time, it is possible that the other meanings of the term would have held some resonance for the audience of the play. If we posit an amalgam of these perspectives, filtered through the immediate prominence of thanes and thanedom in the play (and the absence of other titles), it seems probable that Shakespeare's thanes would have been expected to be similar to earls or English barons but to rank somewhat lower, bearing more marks of royal service or office-holding and fewer of independent nobility. For example, we might expect to see Shakespeare's thanes' titles being transferred through means other than inheritance more easily than would be the case for a more mature feudal title, while expecting them to have little power to oppose or foil the efforts of the king, unlike the earls and dukes of the English history plays. As we shall see, the play itself shows precisely this relationship, and in fact comes very close to the feudal conception of the title seen in Craig.

Beyond their position in the hierarchy of nobility, there are other signs that suggest Shakespeare's thanes correspond to a specifically feudal model rather than to a more general view of thanes as 'lesser'. The first indication is the treatment of the unnamed thane of Cawdor who precedes Macbeth in that title. Upon hearing of his treachery, Duncan declares 'no more that Thane of Cawdor shall deceive / Our bosom interest. – Go pronounce his present death, / And with his former title greet Macbeth' (1.2.64–6). This moment has received some critical attention: John Kerrigan claims Duncan violates the law of inheritance, while David Norbrook argues that the transfer is legitimate because the law of heritability was not yet established.[31] The play seems to stand between these two positions.

Some thanedoms seem to have been inherited: Macbeth mentions that 'by Sinel's death, I know, I am Thane of Glamis' (1.3.71), and Sinel is the name of Macbeth's father in Shakespeare's sources.[32] But at the same time no one seems bothered by Macbeth's sudden elevation to Cawdor, and it was understood in the seventeenth century that the inheritance of thanedoms had not been automatic. It was widely believed that at the time of Macbeth's reign in the eleventh century an inherited title was a special privilege.[33] In transferring the thanedom of Cawdor to Macbeth, then, Duncan only violates a norm if we believe medieval Scotland to be a mature feudal state at the beginning of the play, where all the thanedoms would be heritable. If we take it to be otherwise, Duncan's action is perfectly normal: since the thane of Cawdor is condemned, his thanedom is available to be awarded to Macbeth. Since, as Craig attests, Scottish thanedoms were often given in exchange for meritorious military service, the transfer of an estate to a man who deserved such a reward would be a fitting solution to the problem of a treacherous thane (205).

Taking this perspective into account also helps clarify the situation surrounding the delivery of the thanedom of Cawdor to Macbeth. When Angus and Rosse seek out Macbeth to tell him of his good fortune, the interaction at first seems a bit strange. Angus insists that they come 'only to herald thee in to [Duncan's] sight, / Not pay thee', while Rosse adds that 'for an earnest of a greater honour, / He bade me, from him, call thee Thane of Cawdor' (1.3.103–4, 105–6). Maurice Hunt has drawn attention to oddness of this moment, claiming that this scene implies that 'the entity "Thane of Cawdor" thus amounts to little more than the greeting Duncan specifies'.[34] However, I argue, what Angus and Rosse say derives from a specific aspect of the early feudal system: the delay between the delivery of a title and the possession of its lands known technically as 'improper investiture'.[35] Angus and Rosse here signal to Macbeth that Duncan himself will later provide the actual delivery of the lands while they are simply the messengers of the transfer of the rank and title.

Interestingly, two of them come to deliver this news, even though Duncan appears to give the charge to Rosse alone (1.2.65–7). This would have made the transfer legal: Angus's arrival (along with Banquo's presence) would ensure the presence of sufficient witnesses for the investiture to hold.[36] The use of multiple witnesses for this kind of event strengthens the overall sense that Shakespeare here seems to be working out a real legal and political system, one with a distinct sense of how investiture works.

The curious status of Banquo also supports the idea that Shakespeare's thanes are feudal ones. In Shakespeare's sources, Banquo is called a thane, but in the play he is one of the few adult male characters who are not given that title. This matters because he is a particular kind of thane in the sources: a steward, not a baron. Buck's eclogue specifically called Fleance, Banquo's son, a thane in this sense.[37] In Holinshed and in Hector Boece's *Chronicles of Scotland*, Banquo collects taxes on Duncan's behalf, acting more like an officer of the crown than a noble.[38] Most explicitly, John Leslie's *De Rebus Gestis Scotorum* describes Banquo as 'regium ... Thanum', king's thane.[39] This construction is typical of the description of lesser thanes, and not of the feudal thanes. Selden, for instance, cites 'kings thane' for the Anglo-Saxon type of thane, and 'quaestor regius', king's magistrate, for the type that were primarily stewards, while giving the baronial thanes no such possessive modifier.[40] I would suggest that Shakespeare understood Banquo to be one of these lesser kinds of thanes, and removed his title – leaving him the only major male Scottish character in the play *without* a title – in order to maintain Banquo's slightly lower status without making it explicit. If Shakespeare were not aware of the differences between these types of thanes, it would seem strange that Banquo, one of the few characters explicitly called a thane in his sources, is one of the few not so named in the play. However, once we take into account that Shakespeare's thanes occupy a particular rank and office – one Banquo did not share – it is far less surprising to see him lacking this title.

Other signs in the play, particularly surrounding the theme of loyalty, suggest that Shakespeare made use of a feudal model for thanes. When Macbeth, as king, begins to question Macduff's loyalty, he and his wife discuss sending for Macduff as a first step in dealing with him (3.4.127–8). This moment shows us the Macbeths's paranoia, but it also corresponds to the feudal requirement that a formal summons was required before a title could be revoked.[41] In the opposite direction, Macduff's unwillingness to serve Macbeth is justified in Craig's terms because vassals could refuse to serve if the lord was known to be in the wrong, even in a case where the superior fought in self-defence.[42] This kind of negotiation around formal and informal requirements of office is appropriate to the strange position thanes were seen to have held: not merely royal officers subject to a king's whim but something more, yet still not possessed of the full independence that, for instance, John's vassals displayed (however wrongly) in *King John*.

But while this last point would only justify a refusal to aid Macbeth, the feudal model also helps us to understand the thanes' active support for Malcolm's claim to the throne. Within the play, this support derives from the perception that Malcolm represents 'the medicine of the sickly weal', and that therefore following him will allow them to 'give obedience where 'tis truly owed' by allying with Malcolm to save their country from the harm inflicted by Macbeth (5.2.27, 26). This relates to the concept we find in Craig that a king who sets about to destroy the country relieves the vassal of his obligations in a way that paves the way for this sort of resistance.[43] This position justifies the thanes in their desire to enact 'our country's purge' (5.2.29). This phrase in turn ties into the frequent use of medical terminology in this part of the play, from the English Doctor and his mention of King Edward curing 'the Evil' in his subjects (4.3.146) to the Scottish Doctor whom Macbeth repeatedly asks for purgatives to heal the land (5.3.52, 55–6). Scotland is sick, and it is clearly the role of the king to heal it, as we see in Edward's example and Macbeth's thwarted desire. Both Macbeth and the thanes lead us to expect this cure to take the form of a 'purge', healing by bloodletting or laxative: that is, by removing what is harmful out of the body.[44] Macbeth hopes this will be satisfied by expelling the invading English; the thanes expect to achieve it by killing Macbeth.

But *Macbeth* itself leads us towards a third option, one already invoked by Macbeth in a different context when he recalls a past moment when 'humane statute purged the gentle weal' (3.4.74). He imagined these statutes putting an end to murder as an acceptable behaviour: although murders have still been committed 'since' (3.4.75), they are now 'too terrible for the ear' (3.4.76). Malcolm will enact this kind of statutory purge through his reforms, ridding Scotland not only of Macbeth and his murders, but of the entire political structure that has made the nation ill.

But before Malcolm's reforms can heal the country, both he and the thanes must be satisfied of each others' loyalty. This makes the mutual testing of Malcolm and Macduff in Act Four, Scene Three, crucial because Macduff is the first thane to back Malcolm. In this scene, Malcolm tests whether Macduff holds the proper feudal attitude about a king whose commands will lead to ruin of the country. The sequence of Malcolm's questions and Macduff's responses is important here. First Malcolm claims 'voluptuousness' and an insatiable sexual appetite, and Macduff replies that 'we have willing dames enough' (4.3.61, 73). Then Malcolm blames himself for 'staunchless avarice', and Macduff tells him 'Scotland hath foisons to fill up your will / Of your mere own' (4.3.78, 88–9). It is only when Malcolm goes beyond mere vices to calling himself a man who 'had I power', would 'pour the sweet milk of concord into hell, / Uproar the universal peace, confound / All unity on earth' (4.3.97, 98–100) that Macduff refuses to consider supporting him, and indeed threatens his life. In the feudal context, we can see that Macduff's breaking point is entirely appropriate. Only the ruin of the country can justify the refusal to serve, or an attack on the king, and neither lust nor greed is sufficient reason for it. However, a king who destroyed concord and peace would be unfit, and his nobles would have a positive duty to resist him in order to restore that concord and that peace.

But if Malcolm is testing Macduff, Macduff is also testing Malcolm, and Malcolm too must at some point give the right answer. His crucial response is the assurance that 'what I am truly / Is thine and my poor country's to command' (4.3.131–2). Here he expresses a willingness to do whatever Macduff and the Scots think is necessary for the well-being of the nation. A concern for the state as a whole is as central to his affirmation as it was to Macduff's horror. Only when both sides are satisfied can they proceed together to defeat Macbeth and produce Malcolm's statutory 'purge' of Scotland's ills.

To see how Malcolm's reforms will heal the state, let us examine just what those reforms are actually intended to accomplish. We have already explored the varied meanings of 'thane' in early modern England; now we must see how one differs from an 'earl'. Once again, we find Shakespeare turning to a feudal model. Unlike the baron-thanes, there was no distinctively Scottish definition of earl. Rather than a distinctively Scottish limited grant of jurisdiction, an earldom was a full and complete feudal title (213). Also unlike a thanedom, it was always heritable.[45] The shorter version of this, expressed by Lambarde, was that while a thane might be many things, an earl was always a nobleman.[46] And as such, earls had more rights than thanes.[47] In other words, by making his thanes earls, Malcolm takes Scotland from the youth of feudalism into its maturity.

This change has the potential to heal Scotland in several ways. First, it reduces the potential for tyranny by strengthening the positions of the nobles and reducing reliance on individual royal judgement and trust. We can see this vision of the importance of earls in Giovanni Botero's *Traveler's Breviat*, which describes various Asian nations as 'tyrannicall' because 'They knowe not what an Earle ... meaneth'.[48] Rather than having a hereditary system, the king 'giueth al magistracies and honors', and the nobles, such as they are, 'dispatch no matter of weight without his priuitie'.[49] These conditions for tyranny are present in thane-filled Scotland and are precisely what Malcolm intends to fix. The new earls are hereditary lords, with full power over their lands and the freedom to know that their heirs will inherit after them.

They are also all now royal counsellors by virtue of their earldoms. When Duncan 'built / An absolute trust' (1.4.13–14) on the (first) disloyal thane of Cawdor, and then chose Macbeth to receive that title, he selected counsellors for himself, and did so poorly. Under Malcolm's new system, all his earls will be bound to give him advice, allowing him to hear new voices.[50] As such, it reverses Macbeth's paranoid unwillingness to trust anyone or hear advice, since the bonds of help and counsel are mutual and reciprocal. This remains true even if, as in *King John*, the king is not always bound to act upon the counsel he receives.

The dangers of royally inspired murder and warfare that Malcolm himself had proposed to Macduff are also defused by this change. In a true feudal arrangement like an earldom, only one's own active malfeasance could dispossess a lord (213). This would make Malcolm's threat to destroy the Scottish lords for wealth (4.3.84) more difficult, if not impossible, since the earls would hold all rights over their lands, not just the right to enforce the king's law. It would also mean that a king would find it much harder to destroy the 'universal peace', since substantially less power would be concentrated in his hands, and his earls would be even more clearly bound to disobey him if he attempts the ruin of the country (4.3.99). This sense of limitation speaks to Botero's point that a king without earls is obeyed 'not as a king, but rather as a God', but one with earls is served in a more restricted way that is less conducive to tyranny.[51] Here, I argue, Malcolm substantially decreases the degree to which the fate of Scotland lies in the hands of the king alone and increases the collective power of the former thanes.

Malcolm's reforms also answer the native Scottish desire to 'receive free honours' (3.6.36), that is, the desire to have titles freely given by the king to ennoble and empower his thanes, instead of being kept under royal control as a play for power. They also satisfy another potential meaning of 'free' in this context by producing titles not bound to the king's pleasure but held independently. A similar impulse once featured in Duncan's promise – never fulfilled because of his murder – that 'signs of nobleness, like stars, shall shine / On all deservers' (1.4.41–2). Malcolm at first sounds as if he will, like his father, leave this task for the future: 'we shall not spend a large expense of time / Before we reckon with your several loves' (5.9.26–7). His invocation even echoes his father's, calling on his 'thanes and kinsmen' as his father called on his 'sons, kinsmen, thanes' (5.9.28, 1.4.35). But, in keeping with the wider distribution of trust among all the nobles noted above, Malcolm omits his father's reference to 'you whose places are the nearest' (1.4.36). Moreover, while Duncan left the delivery of his promise for later, Malcolm's audience has only to wait a single line to hear themselves declared earls. Malcolm thus fulfils the promise his father had made, as well as his own, but does so in an innovative way. He does not pile up existing honours in multiples, as Duncan did in rewarding Macbeth by joining the thaneship of Cawdor to that of Glamis, but instead creates and awards a new honour, one that heals the damaged state structurally at the same time that it rewards his followers.

Given these changes to the state, we can see that Malcolm's reforms are not an 'absolutist' change, or one aimed at 'reducing the aristocracy'.[52] Rather, they invite the aristocracy to be a part of the new political structure in a more sustainable way, as equal royal counsellors who no longer hold their titles at the king's pleasure. The purpose of this is not to produce 'a return to, a cycle of, tyranny and violence', as Sharon O'Dair suggests we see at the end of the play, but a breaking of the cycle that we have already seen in the reigns of Duncan and Macbeth.[53] Malcolm's reforms have concrete consequences that are directly aimed at the needs of the Scottish state.

Close attention to the heightened significance of Malcolm's reforms helps distinguish the historicism of setting from Hutson's work on circumstances. Hutson identifies a mode of legal-rhetorical thinking in the early modern period interested in the conditions under which events happen and are understood – circumstances – which she then applies to Shakespeare's dramatic creations.[54] Included among these circumstances are when and where an action occurred, questions with obvious relevance to the issue of setting, which is all about time and place. But when Hutson examines this mode of thinking, the issues of when and where that are revealed are more local and limited than they are in my consideration of the historicism of setting. 'When' becomes an issue of relative timing of events within a narrative, part of a series of 'time-related topic questions' along with 'how long?' or 'how old?' rather than a broader question of where in history a play takes place.[55] Similarly, 'where' becomes a question of relative location, related to issues of 'absence' and 'movement', rather than an issue of what political state the action is located within.[56] Obviously these questions are still linked. To answer how long something has been going on, one must know what time it is, just as to answer where we are going we must know something of where we are and have been. But for Hutson these issues are contingent, a part of the action being presented rather than of the conditions that shape that action. Likewise, they are always rooted in perceptions of the plot, but not necessarily in knowledge or assumptions about the time and place of the setting.

When it comes to *Macbeth*, in particular, this means that she looks to views of the contemporary Renaissance English and Scottish states, and not the medieval ones: to James VI and Buchanan's contemporary political tracts and not to Lambarde or Craig.[57] Ironically, this means that our friend Robert Snagg's preface makes an appearance in Hutson's reading of *Macbeth*, as part of a reading of early modern Scottish political thought as less legally centred than its English counterpart.[58] This leads Hutson to the odd conclusion that there is an 'absence of any identification of the monarchy with the laws and customs of the country' in *Macbeth*.[59] This shows the difference between Hutson's 'circumstances' and the historicism of setting, given what I have argued about the centrality of those laws and customs, as expressed in the political structure of the Scottish state, to both Malcolm's reforms and

Duncan's and Macbeth's failures. In the historicism of setting, the questions of when and where set conditions that point us towards the non-early modern or non-English political and social milieu through which we should interpret the action; for Hutson, they are relative questions we ask about the action within a more local early modern context. Thus for Hutson, the Macbeths's unchecked violence means that there is no 'politically viable state' at the end of *Macbeth*,[60] while I propose that looking at Malcolm's reforms through the lens of the historicism of setting shows us that one has just been established.

Malcolm's political reforms are not limited to the establishment of the earldoms. He also makes two other specific, intertwined promises: 'calling home our exil'd friends abroad / That fled the snares of watchful tyranny', and 'producing forth the cruel ministers / Of this dead butcher, and his fiend-like Queen' (5.9.32–5). These combine to indicate an entire turnover of royal advisors and functionaries. Malcolm's 'friends', his allied earls, will replace Macbeth's 'ministers' as the new Scotland replaces the old. Since the only 'ministers' of Macbeth we see are messengers, murderers and Seyton, it is no wonder that Malcolm calls them 'cruel'. Yet we know Macbeth has other ministers. Earlier in the play he told Lady Macbeth he had 'a servant fee'd' in every noble house (3.4.130). The absence from the stage of these other 'ministers' of his contributes strongly to the sense that the Macbeths act alone. But whether or not any ministers of Macbeth's appear onstage, the turnover Malcolm promises contributes to the theme of changing royal counsel implied by the change from thanes to earls. Malcolm will listen to new voices, and they will not include the voices that spoke to the tyrant Macbeth. Nor will they be the same advisers that served Duncan, or at least they cannot include the two dead disloyal thanes of Cawdor who betrayed his trust.

At the same time that Shakespeare emphasizes the positive potential of Malcolm's reforms for healing Scotland, he reduces the negative effects with which they might be associated. One such association that I suggest Shakespeare purposely avoids is the narrative of Anglicized decline presented in his major chronicle sources, Holinshed, Boece and Buchanan. These authors agree with *Macbeth*, and with the other sources on Malcolm III's reign available in the period, that Malcolm introduced the title of earl into Scotland.[61] Unlike the other sources, however, and unlike

Macbeth, each of these authors adds a moral condemnation of the new titles. Boece refers to the 'vane glore & ambution of honouris' (connected in his mind to 'the arrogance and pride of Inglismen') as the cause of the introduction of 'new names of nobilite', including earls.[62] In the 1587 Holinshed, this becomes a 'vaine shadow of the Germane honor and titles of nobilitie', once again linked to 'the English maner'.[63] For Buchanan they are 'new and foreign [i.e. English] titles of distinction', and thus 'barbarous'.[64] In the chronicles, therefore, Malcolm's action is intimately linked to the supposed decline of Scottish manhood and the introduction of what Shakespeare's Macbeth calls 'English epicures' (5.3.8), even though over the course of his long reign he eventually becomes a good king.

Just as Macbeth's insult is robbed of its power by its speaker and its timing – Macbeth hurls it in the moment he discovers the thanes have abandoned him and joined Malcolm and his English allies – Shakespeare more generally avoids and even reverses his narrative sources' condemnation of this aspect of the transition between Macbeth and Malcolm. In *Macbeth*, Malcolm's creation of earls does not represent a reduction in Scottish manliness; instead, the end of the play sees the restoration of a healthy model of manliness alongside the political reforms. At the same time, those political reforms serve primarily not as an Anglicization of Scotland but as a reform of the Scottish system that responds to the country's own political and social needs.

On the issue of manliness, it is clear in the world of *Macbeth* that Macbeth is wrong about the 'English epicures'. Siward, the primary English character, is a Stoic, not an Epicurean, and as such takes the death of his son in battle with equanimity: 'Why then, God's soldier be he! / Had I as many sons as I have hairs, / I would not wish them to a fairer death: / And so, his knell is knoll'd' (5.9.13–16). Instead of Siward, it is the Scots, Rosse and Malcolm, who express sorrow for young Siward's loss, and even that sorrow is restrained: 'he's worth more sorrow, / And that I'll spend for him' (5.9.16–17). Young Siward himself fights manfully (if ineffectively) against Macbeth, never giving in to fear; he has 'his hurts before' (5.9.12). These two Englishmen, the Siwards, are a direct counterexample to the idea that Malcolm's English ties produced a reduction in Scottish manliness. No Scot in the play is presented as being as bluff, honest and courageous as they are. But the question of the changing Scottish character under Malcolm and Macbeth goes beyond the direct comparison between Englishmen and Scots and touches on the larger discourse of manhood and manliness in the play.

While manliness in *Macbeth* is frequently discussed in relation to the act of sex itself,[65] the discourse I refer to centres on the expression of gender roles in the play. The characters repeatedly debate what manliness means: who is a man, what actions are manly, what men should be and do. In these moments, we can identify two models of manliness in competition throughout the play. The Macbeths's manliness relies on an aggressive masculinity that distances them from a more positive model of manliness that emphasizes the coexistence of aggressive and nurturing instincts in the whole person. Ultimately, the more inclusive category is triumphant, a victory that joins with Malcolm's political innovations to produce a Scotland in which masculine ideals and political reality are at last in harmony.

The Macbeths's version of manliness is inherently secretive and violent. Lady Macbeth dares Macbeth to 'Be so much more the man' (1.7.51) through Duncan's murder, and he in turn challenges his hired murderers to show where they stand in the 'rank of manhood' (3.1.102) when asking them to kill Banquo. In addition to violence, a key factor in this model of manly action is secrecy, the insistence that 'false face must hide what the false heart doth know' (1.7.83) and the need to 'mask[] the business from the common eye' (3.1.127). Committing this secret violence is deeply connected to the rejection of the feminine: first through Lady Macbeth's desire to be 'unsex[ed]' and have her 'woman's breasts' lose their 'milk for gall' as she plots Duncan's murder (1.5.41, 47, 48), then through her expressed willingness to commit infanticide (1.7.54–9) and Macbeth's admiring desire to have her 'bring forth men-children only / For thy undaunted mettle should compose / Nothing but males' (1.7.73–5).

But this violent model of masculinity that rejects the feminine fails. Duncan, as several critics have suggested, began the play by modeling a different, more inclusive version of masculinity.[66] He is shown as possessing a mix of traditionally masculine and feminine attributes and, I argue, serves as a model for the sort of manliness that makes use of the entire scope of human emotion and ability. Malcolm and Macduff in turn restore this softer version of masculinity when they triumph over Macbeth. As William Liston has noted, Macduff's statement that he will 'feel it [his family's murder] as a man' (4.3.224), along with Malcolm's later approval that 'this tune goes manly' (4.3.238), places us back in a world with 'a larger and more encompassing definition of *manly* [and of *man*]'.[67] I take this to be not just a general return to a less violent masculinity but an explicit rejection of the Macbeths's model, coming as it does both in a moment of reported infanticide (with Macduff's actual loss of his children mirroring Lady Macbeth's imagined one) and immediately after a discussion of the potential for rebellion and regicide.

I argue that we see the culmination of this expansive model of manliness, and the rejection of the Macbeth's narrower one, in Malcolm's final speech. There, he speaks of what 'would be planted newly with the time', recalling Duncan's earlier language of fertility – particularly the idea that he 'ha[s] begun to plant' Macbeth and Banquo in his heart (5.9.31, 1.4.28). Malcolm shares his father's willingness to embrace the nurturing side of his humanity, but does so in a new political context in which such nurturing can have its full effect. Duncan plants individuals within the king's own grace, sometimes to good effect, as with Banquo, and sometimes bad, as with the two thanes of Cawdor. Malcolm plants social change on a larger scale: the calling back of exiled friends and the removal of evil ministers. Duncan's 'plantings' could not help but reflect the old Scotland, in which every political action mattered only in terms of individuals' relations to the king. Malcolm, by contrast, structures his planting in terms of large-scale systemic change. Even as he speaks to individuals of their 'several loves' and his 'exiled friends' (5.9.27, 32), his actual solution is general, not individual. He thus joins a broad perspective on political change with the properly nurturing, incorporative model of the male self that does not fear its feminine side or require putting on a public face different from his own. He rejects both the system in which both Duncan and Macbeth operated and the model of masculinity that Macbeth has represented.

These changes are more closely related than they might otherwise seem. The model of manliness Duncan and his son represent is one that emphasizes the importance of the entire self working together in harmony. Malcolm's political change ushers in this sort of collective response on the national scale. Like the unified masculine and feminine aspects of a proper man, the earls and the king share responsibility for the kingdom in a way the thanes and king did not. This political change also serves as a pledge of Malcolm's allegiance to his father's kind of emotionally open masculinity. By bringing together these more unified approaches to masculinity and to political organization, Malcolm produces a Scotland that is fundamentally healthier than it was at the beginning of the play. The king is no longer isolated in power, and his manliness is no longer an isolated part of his soul. This leaves no room for Holinshed's, Boece's and Buchanan's belief that the introduction of earls ruined Scottish manhood. Instead, the change reinforces the positive model of manliness already present in Scotland under Duncan.

Just as Shakespeare rejects his narrative sources' perspective on changing Scottish manliness, he also reduces their emphasis on Anglicization. Kerrigan rightly points out that Malcolm's explicit reference to the title's novelty in Scotland specifically implies a contrast to other polities, where there are already earls (5.9.29–30).[68] However, unlike his sources, Shakespeare does not make this a reference to England. It is important to note that there are no English earls in *Macbeth*, only Scottish ones. Siward is given no title beyond the name of his territory, Northumberland. This usage contrasts strongly with Holinshed, in which Siward is identified both in the text and in the marginal annotations as an 'earle'.[69] The kind of continental humanist context that produced Craig's work would suggest a French, German or Italian context for the new earls, and indeed Craig traces the creation and institution of the title to Charlemagne and his successors, using Lombard texts originally interpreted by French scholars (325–7). Craig even argued explicitly that feudalism came to Scotland before it came to England because of traditional Scottish connections with France, which would imply a French context for Malcolm's reference, rather than an English one.[70]

Another possible non-English context for the creation of earls comes from the nature of the word 'earl' itself. The word is Danish, as is the word 'thane'; Lambarde's Saxon documents used both. The Danish roots of the word were much discussed in the period, though of course it is difficult to know how far such knowledge would have penetrated. William Camden derived 'earl' from the Danish and Saxon 'ear' or 'ar', meaning 'honor',[71] while Cowell calls it a 'word made by the Danes'.[72] John Speed's geography of Britain even differentiated between the Saxon title of ealderman and the specifically Danish title of earl.[73] Danish, though, was spoken not only in early medieval England because of the Saxons, but also in and around Scotland and Ireland as well. Holinshed describes Malcolm II, Duncan's father, as spending most of his reign fighting off Danish incursions from the islands surrounding northern Scotland, while Malcolm III himself had to fight an insurrection in those same lands.[74] The 'Kernes and Gallowglasses' from the 'western isles' who fight with the rebel Macdonwald in Act One of *Macbeth* would have come from these Danish strongholds (1.2.12–13). It is from just this sort of cultural contact that 'thane' also entered into Scottish use.

More generally, the historiography of feudal earls originated with French and Italian scholars more than it did with English ones (although continental earls were usually called counts, *comites*, as Craig does). Thus even if Shakespeare and his contemporaries were unaware of Craig's historiography of feudalism, the larger intellectual context of the newly developing understanding of feudalism in the period would have pointed to the probability of a non-English origin for the title. Therefore, while it is unquestionably true that Malcolm, as nephew to Siward and friend of Edward the Confessor, has a closer relationship to England than Macbeth had, the introduction of earls at the end is not Anglicizing in and of itself. In fact, it could be seen as an innovation that bypassed any English example and looked to the continent for inspiration.

I suggest that this may help to explain why the end of the play does not appear to have been viewed as politically dangerous at the time. Critics have suggested the depiction of a 'blanket dispersing of English titles to Scottish lords' ought to have seemed controversial under James I, who had been accused of doing something similar himself.[75] But Malcolm's structural reform is not analogous to James's personal favouritism, since it is a response to specific threats already established within the play, and the title 'earl' is not marked as distinctively English in the play.

Furthermore, Malcolm's other reforms point towards a relative decrease, not an increase, in English influence. The 'exil'd friends abroad' that Malcolm promises to recall are unlikely to be those who fled to England. Those friends have already come back with Malcolm's army, as we see in the cases of Rosse and Macduff. Instead, Malcolm is promising to bring back the friends who went to other lands, such as Donalbane, who went to 'Ireland' (2.3.139), or Fleance, whom Holinshed describes as fleeing to 'Wales'.[76]

Their return would dilute the impact of the English refugees who have returned with Malcolm by introducing other, countervailing influences to the state. Malcolm's introduction of earls is simply the first part of an entire package of reforms, which combine to change the Scottish state in ways that go well beyond merely making it a mirror of England. Shakespeare does not give us a Malcolm who rules like Duncan, like Macbeth, or even like King Edward of England. Instead he gives us a Malcolm who uniquely identifies and corrects Scotland's own pre-existing problems.

Ultimately, the value of Malcolm's reforms is specifically tied to the nature of thanes and earls. Without this context, we might imagine, with Lukas Lammers, that Malcolm's 'alleged restoration of order seems fragile or even futile' and 'the very lines that promise change also echo the play's past', or with Hutson that Scotland is a land of 'radical political instability'.[77] After all, we have seen kings promise titles and reforms before, and the disappearance of the distinctively Scottish thanedoms might seem ominous if we imagine earldoms as a spectre of Anglicization. But once we recognize the distinctive, targeted nature of Malcolm's reforms, and their particular connection to the troubles that have dogged Scotland throughout the play, we can see that change here triumphs over repetition: that Malcolm has clearly identified not an opportunity to make Scotland more English, but a chance to make Scotland more itself and heal the damaged state.

The final speech in which Malcolm makes these reforms is one of Shakespeare's major innovations in the play, drawing not only on this model of feudal thanage but on two other substantial changes Shakespeare made from his sources: the removal of Macbeth's period of good rule, and the excision of his heir. Each of these changes has significant implications not only for the moment of Malcolm's ascension, but for the character of Macbeth. Shakespeare's portrait of Macbeth is more domestic, more isolated and more self-focused than Holinshed's is, and the difference arises from the very changes that give weight to Malcolm's reforms.

In Boece's and Holinshed's accounts, Macbeth did not become a tyrant immediately upon his coronation. Instead he initially governed 'in Iustice', such that if he had 'continued in vprightnesse of iustice as he began, till the end of his reigne, he might well haue béene numbred amongst the most noble princes that anie where had reigned'.[78] He issued a just code of law, which both sources reproduce at length, and which Craig uses as a source to prove the existence of barons in Scotland (101).[79] It is only after ten years of good rule that he becomes the tyrant that Malcolm overthrows.[80] After this change in Macbeth, Shakespeare and his sources are once again close, but the initial ten years of good governance are entirely absent from Shakespeare's play. If anything, they are given to Duncan, who appears as an older, wiser and better king than he is in the chronicles.

This change might stem from dramatic convenience, since it is probably easier to portray a Macbeth who does not turn from Duncan's murder to become a good king only to return to murder Banquo a decade later. Yet Shakespeare did not shy away from such sudden reversals in his other plays. Richard III changes emotions rapidly and frequently, and though he remains a tyrant often shows a different face to the world, while the Leontes at the beginning of Act One and, more importantly, Act Five of *Winter's Tale* has seemingly little in common with the Leontes of Acts Two and Three. Shakespeare could have written the changing Macbeth his sources gave him, and made as memorable a character. But he did not. And I suggest that he did not because of what those ten years represented in his sources: the correction of the ills of Scotland, and the rectifying of 'all enormeteis that fell be febyll ad|ministration of king Duncane'.[81] In the chronicles, the troubles under Duncan and those under Macbeth are separate problems, with separate causes and solutions. Shakespeare eliminates Macbeth's ten-year reign of justice in order to bring those troubles together and make them a continuous whole, while transferring the 'enormities' to Macbeth. He then transposes the healing of the country from Macbeth to Malcolm. In Holinshed's account, Macbeth makes 'holesome laws and statutes for the publike weale of his subiects',[82] helping to cure the state after Duncan's mismanagement. Shakespeare has Macduff echo this word while wondering when Scotland will see its '*wholesome* days again' (4.3.105) (emphasis mine), but Macduff is speaking of Macbeth's errors rather than Duncan's. Shakespeare's Macbeth participates in precisely the troubles that Holinshed's Macbeth attempts to cure.

By making these changes, Shakespeare produces a single tragedy out of the chronicle Macbeth's double one. He is not the valiant man struggling against the system but betrayed by his own impulses that we have seen in *King John*. Instead he is a man who lets his private ambition, lashed on by his wife, overwhelm his loyalty, his good sense and his understanding of virtue. To this end, Shakespeare transforms Duncan from a young and feeble king in the sources to an older, wiser man who 'hath borne his faculties so meek, hath been / So clear in his great office, that his virtues / Will plead like angels, trumpet-tongu'd, against / The deep damnation of his taking off' (1.7.17–20). Boece's and Holinshed's Macbeth would never have spoken so well of his victim because their Duncans had committed so many 'enormities and abuses' for Macbeth to solve, including a number of 'seditious attempts', from which 'much trouble dailie rose in the realme'.[83] While Scotland under Shakespeare's Duncan underwent difficult times, given the crisis with which the play starts, there is no suggestion that this results from Duncan's misrule. The political unrest appears to be less a commentary on Duncan's leadership and more a result of the systemic insecurity of the state before Malcolm's reforms. For all of Shakespeare's Duncan's virtues, his Scotland is in trouble, no less than is Macbeth's. Malcolm's reforms solve these structural problems by tying the nobility more closely to the state, thus reducing both internal unrest and the opportunity for foreign invaders to obtain support from disaffected lords, as both Norway and Malcolm did.

If Shakespeare differs from his sources by making his Macbeth uniformly tyrannical, it is unsurprising that he also differs from those same sources by ending Macbeth's faction with Macbeth's death, or perhaps it is better to say by removing that faction entirely. Shakespeare's Macbeth plots his regicide with his wife only, whereas in Holinshed there is an entire 'conspiracy to murder Duncan', including Banquo and others, as Henry Paul has pointed out.[84] Certainly Paul is right that one of the reasons this is absent from Shakespeare's play is a desire to show James I's ancestor, Banquo, in a better light. Yet I would note that Shakespeare removes not only Banquo's involvement but also the entire conspiracy. The Macbeths of *Macbeth* have no factional supporters to spur them to the crown, only themselves.

In this Shakespeare borrows from Holinshed and Boece but not from the history of Macbeth. Instead, this material is taken from the earlier murder of King Duffe by Donwald, who was 'kindled in wrath by the words of his wife', and 'determined to follow hir adluise in the execution of so heinous an act' as killing Duffe at their home.[85] Macbeth in Holinshed also acts at his wife's urging,[86] but she is not involved in the actual murder plot itself, which is planned by Macbeth, Banquo and their friends. Shakespeare places Lady Macbeth at the centre of the murder plot, as in the story of Duffe, but removes the servants who did the actual killing, after Donwald and his wife put Duffe's guards to sleep.[87] Shakespeare therefore achieves a double reduction in the number of conspirators, first from a wide swath of the nobility down to the Macbeth household via the Duffe story, and then from that whole household down to only its two primary members: Macbeth and Lady Macbeth. Shakespeare creates the entire character of Lady Macbeth out of the mere hint in Holinshed (and, as Ryan Davidson has noted, possibly in William Stewart's *Buik of the Croniclis of Scotland*[88]), and gives her to Macbeth as his only co-conspirator. In doing so, he turns a public drama into a private one because Macbeth's only connection is within his marriage. They hide everything from all outsiders, a pathological need tied to their arguments about manliness that drives her insane and leaves him utterly alone. This loneliness comes into focus during the banquet scene. Despite their best efforts, they repeatedly separate themselves from the nobility at the table, and ultimately from each other.

Shakespeare emphasized Macbeth's isolation at the end of the play through another change from his sources. His Macbeth is left at the last only with 'constrained things, / Whose hearts are absent too' (5.4.13–14). He has no true believers, no diehard allies, except himself. His wife dies, leaving him no family and, crucially, no heirs. Boece, Holinshed and Buchanan all tell that story differently. In their accounts, Macbeth's supporters remained strong enough to crown another king after Macbeth's death (the doomed Lugtake[89]) though not strong enough to defeat Malcolm. Lugtake was, as Holinshed writes, 'either the sonne, or (as some write) the coosen' of Macbeth, and his supporters were those who still backed the claim of the now-slain Macbeth.[90] Malcolm and Macduff were able to defeat this new threat rather quickly, but the episode suggests a different picture of the Scottish response to Malcolm than is found in *Macbeth*.

By isolating Macbeth in this way, Shakespeare gives him only one real connection at the end: to the audience. We and we alone know how he thinks, why he acts and the price he has paid to become what he has become. In the play's final act he becomes a version of the man who does not belong in his world, not for the reasons we will later see for Caius Martius but to a similar effect. Holinshed's Macbeth is not a tragic figure; his struggle is neither lonely nor doomed, merely unsuccessful. Shakespeare's Macbeth is all three because Shakespeare has removed every support he might have had. Macbeth's willing followers – and successor – do not exist, and by the end, even Lady Macbeth is gone.

Macbeth's isolation makes him an extreme avatar of the political system that Malcolm will replace. In that system, the thanes administer the king's justice but all power ultimately sits in his hands. The king is truly alone in power at the centre of the state. Macbeth's troubles mirror this, as he becomes less and less able or willing to place trust in anyone or delegate any authority to others.[91] At the same time, as we have seen, his use of a violent, secretive model for manliness isolates him from those he might have relied on, including Lady Macbeth. As Macbeth's psychological walls close in, he becomes almost a parody of the kind of king that the Scottish political system seems designed to produce: self-willed, untrusting and therefore weak. That *Macbeth*'s Duncan is not such a king is a testament to how much Shakespeare changes the character that he found in his narrative sources in order to emphasize Macbeth's own problems. But Macbeth himself certainly is this kind of a weak king, despite his physical prowess. Macbeth's violent masculinity led him to murder his only friend, Banquo, while Malcolm and Macduff, through their mutual testing and their shared model of manliness, create a bond Macbeth can no longer equal. By isolating Macbeth in this particular way, Shakespeare makes Malcolm the antithesis of everything Macbeth stands for, increasing the sense at the end of the play that the old order has been swept entirely away. Malcolm's reforms will make it impossible for a king to be this isolated, just as the return to Duncan's sense of manliness will prevent much of the process by which it occurred.

Macbeth's isolation is only the largest of the changes Shakespeare makes to the end of the Macbeth story. Besides eliminating the Lugtake episode and what it implies about support for Macbeth, Shakespeare changes the chronology of Malcolm's victory, putting the establishment of the earls before the coronation, and removing the interval after the coronation during which Malcolm called a parliament to oversee his changes to the state.[92] These omissions are all related, since it was during that time that Lugtake's supporters regrouped and organized themselves. Shakespeare also removes the special honours given to the earls of Fife – that is, Macduff and his descendants – which gave them greater authority within their lands than the rest of the earls as well as giving them certain ceremonial rights and privileges.[93] By removing these, Shakespeare ensures that Malcolm's reforms will appear equal and unbiased, avoiding the dangerous 'absolute trust' that his father had misplaced onto the thane of Cawdor (1.4.14) while retaining the possibility of placing a general trust in all the earls. The same logic applies to the fact that Shakespeare's Malcolm changes all his thanes to earls, while Holinshed's changed only most,[94] leaving others still as thanes. These changes align Malcolm's reforms more closely with the model of feudal maturation, in which mixing thanes and earls would be a strange mixture of different ages of feudal tenure. Even without direct consideration of this model, however, the change of all the thanes into earls certainly strengthens the sense within the play that Malcolm has fixed the whole system, not just part of it. Tracking these changes to Malcolm's reforms shows that Shakespeare idealized the reforms by making them both universal and uniform, thus turning them from controversial changes accused of damaging the ancient Scottish manliness into a cure for the ills that plagued the Scottish state in *Macbeth*.

These changes also serve to isolate Macbeth and turn him in upon himself. In the histories, he is a complex *ruler* who solved many problems but created just as many, and whose supporters believed enough in him to remain loyal beyond his death. Shakespeare makes him a complex *man* instead, one whose internal rather than external life interests us, and whose primary relationship is not to his country but to his wife. In making *Macbeth* a feudal play, Shakespeare made Malcolm a reforming statesman. But he also made Macbeth a tragic figure.

In both *Macbeth* and *King John*, then, we can see Shakespeare navigating carefully between two competing narratives about the setting and making choices between them. In each case, he chose not to tell the story as he would have found it in his chronicle sources, especially Holinshed: the Magna Carta does not appear in *King John*, and the end of *Macbeth* is not a spectacle of Anglicizing weakness. Instead, he looked to other ideas about each setting circulating in the period and used them to craft plays that draw our attention to the struggles of their main characters, with John straining at the restrictions imposed by counsel and Macbeth finding himself isolated in a violently flawed vision of manliness. At the same time, the ending of each play is more optimistic: Prince Henry's leadership will keep England true to itself, and Malcolm's reforms purge Scotland's cycle of disorder. Thus, we can see how the historicism of setting gives us insight into Shakespeare's dramatic and political imagination at work as he weaves together multiple complex historiographical narratives to elevate each play.

PART TWO

The European past: Ancient Rome

4

Julius Caesar, factions and the end of the Roman republic

While the English and Scottish past was a contested space in which Shakespeare had to navigate between multiple historical accounts, his depictions of the European past in his ancient Roman plays were able to draw on more consistent narratives with less variation. This is not to say that Roman history was not much-debated and much-discussed in early modern England. Rather, it is to point out that despite that debate, there was more consensus within early modern England about the political nature of these two republican Romes than there was about the England of *King John* or the Scotland of *Macbeth*. In these plays, then, we can see how Shakespeare puts his own spin on the political structures he found in different eras of Republican Rome, drawing on the common assumptions about politics in those eras prevalent in early modern England.

Politics in the Rome of *Julius Caesar*, for instance, hinges on the existence of predetermined factional divisions within the Roman republic. These in turn give new significance to the play's frequent use of the terms 'friend', identified here with political affiliation, and 'lover', associated with the personal affective relationship we usually identify as friendship. By tracking the factions through the use of love and friendship in the play, we can better understand Caesar's death and the public response to it, the quarrel between Brutus and Cassius in Act Four, and the ominous overtones of the play's ending.

The Roman political structure in Caesar's day had been warped by the events of the civil wars in the generation before into a kind of institutionalized factionalism. Political infighting, which often took the form of actual military combat, was between factions, not individuals, and frequently continued beyond the death of a given factional leader. The significance of these factions played a major part in the early modern English understanding of the Roman civil wars, and I will show that *Julius Caesar* assumes this political situation as a basis for its exploration of Caesar's Rome. In particular, I argue that the play identifies Caesar and his allies with a specific faction ultimately derived from Marius that was opposed to another faction ultimately derived from Sulla.[1] These factional politics are best understood in conjunction with early modern English accounts of Caesar's time: both Shakespeare's direct narrative sources, which are naturally relevant, and others circulating in the same literary culture, which give us insight into the assumptions available to Shakespeare and his contemporaries. The primary direct source for *Julius Caesar* is Thomas North's translation of Plutarch's *Lives of the Noble Greeks and Romans*.[2] There are multiple *Lives* that bear on the events surrounding *Julius Caesar*: the *Life of Caesar*, of course, but also those of Caius Marius, Sulla, Crassus, Pompey, Marc Antony, Brutus and Cicero. Together, they tell a consistent story about the events of the Roman civil wars, the importance of faction to those wars and the nature of those factions.[3] That story traces the civil unrest in the Roman republic from Lucius Cornelius Sulla's victory over Caius Marius to the rise of Pompey, Crassus and Caesar after Sulla's death, and then the disintegration of that triumvirate and the triumph of Caesar.

Within that narrative, which is told with minimal variations in each of the relevant *Lives*, North's translation of Plutarch emphasizes the factional nature of the wars. North uses the term 'faction' for the political groups under discussion whenever Plutarch steps back from the details of an individual biography either to examine Rome as a whole or to set the stage for the next part of a *Life*.[4] In this way, he casts factions as the basic unit of Roman political life. These factions are continuous, lasting long after their founders' deaths. The best example of this comes from the *Life of Caesar*, in which Sulla responds to his advisors' recommendation that he spare Julius Caesar by telling them 'that they did not consider that there were many Marians in that young boy'.[5] Because Caesar was

Marius's nephew, he was a potential leader of the Marians and therefore contained 'many Marians'; even though Marius himself was already dead, his faction could live on through Caesar. Sulla's faction likewise persisted after his death. His lieutenants included 'Pompeius, Crassus, Metellus, and Seruilius', and, as already noted, Pompey and Crassus remained in power after Sulla's death, later splitting power with Caesar's Marians.[6] Although some of Crassus's followers may have joined Caesar after Crassus's death, the continuity remains clear in North between the Sulla-Pompey and Marius-Caesar factions. In turn, Cassius and Brutus are identified as members of Pompey's faction pardoned by Caesar after his victory, extending the factions into the period depicted in *Julius Caesar*, and Cassius calls on Pompey's memory to aid him in the assassination.[7]

Although these factions proved persistent, North portrays them as a relatively new feature of late republican Rome, a 'chaunge and alteracion of gouernment'.[8] Key to this 'chaunge' was the institution of the spoils system, whereby members of the victorious faction were rewarded with the positions and wealth of the defeated, and the latter were excluded from office.[9] For North and Plutarch, the institution of the spoils system was part of a larger whole: the rise of the factions in the Roman political structure.

Of course, North's Plutarch was far from the only early modern English text to treat the theme of factionalism during the Roman civil wars, or even the only translation of a classical text to do so. The same theme emerges from contemporary translations of Livy,[10] Suetonius,[11] Tacitus,[12] Appian,[13] Eutropius[14] and Lucan.[15] In all these translations, we find the same theme echoed that we found in North's Plutarch: the importance of a continuous factionalism to the conflicts of the late Roman republic from Sulla and Marius all the way through to Octavius, Antony and Lepidus.

Nor was this theme confined to translations alone. I could, for instance, have written this entire section out of the work of just one man, Lodowick Lloyd, a prolific author who between 1590 and 1607 published five books that touched on the Roman civil wars and the significance of faction.[16] Lloyd's repeated references to the Roman civil wars, like the translations previously discussed, emphasize the factional nature of the conflict and the continuity from Sulla and Marius to Brutus, Antony and Octavius. His perspective is perhaps best summarized in *The Practice of Policy*: the Roman state was 'deuided by factions, from Sylla to Caesar, from

Caesar to Augustus, sometime running from Caesar to Pompey, and from Pompey to Caesar, vntill they and their factions were slayn by the sword, and their countrey welnigh destroyed'.[17] This view is precisely what we would expect from a careful early modern reader of the ancient historians. It is also worth noting that although Lloyd names the factions by their leaders, he does not see the existence of the factions as dependent on those leaders' presence. In the *Stratagems of Jerusalem*, he refers to Carbo, Marius's successor, as 'the head and chiefe of all Marius faction, the onely enemie of Sylla', making it clear that, in his mind at least, the faction survived Marius's own death.[18]

Lloyd was merely the most prolific early modern English recapitulator of the Roman civil wars and the Caesar story. William Fulbecke compiled a history tellingly titled *An historicall collection of the continuall factions, tumults, and massacres of the Romans and Italians during the space of one hundred and twentie yeares next before the peaceable empire of Augustus Caesar*.[19] This 'perennial factionalism, civil war, and the breakdown of the republic' was likewise the theme in Sallust's work, who Freyja Cox-Jensen has found was the most printed Roman historian in England during the sixteenth century, just ahead of Livy and Plutarch (though Plutarch outstripped his popularity towards the end of the century).[20] Other writers throughout the period similarly engaged with these topics, in histories,[21] commentaries,[22] essays[23] and advice books.[24] These books cited, or failed to cite, a variety of sources, used the Roman stories for a variety of purposes, and couched their commentary in a variety of terms. Yet two common themes run through them all, as they do through the translations and through Lloyd's various works: the importance of 'faccious dealyng' in the period, and the continuity of the wars from 'Marius and Silla' to 'Pompeius and Caesar', and on through 'the Triumvirate of Octavius, Antonius, and Lepidus, against Cassius and Brutus'.[25] As D. Alan Orr has shown, similar themes, particularly including the 'heavily factionalized' nature of late Republican Rome, were dramatized in Thomas Lodge's *The Wovnds of Ciuill War* in the early 1590s.[26] As such, it does not matter so much whether Shakespeare (or his audience) had read any individual one of these texts as a source (though the general consensus is that he used at least North's Plutarch): these assumptions about continuous factional strife circulated broadly in the period and would have been widely available to both the playwright and his potential audience. As Cox-Jensen has observed, early modern English readers used a wide variety of texts to inform themselves about ancient Rome,[27] and these texts spoke with remarkable uniformity about the dangers of faction in Caesar's time.

I argue that this general early modern understanding of the factional divisions of late republican Rome grounds the political world of *Julius Caesar*, and the characters respond to the dangers it presents. In particular, I suggest that these factional divisions and their history create the effect of 'representing a Rome which is ... ancient' that Colin Burrow has identified in the play.[28] Part of producing a Rome that is a 'distinct cultural field' from early modern England is giving life to 'its own idea of the past' and thus representing a Rome experiencing its own nostalgia for an already past world.[29] This is an effect we will see Shakespeare make even greater use of in *Coriolanus*, but it is already present here. As a result, when various characters' awareness of the dangers of factionalism manifests itself in a constant yearning for the early republic, that nostalgia strengthens the play's own sense of its Caesarean Rome. That past political world haunts *Julius Caesar* as surely as Caesar's own ghost. Brutus and Cassius each conjure up the verbal spectre of Marcus Junius Brutus, Brutus's tyrannicidal ancestor, and the idealized memory of the earlier Republic is never far from the conspirators' minds. Yet the world of *Julius Caesar* is not that world. It is the fallen, factional world of the late Republic.

Julius Caesar reminds us of that factional reality from the very beginning. The tribunes who break up the plebeians' celebrations for Caesar in the first scene bring up the civil wars, asking the crowd, 'knew you not Pompey?' (1.1.38).[30] Although addressed to the plebeians, the question might equally apply to the audience, for whom a knowledge of Pompey would indeed be useful. The tribunes then deride the celebrations because they come as a result not of a foreign victory but of a domestic, factional one: Caesar 'comes in triumph over Pompey's blood' (1.1.51–2). 'Pompey's blood' technically refers to Pompey's sons, over whom Caesar held his triumph, but it also carries the implication that Caesar is triumphing directly over Pompey's death. By extolling the memory of Pompey to the plebeians and rejecting Caesar's celebrations in Pompey's name specifically, the tribunes immediately recall for us the factional history of Rome and its relevance to the play.

Having brought up the factions, *Julius Caesar* does not allow us to forget them. Caesar's entrance brings the appearance of harmony and triumph, but his exit leaves Cassius and Brutus onstage. They immediately remind us of the divide underlying the state, both through the content of their conversation and through their refusal (like that of the tribunes) to join in the general festivities. It is quickly clear that Cassius is already working against Caesar and impatiently awaits Brutus's participation. He tests Brutus repeatedly, and tells the audience that he plans to push him even further by anonymously giving Brutus forged letters that continue to urge him towards Cassius's opinion (1.2.316). Initially this might seem to imply that we see Cassius creating a conspiracy against Caesar out of whole cloth, starting in this moment.

But Brutus is not the only target of Cassius's intrigues, and that further context is crucial. We next see him bring Caska into the fold, who begs him to 'be factious for redress of all these griefs' (1.3.118) – that is, to form a faction. In response, Cassius informs him that the faction already exists: 'I have moved already / Some certain of the noblest-minded Romans / To undergo with me an enterprise / Of honourable dangerous consequence' (1.3.121–4). This is news to Caska; it is also news to the audience. Cinna's entrance confirms Cassius's statement, as we suddenly discover in a few lines the other members of the faction: 'Cinna', 'Metellus Cimber' and 'Decius Brutus and Trebonius' (1.3.133, 134, 148). We realize that we are not witnessing the beginning of a conspiracy but the last stages of its formation. These previously unknown men 'are the faction' (2.1.77), as Brutus says, and they are joined together before we even know it.

I suggest that identifying this moment as one of purely individual persuasion, as Jan H. Blits does, marks an overemphasis on individual rather than collective decision-making and particularly on Cassius's particular influence and importance to the creation of this group.[31] Cassius is not here revealing that he has individually pressed every member of his group in the same way that we have seen him approach Brutus. Rather, he is establishing himself as one of the heads of an already extant faction within the state, one that Brutus will be part of as well.

The opposing faction is equally predetermined. Shortly after Caesar's death in the third act, we see Mark Antony speaking to Octavius Caesar's servant; Octavius himself arrives in Rome in the next scene. After only one intervening scene, Antony, Octavius and the previously unmentioned Lepidus are already selecting which enemies to proscribe (4.1.1). Some of this reflects Shakespeare's usual compression of time, but the triumvirs can move so swiftly precisely because they are already allies, and step smoothly into the power vacuum after Caesar's death. Brutus spared Antony because he believed him 'but a limb of Caesar' (2.1.164). However, it would be closer to the truth to say they were both 'limbs' of something larger than themselves, something that did not die with Caesar but lived on through Antony and his fellow triumvirs. This is the faction of Caesar and Marius, just as Cassius's faction is that of Pompey and Sulla. It is no accident that Antony goes to meet his fellow triumvirs 'at Caesar's house' (3.2.254), any more than that the conspirators await Cassius 'in Pompey's Porch' (1.3.126). These physical locations serve to ground the play's politics in the physical manifestation of factional Rome, as each stands in the literal footsteps of their predecessors. It is from these two preexisting factions that the 'fierce civil strife' that Antony predicts will emerge (3.1.263). Their presence is palpable throughout the play as a critical element in the political calculus of Rome.

This deep factional division exists in the play's language as well as in its action. Consistently, those who share a faction are referred to as 'friends', while those who are linked only by ties of personal attachment, or what we would usually call friendship, are referred to as 'lovers'. Two men can be both 'lovers' and 'friends', as Cassius and Brutus or Caesar and Antony are. However, the two words represent distinct relationships. All of the characters in the play understand this distinction except Caesar – a point to which I will later return.

Shakespeare's treatment of the words 'friend' and 'lover' corresponds to the difference between two uses of the term 'friend' prevalent in both early modern England and the classical past. The first is the meaning that 'friendship' still has in modern English: a bond of mutual affection outside the family. This sense of 'friend' was widespread in Renaissance England, as a generation of recent scholarship has shown.[32] Importantly for *Julius Caesar*, this emphasis on the importance of affective friendship, especially among males, derived from early modern readings of Cicero's *De Amicitia* (*Of Friendship*), and as such was closely associated at the time with classical, and specifically Caesarean, Rome.[33]

But there was always another side to friendship, even for the Renaissance English. This is what Tom MacFaul has called the 'specialized meaning in a political context' of the word 'friend', one that is 'stripped of its affective component'.[34] What I take MacFaul to mean by this is that in certain political cases – like the one we encounter in *Julius Caesar* – 'friend' took on a more limited meaning that identified merely an association for political ends. Shakespeare himself had employed this more political meaning in both *King John* and *Macbeth* (as we have seen) and in his earlier Roman play *Titus Andronicus*, especially in the first scene in which both Bassianus and Marcus Andronicus signify political followers by the use of 'friends' as well as of 'faction'.[35] We see it again in *Julius Caesar*.

I believe it is precisely because the exclusively political resonance of 'friend' is so important to *Julius Caesar* that the play makes such liberal use of 'love' and 'lover'. The root of *amicitia*, friendship, is after all *amor*, love. Shakespeare displaces the affective content of 'friend' onto 'lover' in order to distinguish between the two types of relationship. Affective friendship is not absent from the play; it is simply called by another name. I suggest that this distinction may be derived from North, who sometimes refers to allies within a faction as 'friends': 'Caesar's frendes', 'Pompey's frendes', 'Cassius ... his frendes'.[36]

In North the lines are somewhat blurred between friendship and faction, since Cassius's friends are both factional conspirators and personal confidants, and Caesar and his friends also share both political and personal bonds. But there are hints, especially in the case of Pompey, of the meaning Shakespeare would seize upon. The Romans who did not flee Rome at Caesar's approach had no personal connection to Caesar, yet Pompey says he would account them Caesar's friends, while Lepidus, one of Caesar's 'chiefest friends', is hardly mentioned in the *Life of Caesar* before he attains that title.[37] In these cases, we see friendship merging into something more like faction, and it is this meaning of friendship that Shakespeare adopts.

A brief examination of the language of association in the play reveals these overlapping but distinct uses of 'love' or 'lover' and 'friend' or 'friendly'. The conspirators are bound by friendship: Cassius tells Caska that Cinna is 'a friend' in order to identify him as a member of their faction, and during their meeting they are all 'gentle friends' (1.3.133, 2.1.170). Even their departure is couched in friendship: 'friends, disperse yourselves' (2.1.221). When they seek to woo Antony to their side after the assassination, Brutus confidently claims that 'I know that we shall have him well to friend', and Cassius plainly asks him 'will you be pricked in number of our friends?' (3.1.143, 216). Antony picks up on this theme and uses the same term against them, convincing them to let him speak at the funeral by first pretending that 'friends am I with you all' and then asking to speak 'as becomes a friend', purposely leaving it ambiguous as to whether he would do so as their friend or as Caesar's (3.1.220, 229).

Antony's quick recognition and adoption of this terminology may be related to his own faction's use of it. When he, Octavius, and Lepidus join to attack the conspirators after Caesar's death, they agree to 'let our alliance be combined, / Our best friends made' (4.1.42–3). Friendship and alliance are synonymous; by making friends, the triumvirs mean rallying their faction to the cause. This manner of speaking is widespread; when one of his troops presents Antony with Lucilius, thinking him to be Brutus, Antony assures the man that 'this is not Brutus, friend' (5.4.26). This soldier has never appeared before, and does not even have a name. Antony calls him 'friend' not because they are close but because they share a faction. That this factional language of friendship is used by both factions in the play belies Andrew Hadfield's claim that there is 'no shared public culture' in *Julius Caesar*.[38] The two sides share a common culture and terminology even as they disagree about which side ought to rule.

The bond of affection signified by 'love' and its attendant terms also appears frequently in the play, both between and within factions. Cassius knows that Caesar 'loves Brutus' (1.2.312) and that Antony has an 'ingrafted love' for Caesar (2.1.183). Brutus, although he would not have Caesar become king, insists 'yet I love him well' (1.2.82). When trying to warn Caesar about the conspirators, Artemidorus writes to him as '*Thy lover*' (2.3.9). In signing his letter '*Thy lover*' rather than '*Thy friend*', Artemidorus signals that his action derives from admiration of Caesar's 'virtue' rather than from any factional affiliation (2.3.12). Indeed, this makes Artemidorus's failed effort to save Caesar's life all the more tragic. He will not benefit politically from Caesar's survival, for he is not of Caesar's faction. He simply wishes to see a virtuous man live; his reward is to be ignored and watch the assassination helplessly. In all of these cases of 'love', it is the affective relationship that Shakespeare emphasizes, not the political. The lover bears the beloved in his heart but does not express a political position by admitting his love.

In the immediate wake of Caesar's death, soon after Artemidorus's attempted intervention, Shakespeare underscores the significance of the distinction between friendship and love in the contrasting speeches that Brutus and Antony deliver at the funeral. Both Brutus and Antony deploy the languages of love and friendship to work the crowd, but Antony co-opts the crowd more effectively, turning it into a mob that aligns with his faction and goes out to destroy his political opponents. The key differences between the two speeches occur in their respective first lines. Brutus begins 'Romans, countrymen, and lovers' (3.2.13), while Antony instead opens with 'friends, Romans, countrymen' (3.2.74). These two lines differ in two vital ways: the change from 'lovers' to 'friends', and the re-ordering of the terms. These changes produce speeches that point to drastically different ends.

Brutus hopes to calm the crowd and explain the conspirators' actions by claiming that they acted in order to preserve and restore Rome. To that end, he identifies his audience as Romans first, then his countrymen, identifying himself as Roman too, and then finally expresses his desired relation to them: he wishes them to be his 'lovers'. He called the people 'friends' when he first entered the square (3.2.2) because he believed they were on his side. But when it comes time to address them formally, he no longer speaks to their political leanings. Instead, he wishes them to be his 'lovers', that is to think well of him and to wish him well. This introduction could be said to summarize his speech; he wants the people to excuse Caesar's murder and love him (and of the rest of the conspirators) because of their identity as Romans and their belief that he too is a Roman, acting in the best interests of Rome. He has no future plans to mobilize the people as allies.

Antony, by contrast, intends to convince the crowd to act on his side against Brutus and the conspirators. He cunningly begins by assuming that he has already succeeded, calling the people his 'friends' before he has convinced them to be so. At this point, the crowd has already taken Brutus's side. It is therefore a major risk for Antony to begin by terming the people 'friends'. But it is a calculated risk. He will bring them around to his side in large part by treating them as if they were already there. Only after he has claimed them as 'friends' does Antony go on to call them 'Romans, countrymen', positioning himself and them just as Brutus had relative to Rome. This secondary move empowers the irony of his later praise of Brutus and the conspirators. As with Brutus's speech, Antony's first lines are a microcosm of the whole, but unlike Brutus, Antony has crammed two distinct messages into a single line.

The longer speeches make heavy use of the distinction between friendship and love. Brutus speaks of his 'love to Caesar', including the famous line 'not that I loved Caesar less, but that I loved Rome more' (3.2.19, 21–2). He promises 'tears, for his love … and death, for his ambition' (3.2.27–8). But his only reference to friendship emphasizes the fact that he is not Caesar's friend: 'if there be any in this assembly, any dear friend of Caesar's, to him I say, that Brutus's love to Caesar was no less than his' (3.2.17–19). Here Brutus imagines someone who is a friend of Caesar's and is also bound to him by ties of love – a 'dear friend', introducing an affective term alongside 'friend'. He speaks to that imagined man of their shared love for Caesar. But only that man, and not Brutus, can call Caesar 'friend'. Brutus's love cannot participate in the political sense of friendship, or else he would not have murdered Caesar.

In conveying his twin loves of Rome and Caesar, Brutus emphasizes an aspect of love that makes it fundamentally distinct from friendship: its comparability. Political friendship is binary; it cannot be more or less. Love, however, exists in degrees. Brutus tells his hypothetical dear friend of Caesar's that 'Brutus's love to Caesar was no less than his' and justifies himself by explaining 'not that I loved Caesar less, but that I loved Rome more'. In this moment, the ability to compare loves turns into the necessity of ranking them because loves inevitably come into conflict.[39] By contrast, friendship, representing factional affiliation, not only cannot be compared because it is only either present or absent, but need not be compared because all one's friends are also friends. Brutus's love for Caesar, while 'no less' than that of the dearest of friends, is an insufficient guard for Caesar's life because it must compete with Brutus's love for Rome. Friendship would have brought Caesar safety from Brutus; love brings only 'tears' (and 'death'). Antony will echo this thought when he points out the hole 'the well-beloved Brutus' made in Caesar's breast (3.2.174).

Like Brutus, Antony underscores his love of Caesar, but unlike Brutus he combines that love with an emphasis on political friendship that becomes his primary focus. He says that Caesar 'was my friend, faithful and just to me', and calls himself one 'that love[s] my friend' (3.2.86, 212). Throughout the speech, he repeatedly invokes love, but only love for Caesar, reminding the people that 'You all did love him once' (3.2.103) and telling them that 'Caesar thus deserved your loves' (3.2.229). He structures his own relation to the people around friendship, not love; the people loved Caesar, but they will be Antony's 'friends' (3.2.141, 203, 228). The repeated word stresses the relation between Caesar, Antony and the crowd that Antony wants them to have in mind – that their love for Caesar should motivate them to be Antony's allies – and it works.

Before we turn further to the civil war that follows Antony's speech, we must consider further the Rome in which that speech is made. Antony's faction is Caesar's faction, but Caesar himself threatens the factional order in two different but related ways. Caesar believes that he has transcended factions and brought peace to the civil wars, that there is no distinction between those who are his friends and those who love him. The conspirators, on the other hand, fear that his victory has broken the factional order that had existed previously, and seek by killing him to restore Rome, though they do not all agree on exactly how the assassination will do so, or what Rome it will restore.

Caesar is the only character in the play who mistakes his lovers for his friends, confusing the two categories and opening himself up to the conspiracy. Decius Brutus, in luring Caesar to the Senate, speaks of his 'dear, dear love' for Caesar and tells him that 'reason to my love is liable' in his explanation of Calphurnia's dream (2.2.102, 104). He is careful not to speak of friendship. Trebonius does mention friendship in the same scene, but not as Caesar's friend: it appears in an aside in which he admits that Caesar's 'best friends shall wish I had been further' from Caesar (2.2.125). Caesar, however, includes the whole company all in his vision of friendship: 'good friends, go in, and taste some wine with me, / And we, like friends, will straightway go together' (2.2.126–7).

There is strong dramatic irony in these lines no matter how we take the word 'friend'. But I suggest that it is crucial that this is the only time when 'friend' is applied to someone clearly of the other party without deception on the part of the speaker. In Caesar's misapplication of the term, I suggest, we see him claiming to be beyond the factional use of the word by his fellows. He, and he alone, can remake men's allegiances linguistically because he has transcended faction. This side of Caesar, the side that sees himself as beyond his fellow men, is much commented on, usually with reference to Caesar's belief that he is beyond mortality.[40] I see this belief in transcendence manifesting not just in his self-conceit but in his practical relation to the politics of the play. Caesar believes he has transcended faction as well as human weakness.

This does not mean that he is completely insensible to political danger. He points Cassius out to Antony for special attention as a potential threat. But his reasons for distrusting Cassius are personal, not factional: Cassius's 'lean and hungry look' (1.2.193) and the thought that 'Such men as he be never at heart's ease / Whiles they behold a greater than themselves' (1.2.207–8). Caesar has no thought that Cassius might be part of a larger faction ranged against him. For him, Cassius is merely an individual, 'the man I should avoid' (1.2.199). It is Cassius's personal ambition that Caesar distrusts, not his presence in an opposing faction. Ultimately, he downplays even that threat because of his belief in his own transcendence: 'I rather tell thee what is to be feared / Than what I fear: for always I am Caesar' (1.2.210–11). This is the same overconfidence in the strength of his position that we witness in his refusal to read Artemidorus's letter. Believing himself to be beyond the factional infighting from which his power emerged, Caesar no longer takes the precautions other men might need.

Caesar is not the only one who thinks that his rise to power has overturned the factional order. His opponents believe it too, but unlike him they fear it. They see in Caesar the end of the political order they are used to inhabiting and thus a fundamental threat. They represent this through the image of Caesar as king. For them, the dissolution of faction becomes the dissolution of the Republic itself. Until after Caesar's death, the only characters who speak of Caesar's potential kingship are conspirators. Cassius and Brutus express dismay at the idea of Caesar as king; Caska reports that Antony offered Caesar a crown and worries that the Senate means to choose him king; and Decius Brutus tells Caesar that the Senate will crown him. Even after Caesar's death Antony only partly confirms Caska's story, while maintaining Caesar's own innocence of ambition: 'I thrice presented him a kingly crown, / Which he did thrice refuse' (3.2.97–8). All the other references in the play to kingship are in the mouths of the conspirators.

This distancing effect between Caesar and the desire for a crown functions whether or not audiences are aware of Shakespeare's actual sources for the scene. However, it is noteworthy that Shakespeare created the effect by significantly altering his sources. In North's Plutarch, the 'couetous desire he had to be called king' is Caesar's great sin, the reason why the plebeians turn against him.[41] Plutarch's Caesar had a series of events staged to test the waters around his potential kingship. He was met by emissaries from the city of Alba 'who called him king', to which he responded 'he was not called king, but Caesar'.[42] He then had Antony offer him a crown, which he twice (not thrice) refused; when he found the people approved his refusal, he gave up the scheme.[43]

Shakespeare retains elements of both these episodes. His Caesar calls himself Caesar incessantly, almost to the point of self-parody, as several critics have noted.[44] Shakespeare also includes the presentation of the crown. But in both cases, Shakespeare makes a crucial change: he obscures any direct connection between Caesar himself and kingship. He does not include the incident with the greetings from Alba, merely taking Caesar's odd verbal tic of referring to himself in the third person from that exchange, and the presentation of the crown takes place entirely offstage. Only the cheers that attend on Caesar's refusal of the crown are audible in the relevant scene and they are misinterpreted: Brutus 'fear[s] the people / Choose Caesar for their king' and 'do[es] believe that these applauses are / For some new honours that are heaped on Caesar' (1.2.79–80, 132–3). Like Brutus, the audience only hears of the events from Caska afterward. By refusing to show this moment, but instead placing the story of the crown in Caska's mouth, Shakespeare distances Caesar from the desire to be king, since our only knowledge of that desire comes from Caska, a member of the opposite faction. A natural scepticism about the accuracy of Caska's account of Caesar's motivations sets in when Cassius makes sure that Brutus ask Caska, and no one else, about what has happened (1.2.178). Where Plutarch presented an explicit account of Caesar's desire to be king, Shakespeare positions his audience to see that desire only through the lens of the conspirators' ill will.

This does not mean that Shakespeare's Caesar does not desire to be king. We have already seen his own belief that he stands above the factions, and he did have Antony offer him the crown. But Shakespeare's alterations to the circumstances surrounding that desire suggest that Caesar's ambition to be king is not a publicly acknowledged fact in *Julius Caesar*, as it is in Plutarch, which implies in turn that concern about Caesar's ambition separates the conspirators from the plebeians they claim to represent, rather than uniting the two as it does in Plutarch's narrative. It is useful, then, to investigate what the conspirators mean when they worry about Caesar becoming, or desiring to become, king.

Significantly, Brutus has a different idea of what kingship means than his allies do. For Cassius and the other conspirators, Caesar's potential kingship must be avoided so that the factional system can continue and they can rise. Cassius imagines kingship as a diminution and elimination of all others: Caesar 'doth bestride the narrow world / Like a colossus, and we petty men / Walk under his huge legs and peep about' (1.2.134–6). In Cassius's mind, Caesar's kingship will shrink all others into nothingness: 'When went there by an age, since the great flood, / But it was famed with more than with one man? / When could they say, till now, that talked of Rome, / That her wide walks encompassed but one man? / Now it is Rome indeed, and room enough, / When there is in it but one only man' (1.2.151–6). This is a fantasy of dissolution and diminishment; Cassius has not actually found Caesar tyrannical, but rather looks forward with his imagination to the potential of kingship. He sees a monarchy as a world in which there is no one else but the king. However, the ideal world to which Cassius compares this terror is not one of broad egalitarianism. It is a world of great men: '"Brutus" will start a spirit as soon as "Caesar"' (1.2.146). But 'Brutus' is no average name. It is itself a name to conjure with, a name that destroys kings as it would devils (1.2.158–60). In this argument, Brutus is special, just as Caesar is, and Cassius is emphatically not suggesting a system in which they are merely the equal of any Roman. Instead, his version of Rome is one that is 'famed with more than with one man', a Rome in which there are at least two factions, each led by men who should be famed. He has picked out Brutus as the man for his faction, a choice we later hear Cinna echo when he wishes that Cassius 'could / But win the noble Brutus to our party' (1.3.140–1). This perspective on Rome is mirrored in Caska's request that Cassius 'be factious for the redress of all these griefs' (1.3.118). The conspirators' shared position is that

Caesar's potential kingship threatens the existing factional division by threatening to replace the presence of at least two competing heads of factions with the domination of a single man.

Brutus does not agree with this perspective, as we can see in their argument about how to treat Antony after Caesar's murder. Cassius suggests killing Antony because 'we shall find of him / A shrewd contriver. And you know his means / If he improve them may well stretch so far / As to annoy us all' (2.1.156–9). Cassius here imagines exactly what does in fact occur after Caesar's death: Antony taking over Caesar's faction and destroying the conspirators. 'His means' here is not merely Antony's personal wealth or skill but his factional connection. Cassius's fear results both from his understanding of the factional politics in which he operates and from his awareness that while destroying Caesar may eliminate Caesar's potential kingship, it will not eliminate his faction.

Brutus, however, wishes to treat Antony more kindly because he views kingship as a different matter from factionalism entirely. Like Cassius, he sees kingship as separating the king from all men below him: having climbed the ladder of ambition, 'he then unto the ladder turns his back, / Looks in the clouds, scorning the base degrees / By which he did ascend' (2.1.25–7). But unlike Cassius, he does not see this in terms of the factional system but in general terms relative to Rome as a whole. He thinks of himself acting for 'the general good' and 'for the general' (1.2.85, 2.1.12). He takes the ambiguous paper that Cassius has thrown into his window, which says 'shall Rome, et cetera', and reads it as 'shall Rome stand under one man's awe' (2.1.47, 52). He then apostrophizes Rome in his answer: 'O Rome, I make thee promise' (2.1.56). Again like Cassius, he has imagined a king as a single entity overshadowing all, but, unlike Cassius, Brutus has not imagined himself delivering a divided factional Rome from this threat, but a single unified Rome. Brutus's imagination picks up on Cassius's reference to his ancestors not as a sign that Brutus should lead a faction but as a reminder of the earlier republic, established when 'my ancestors did from the streets of Rome / The Tarquin drive, when he was called a king' (2.1.53–4). It is notable that where Cassius had imagined 'a Brutus once' who did this (1.2.158), Brutus calls on 'my ancestors'. Even in his historical vision, Brutus sees himself as standing for the multitude, where Cassius sees an individual worthy of leading a faction.

This difference in imagination feeds Brutus's refusal to kill Antony. It is only because he sees Caesar as a single man standing above the whole of Rome that he can miss or ignore the idea that Antony will control Caesar's faction after his death. For Antony to be 'but a limb of Caesar', who 'can do no more than Caesar's arm / When Caesar's head is off', Brutus must imagine him not as part of a faction but as a toady to a king (2.1.164, 181–2). Brutus is making the same mistake as Sulla's advisors did: there are many Caesareans in that Antony. But Brutus does not believe this because he has divorced the issues of faction and kingship in his mind. To imagine the conspirators as 'purgers, not murderers' is only possible if we share Brutus's vision in which all Rome stands as one against the spirit of Caesar (2.1.178). In this view, Caesar is a foreign object contained within an otherwise uniform Rome. Here we see Brutus thinking about Caesar as the thanes and Macbeth thought about Scotland's wars as a 'purge' – and like them, his political imagination lags behind the play's conception of how politics works. If we, like Cassius and the early modern English, see instead a Rome divided into factions, we can see how Brutus's vision will fall short: Caesar's faction will avenge him. Thus while I agree with Worden that Brutus seems to lack an effectual 'constitutional programme' for Rome,[45] I would suggest that this does not make him typical of Shakespeare's Rome, but unusual; his misunderstanding of Rome's factions differentiates him from his fellow Romans.

Brutus's failure to engage properly with the factional structure of Rome weakens the conspiracy. We have seen how this belief leads him to veto the murder of Antony, as well as how his speech to the people after the assassination is outshone by Antony's more effective use of the rhetoric of friendship. It is worth noting too that it is Brutus's fault that Antony gets to make that speech. After the conspirators have attempted to subvert Antony to their side, Cassius begs Brutus 'do not consent / That Antony speak in his funeral' (3.1.232–3). Brutus overrules him because he believes that giving Caesar 'all true rites and lawful ceremonies' will 'advantage more than do us wrong' (3.1.241, 242). This belief can only be held by someone, like Brutus, who imagines a Rome unified against Caesar's spirit. Cassius and Antony both understand that the factional division of the city is too explosive for this course of action to be safe for the conspirators. Brutus's inability to see that the factional divisions are still present and important makes him blind to the danger Antony's speech poses, and exposes the conspirators to destruction.

That destruction is hastened by the swift action of the other faction. Here again it is worth noting that Shakespeare modifies his sources to heighten the effect. In Plutarch's version of the story, there was a short period after the death of Caesar in which Octavius and Antony were enemies, even fighting a battle against each other.[46] Shakespeare eliminates this altercation; Antony is in constant communication with Octavius throughout. The two leaders are clearly aligned: Antony first sends Octavius a warning about the dangers of Rome and later expresses his joy when Octavius arrives (3.1.288–9, 3.2.256). In both cases, the mood is one of openness and cooperation, with a sense that the two already know that they will be working closely together.

And so they do. In Octavius's first scene, separated from the funeral only by the lynching of Cinna the poet, we see the triumvirate (these two and the newly appearing Lepidus) already proscribing those in Rome they have condemned to die. In Plutarch, this took three days and substantial negotiation; in Shakespeare it does not last ten lines (4.1.1–6).[47] That does not mean the moment is not important to *Julius Caesar*. Rather, the swiftness with which the proscriptions happen joins with the elimination of the dissension between Antony and Octavius to create a situation in which Caesar dies, is mourned and is replaced as leader of his faction in the space of a single, fast-paced act.

Cassius predicted this outcome earlier in the play. One effect of reading *Julius Caesar* with factional politics in mind is that we come to see how deeply Cassius understands Rome, and how central he is to the play. He knows how the factional politics will play out; it is Brutus, disregarding Cassius's warnings, who causes the faction to fall short of its political goals. In this, Cassius is a tragic figure. One cannot help but wonder what happened in the 'other street' where Cassius spoke without Antony to follow him (3.2.3). 'Those that will follow Cassius' would have heard a very different tale from what the audience (and the plebeian mob we follow) heard (3.2.5). Yet whatever Cassius was able to do offstage, Brutus has undone by allowing Antony such free rein. I agree with Michael Platt that 'Cassius needs Brutus more than Brutus needs Cassius',[48] because as Platt points out, he does not have the political standing to lead the conspiracy alone. But this is a tragic flaw in the world of faction, because as a result of his need Cassius's correct political instincts must give way to Brutus's incorrect ones.

This need is personal as well as political. Cassius and Brutus are the prime examples in the play of those who are both friends and lovers, both politically aligned and personally close at the same time. But their relationship shows the difficulty of maintaining both bonds at once. Cassius reveals early on that he is willing to deceive Brutus for political ends, writing 'in several hands' in order to pretend his messages come 'from several citizens' (1.2.315, 316). He plays upon Brutus's knowledge that they are both friends and lovers – that he is, as he tells Brutus, 'your friend, who loves you' (1.2.36) – to work upon him, in order that Brutus's 'honourable mettle may be wrought / From that it is disposed' (1.2.308–9). In this moment, we see one of the two bonds between them come before the other: friends should not lie to friends, since they share interests, but lovers may lie to lovers, as Brutus does later to Caesar. And what better reason to lie to a lover than to turn them into a friend?

After the assassination, the tension between the two bonds develops further. Cassius and Brutus have a falling out, one which seems half caused by the expectations of their alliance and half by the expectations of their love. Indeed, the terms for the two mix together. Lucilius tells Brutus that Cassius received him 'with courtesy and with respect enough' (4.2.15) that is, with the proper political forms, but nothing more: 'not with such familiar instances / Nor with such free and friendly conference / As he hath used of old' (4.2.16–18). He mingles the expectations of love and party, implicitly attaching an affective meaning to 'friendly' by associating it with 'familiar' and 'free'. Brutus's response combines the two discourses even more explicitly; he calls Cassius 'a hot friend, cooling' and warns Lucilius of what happens 'when love begins to sicken and decay' (4.2.19, 20). Brutus shows the difficulty of keeping two bonds with the same man separate. Cassius was not merely a 'friend', but a 'hot friend', a man tied to Brutus by both the heat of 'love' and the tie of friendship. The two relationships are still distinct; a hot friend cooled is still a friend, if not a lover, and Cassius still used Lucilius respectfully, if not familiarly. But changes in one relationship imply the possibility of changes in the other: hence the lack of 'free and friendly conference'.

This possibility becomes explicit in the following scene when Cassius and Brutus confront each other. Their quarrel stems from different expectations of how their love and their political alliance should interact. Cassius expects Brutus's love to soften his attitude towards Cassius's officers because of Cassius's letters (4.3.2–5). But Brutus believes that he has already expressed his love by restraining himself from chiding Cassius directly for the fault (4.3.15–16). Cassius believes that love functions in the relationship between the men and will allow him to convince Brutus; Brutus believes that it functions internally within himself, as a restraint against his chastisement of Cassius. Because they have different expectations, they are each disappointed; Brutus cannot believe that Cassius would try to write to change his mind, and Cassius thinks that Brutus's personal restraint is insufficient. Each assumes that love and political alliance interact, but they cannot agree on how.

The quarrel that follows stems directly from this disagreement about the boundaries between the political and the personal. According to Brutus, Cassius refused to give Brutus money to pay his soldiers; Brutus treats this not as a political decision but as a personal one: 'was that done like Cassius? / Should I have answered Caius Cassius so?' (4.3.77–8). Cassius denies the charge, and in the process breaks down the last barriers between 'friend' and 'lover'. He says 'a friend should bear a friend's infirmities, / But Brutus makes mine greater than they are', then accuses him directly and personally: 'you love me not' (4.3.85–6, 88). In this moment, Cassius expresses his sense that both of their relationships have fallen apart simultaneously. He believes 'a friendly eye could never see such faults', and that he himself is 'hated by one he loves … / … and all his faults observed' (4.3.89, 95–6). In this moment, Cassius offers to let Brutus kill him: 'strike as thou didst at Caesar: for I know, / When thou didst hate him worst, thou lov'dst him better / Than ever thou lov'dst Cassius' (4.3.104–6). Here we see the comparability of love raise its head again; because Brutus and Cassius are speaking of love and not merely friendship, the issue of degrees of love inevitably arises. Just as inevitably, Caesar is again the subject. But in making this comparison, Cassius sidesteps the obvious point that Caesar was not Brutus's friend, and that it was that lack of friendship (not lack of love) for which Brutus killed him.

Brutus, of course, refuses to kill Cassius and steps back from the brink of the quarrel. Notably, the resolution of the spat comes with the re-assertion of the separation of the two relationships between the men. Cassius and Brutus swear their 'love', but they are not the only parties to the end of the quarrel (4.3.118). Their lieutenants and a poet break in on them, and the poet admonishes them to 'love and be friends' (4.3.130). Brutus and Cassius do not directly acknowledge this dual demand, but this interruption takes them from discussing their love to directing troop movements (4.3.137–8). They then proceed to discuss the political situation and in the process use the term 'friend' once more in a completely political sense, absent any mention of love: they 'have tried the utmost of [their] friends' to raise troops (4.3.212). In the aftermath of their quarrel, they are back to distinguishing between love and politics.

But the earlier breakdown of that distinction is important because it shows the difficulty of holding the two bonds separate. When they are 'ill-tempered' neither Brutus nor Cassius can refrain from collapsing the distinction between their friendship and their love (4.3.114, 115). Yet for their relationship to function properly, the two must remain distinct. When each takes the other's political decisions personally, their relationship breaks down. By showing what happens when Brutus and Cassius blur the line between these two bonds, Shakespeare indicates that the two ought to be separate. Octavius and Antony, after all, have no such problems. The personal and political – the lover and the friend – may overlap, but they cannot collapse, even where they apply to a single person.

Shakespeare gives over the majority of Acts Four and Five to this interplay between Brutus and Cassius in order, I argue, to emphasize the shadow that the early republic has cast upon the conspirators and, by extension, Rome. It is clear in the world of the play that it is dangerous to confuse one's friends and one's lovers. But after the play has spent three acts showing this, it turns to examine what happens when the two relationships are actually mixed, with near-disastrous results. We have already seen that Brutus still yearns for the time when factional distinctions were not necessary, and I believe that these scenes confirm that Cassius does so too. Neither of them believes that they live in that time. But each of them is sufficiently attracted to that sort of personal, factionless politics that they seek to live out that fantasy in their own relationship, even as their attempt results in the disharmony that we see between them.

While both Brutus and Cassius participate in this fantasy, it is Brutus's more explicit adherence to that sort of belief that allows

Antony to call Brutus 'the noblest Roman of them all' after his death (5.5.68). Antony sees that 'all the conspirators save only he / Did that they did in envy of great Caesar', that is, that all of the other conspirators wished to bring down the man who had destroyed their faction (5.5.69–70). Brutus instead killed Caesar 'in a general honest thought / And common good to all' (5.5.71–2). Antony, a supreme political actor who is highly sensitive to faction, admires the opposite political instincts in Brutus. But it is a personal admiration, an admiration for 'his life', not for his action (5.5.73). In this, Antony mirrors Caesar's reaction to the dead Pompey in Plutarch, when he took Pompey's head 'and beholding it, wept'.[49]

Indeed, the end of *Julius Caesar* has much in common with the aftermath of Caesar's defeat of Pompey. Like Caesar, Antony and Octavius take on the attendants of their enemy. Caesar 'curteously vsed all Pompeys friendes' and particularly preferred 'Cassius and Brutus'.[50] In a similar manner Antony, on finding Lucilius, expresses a desire to 'have / Such men my friends [rather] than enemies' (5.3.27–9). In a similar moment, Messala (another of Brutus's men) commends Strato to Octavius: 'take him to follow thee / That did the latest service to my master' (5.5.66–7). Once again, the victors are taking their enemy's followers and attempting to make friends of them. Antony has identified that now there is no faction of Brutus, and thus Lucilius can be Antony's 'friend', while Octavius is doing the same with Messala and Strato.

These changes of allegiance also occur in Plutarch's *Lives*, but Shakespeare compresses the action. Plutarch placed the change of allegiance well after the battle, but in Shakespeare Messala and Lucilius enter with their new masters before they have even found Brutus's body, and Strato is preferred to Octavius immediately (5.5.51 s.d.).[51] Plutarch's Antony and Octavius take time to judge their new companions; Shakespeare's rush headlong into forgiveness and acceptance, like Caesar before them. By mirroring Caesar's magnanimity, Antony and Octavius might seem to be attempting to usher in a new period of calm and peace.

But with the factional prehistory of the play in mind, this instead presages the tensions to come. Caesar's generosity was counterproductive, since it saved his murderers; how then are we to think of Antony and Octavius doing the same? Furthermore, Caesar showed mercy as part of his attempt to position himself as singularly above the factions; the fact that Antony and Octavius both imitate him spells trouble for their future: only one man can be Caesar. Much as Tavares suggests that *Henry V* and *The Battle of Alcazar* end on an anxious note because of the 'presumed shared knowledge of knowing consumers' of the historical future, so too does *Julius Caesar*.[52] The presence of both Antony and Octavius onstage would have served as a reminder of the future: Octavius will become the emperor Augustus, and his war with Antony to become so will once again tear the Roman world along factional lines, as Shakespeare himself would later dramatize in *Antony and Cleopatra*. Not every member of the audience would know that history, though in the 'Latin-soaked culture' of the period (in Stuart Gillespie's words), the narrative would have been extremely familiar to many.[53] But the re-division of Rome into two camps is unmistakeable, especially on a stage where Lucilius now stands with Antony and Messala and Strato with Octavius. It is on this alarming certainty that *Julius Caesar* ends, a note that is most audible when we listen with an ear to the factional prehistory of the play.

5

Coriolanus and the tribunes in the early Roman republic

The conspirators in *Julius Caesar*, especially Brutus, constantly cast their minds back to the early republic, which they identify as a golden age. But as we have seen that vision leads them astray in the rough and tumble world of the late Republic. In *Coriolanus*, Shakespeare himself turns to that earlier time, setting the play in the founding days of the Roman republic. So what did Shakespeare's contemporaries know, or think they knew, about this particular Rome?

I argue that what they knew hinged on the creation of the tribunes in Rome and Coriolanus's inability to accept that change, and that viewing Shakespeare's play through this lens allows us to see the play as one long meditation on what it means for Coriolanus himself to belong – or not belong – in Rome. I suggest that Shakespeare centres the play on the political change created by introducing the tribunes, which occurs offstage during the first scene, and on Coriolanus's reaction to it. This in turn focuses our attention on the tribunes as a disruptive force and on the tragedy of Coriolanus's failed search for a society in which he can operate politically. Coriolanus's troubles result not merely from his own personal failings but from inevitable consequences of this change in the political structure, and his death at the end is ultimately a welcome release from a world that no longer has space for him politically.

Early Republican Rome, and with it the story behind *Coriolanus*, was well known to the early modern English from classical sources and their contemporary translations, if not as omnipresent as the history of Caesar. This story centred on Caius Martius Coriolanus,[1] a patrician who was exiled from Rome at the behest of the tribunes and returned with an invading army, only to be dissuaded at the last moment by the joint appeal of his mother and wife. The story was most closely associated with two major classical histories: Plutarch's *Lives*, in Greek, and Livy's *Ab Urbe Condita*, in Latin. Both of these texts were widely available in Shakespearean England, and each had been translated into English: Plutarch in 1579 by Thomas North, as we have seen in the previous chapter, and Livy in 1600 by Philemon Holland. By examining these translations, some modifications made in translation, and other references to the Coriolanus story in early modern England, I will demonstrate that the versions of the story circulating in Shakespeare's time were clear both that the office of the tribunes was created during Caius Martius's life and that the tribunes were, in turn, responsible for his downfall. I will then show how Shakespeare further emphasizes the importance of the tribunes and continue on to read the play in that light, arguing that the centrality of the tribunes to Caius Martius's troubles in Rome shapes the narrative and emotional arcs of the play, bringing to the fore the questions of how and whether Caius Martius can belong in Rome.

The part of the story *Coriolanus* focuses on begins with the plebeians in revolt. In both North's Plutarch and Holland's Livy, the revolt only ends when the Senate agrees to institute the '*Tribuni Plebis*', the 'Tribunes of the commons'.[2] The patricians solve an immediate crisis by granting an institutional change: the creation of the tribunes. Caius Martius opposes this creation, and, in a later crisis focused on the distribution of grain, he tries to 'take from them their Tribuneshippe'.[3] He wishes to use this opportunity to free the patricians of the 'Tribunes authoritie ouer them' in exchange for the food that the plebeians need in this crisis.[4] For Plutarch's and Livy's Caius Martius, the grain troubles are not really about grain. Instead, they are about the degree of the Senate's political power over Rome, which Martius sees expressed in the status of the tribunes.

The direct result of this in both narratives is that the tribunes are able to use Martius's overaggressive attempt to eliminate their office to exile him from Rome instead. They bring Martius to trial, during which the tribunes remind the people of Martius's desire 'to take the office of Tribuneshippe from them'.[5] He scorns the tribunes, which only inflames their hatred.[6] The tribunes and people combine to cast him out of Rome as a direct response to his political threat.

The common element of both these narratives is that Caius Martius's downfall is intimately linked to his clashes with the newly created tribunes, and in particular his wish to live in a Rome where they do not exist. We can see this understanding of the story emphasized in Holland's translation of Livy's text, where the choices he makes as a translator demonstrate an awareness of the importance of the tribunes and their rivalry with Caius Martius. Holland's detailed alterations demonstrate the receptivity of at least one influential early modern reader to the importance of the tribunes in the Coriolanus story. Examining how Holland shaped the narrative he told gives us a glimpse of the sort of interpretation of the Coriolanus story from which Shakespeare began his own alterations.

Holland subtly emphasizes the importance of the relationship between Caius Martius and the tribunes at two key points. When Caius Martius rises up in the Senate to decry the power of the tribunes, Livy describes him as '*hostis tribuniciae potestatis*', an enemy of the power of the tribunes.[7] Holland instead calls him an 'utter and capitall enemie to the Tribunes power and authoritie', adding the intensifying phrase 'utter and capitall' and expanding *potestatis* into the double 'power and authority' (66). 'Utter and capitall' emphasizes the intensity of this rivalry, while 'power and authority' makes clear that to Holland, it was not merely the degree to which the tribunes *were able to* act in Rome that offended Caius Martius, but the fact that they had the *right* to act: their authority. The Latin *potestas* can be either (and both) of these things, as can the English 'power', but by expanding the single word into the double phrase Holland brings them both explicitly to light.

Holland makes a similar change when the tribunes call Martius to answer for his words in the trial. Livy describes his reaction thus: '*contemptim primo Marcius audiebat minas tribunicias*', at first Martius heard the tribune's threats with contempt.[8] Holland translates this as '*Martius* at the first scorned the Tribunes thundering threats, & gave the hearing, as though he made smal reckoning there of' (67). Once again Holland doubles and expands the meaning of the Latin to develop a specific nuance. Here he extracts both the sense that Caius Martius was rude in his reaction ('scorned') and that he dismissed the tribunes ('smal reckoning'). In addition, he adds the term 'thundering' to the tribunes' 'threats' (*minas*), expanding the impression of the danger they present by introducing the euphonius 'Tribunes thundering threats' at the same time that he emphasizes Martius's dismissal of them. These two additions heighten the contrast between the two parties' attitudes, ratcheting up the tension of their confrontation.

Notably, Holland does not apply this same technique when he describes Caius Martius's relationship with the plebeians as a whole. In between the two moments I have quoted above, Livy describes the people realizing that they would have a chance to judge Caius Martius: '*se iudicem quisque se dominum uitae necisque inimici factum uidebat*', each one saw that he was made the judge and lord of the life and death of his enemy.[9] Holland translates this as 'everie man saw, that he was himselfe to be the judge and lord of his enemies life and death' (67). He does not re-emphasize *inimici* as he had *hostis*, leaving it as simply 'of his enemies', and the double 'judge and lord' is in Livy rather than introduced by Holland. The effect of these two different approaches, concentrated in a small section of the text, is to give a greater sense of the importance of Caius Martius's relationship with the tribunes relative to the Latin original. They are the ones who are 'utter and capitall' enemies, while Martius and the people are merely 'enemies', and their threat is also emphasized.

These minor changes reflect perspectives already present in Livy's original Latin. But the changes build on a tendency in the classical versions of the Coriolanus story: the heavy emphasis on the relationship between Caius Martius and the tribunes as the central element. These changes are significant insofar as they suggest that Holland was alive to the importance of that relationship, an awareness that Shakespeare adopted and built upon.

In *Coriolanus*, Shakespeare expanded this reading of the Coriolanus story, centring the relationship between the newly created tribunes and Caius Martius. But in doing so, he did not react to Holland and North (or Livy and Plutarch) alone, though their translations represent the most complete treatment of the story – and as we have already seen from Cox-Jensen, both Livy and Plutarch circulated widely in the period.[10] Coriolanus's troubled relationship with the tribunes cropped up in summaries and translations of chronicles,[11] in essays and advice books,[12] and as a historical model for contemporary history.[13] It is from such retellings of the story that Shakespeare built his own version, drawing on the hints in all these texts that the true heart of the story lies in Caius Martius's own reaction to these new tribunes.

The most significant difference in Shakespeare's narrative from those that we have examined above is in the timing of Caius Martius's attack on the tribunes. In Plutarch, Livy and the other versions of the story, this is a matter of public policy in response to the people's unrest during a famine. In Shakespeare, the issue is more personal. The attack is a reaction to the tribunes' treatment of him in particular. Shakespeare's Martius takes issue with the tribune Sicinius's use of the word 'shall' in declaring that he (Caius Martius) shall not be consul and rants for over eighty lines (with interruptions) against the institution of the tribunes (3.1.86–171).[14] He calls on those 'that love the fundamental part of state / More than you doubt the change on't' to 'at once pluck out / The multitudinous tongue' (3.1.152–3, 156–7). This 'tongue' should be identified as the 'tribunes of the people / The tongues o'th'common mouth' that he disdained at the beginning of the scene (3.1.21–2). Caius Martius's 'doubt' here takes two meanings simultaneously: both uncertainty and fear. He is calling on those who, like him, 'love' the political structure of old Rome with its senators and consuls – 'the fundamental part of state', implicitly contrasted with the apparently non-fundamental tribunes – to fight back by removing the tribunes, putting aside both their uncertainty that change has come and their fear of that change in order to act swiftly. He concludes by wishing to 'throw their power i'th'dust' (3.1.171). He has grasped the essential nature of his problem: the structural change to the political organization of the state brought on by the introduction of tribunes has made Rome a different place. In his desperate desire to return to the old Rome, he calls for the removal of the tribunes.

This appeal would not be out of place in the other versions of the story, except that it unfolds not as a coherent speech in the Senate in a debate but as an individual outburst of vitriol in reaction to a personal disappointment. Shakespeare's Caius Martius is personally offended by the actions and the attitude of the tribunes, and his desire to abolish them is far less statesmanlike than it is elsewhere. Although his concern is still for the change to 'the fundamental part of the state', the issue that has prompted him to that concern is personal (his own inability to properly acclimate to that change) rather than public (the needs of the patrician class as a whole).

Perhaps because of this, Shakespeare's Caius Martius, unlike Plutarch's, Livy's and the others', appears to be without allies in his desire to rid the republic of its tribunes. Plutarch and Livy in particular both make sure to emphasize that Martius's positions were widely held: that he 'wanne all the young men, and almost all the riche men to his opinion' or that 'many thought' like him.[15] Only in Shakespeare is Martius alone in this position.

Yet ironically Shakespeare's Caius Martius has more reason for his outburst. Where in the other versions of the story his call for the abolition of the tribunes is mere opportunism, in Shakespeare's Caius Martius reacts to a specific exercise (he would say abuse) of the tribunes' authority: their announcement that he will not become consul. Shakespeare's Caius Martius has a specific problem that will actually be solved by the abolition of the tribunes, while the others' are merely finding an excuse for a power play.

This is typical of Shakespeare's treatment of the tribunes. He simultaneously emphasizes their importance to the events of Caius Martius's downfall and makes that importance particular to Caius Martius. Another example of such an alteration is Shakespeare's handling of the character of Menenius Agrippa, whom he uses as a tool to examine the relationship between Caius Martius and the tribunes. Shakespeare's Menenius is able to adapt to the introduction of the tribunes in precisely the way that Martius cannot. They voluntarily give him responsibility for bringing Martius to trial (3.1.331–2). He is foremost among those who counsel Martius on how to address the tribunes appropriately in the trial, telling him 'speak fair', 'only fair speech', 'mildly' and 'calmly' (3.2.71, 97, 145; 3.3.31). And notably, he retains the tribunes' favour even after Martius's exile (4.6.11–13). Menenius is a model of the ability to function politically. Despite the distaste he shows for the tribunes when Martius's army approaches – 'a pair of tribunes that have racked for Rome, / To make coals cheap' (5.1.16–17) – he nevertheless accepts them as part of the system, understands how to handle them, and is able to keep them from seeing the true depth of his disdain until he wishes to make it known. This is precisely the set of skills that Martius lacks, the lack of which leads to his downfall. He thus serves as an example of what Martius could be, but is not – a characterological technique we will see again in *Othello*, where the Duke models effective enquiry for Othello.

Menenius's interactions with the tribunes also expose their hatred of Martius in particular. He is alone with them onstage twice, and in each case the subject immediately turns to Martius. When Menenius engages them in a debate about men's faults, they talk of Martius: 'he's poor in no one fault, but stored with all' (2.1.17). Later, they use Menenius's presence as the occasion to crow that 'your Coriolanus is not much miss'd' (4.6.13). Significantly, his role in provoking these expressions of the tribunes' hatred of Martius, like his function as a potential political model for Martius, is entirely Shakespeare's invention. Menenius appears in Plutarch and Livy only as the messenger to the plebeians during the riots that lead to the introduction of the tribunes. Shakespeare crafts out of that minor functionary a much larger figure, and uses that figure to focus our attention on the personal relationship between Martius and the tribunes.

But why should it matter that our focus is on Caius Martius and the tribunes? Ultimately, these changes reveal *Coriolanus* as a play about belonging: about the way that Caius Martius belongs in Rome at the beginning of the play, and how that belonging has shattered by the end of it. It is about the process through which his sense of belonging drops out from under him; how he tries to compensate, correct and retaliate for those failures of belonging; and how he fails again, this time to his death.

But if *Coriolanus* is about belonging, then we must acknowledge the fact that Caius Martius himself does not seem to belong comfortably in Rome. Within thirty lines of the opening of the play the Citizens have concluded that they will proceed 'against him first', because 'he's a very dog to the commonalty' (1.1.26). We see their reason for such an opinion later in the scene, when he enters and immediately harangues the Citizens as 'dissentious rogues' (1.1.159). It is clear that at least one group of Romans does not wish to be associated with Martius, and that the feeling is mutual.

The sense that Martius does not belong in Rome extends beyond mutual antagonism with the plebeians. The senators may find in him a 'worthy Martius', and his mother may believe him a 'good Martius', but neither of them is comfortable with how he fits into Roman life (1.1.231, 1.3.23). Even to his friend Cominius, he can be 'too modest ... / More cruel to your good report than grateful / To us that give you truly' (1.9.52–4). He cannot bear to hear his deeds retold: he flees the scene when he is being celebrated, despite Menenius's instructions to stay (2.2.75). He has to be argued into asking the plebeians for their votes. Even at the most important point of the play, he refuses to act as he is supposed to: he will not be quiet after the tribunes have informed him that he will not be consul, despite Menenius's urgent 'not now, not now' and the injunction that, if he must speak, he should do so 'mildly' (3.1.64, 3.2.145). He is 'too absolute' to do as is expected of him (3.2.40). Coriolanus may be a paragon of martial prowess and vigorous action but there is always something slightly off about his interactions with others, even in his moments of triumph. He does not belong.

Here it is important to define what I mean by 'belonging'. When I refer to Caius Martius's belonging in Rome here, I am talking about a very limited political sense of belonging that is only one of several types shown in the play. Much as the factional nature of Rome in *Julius Caesar* comes across in the use of 'friend' and 'lover', the complex overlay of belonging to Rome in *Coriolanus* finds expression in the contested status of the word 'Roman'. At a basic level, 'Roman' refers to those who are from Rome in some way; we see it in this sense when Martius talks of the Volscian Aufidius 'piercing our Romans' (1.5.11). But the term quickly acquires other meanings. One can be Roman by acting in a way that reflects the values of the community, as when Cominius commends his men for having 'come off / Like Romans, neither foolish in our stands / Nor cowardly in retire' (1.6.1–3). One can also be Roman simply by birth: Menenius claims not only himself but also Martius as Roman in his visit to the Volscian camp, although they are by then on different sides of the war (5.2.37–8). One can even be Roman by political action: the 'state' is also 'Roman', in Menenius's words, and thus participation in the political community is a mark of Roman-ness (1.1.64).

These different types of 'Roman', like the categories of belonging that they reflect, can overlap and compete. It is possible to be, in Caius Martius's words, 'though in Rome littered; not Romans', and we meet a man who is 'a Roman, and my services are ... against 'em' (3.1.240, 4.3.4–5). The very superabundance of the term in the play, I suggest, points to the idea that we should not move too quickly to assert that there is one 'true *romanitas*' and the others are false.[16] While Caius Martius certainly believes his own Roman-ness is superior to others', the contested status of the word means that he is not necessarily right.

Instead, Caius Martius operates in a world in which his Romanness is a complex compound of multiple orientations towards multiple communities that can all be Roman. I argue that the play is focused on Caius Martius's belonging in Rome as a member of what we might call the 'community of law and political action'.[17] I distinguish belonging to a political society in this manner from belonging to the larger 'sphere of common culture and values'.[18] Caius Martius does not fully belong in Rome in that sense, as he is too much of an outlier in his behaviour. On the other hand, there is also a kind of belonging based on 'common blood and descent'.[19] In this respect, of course, Caius Martius will always belong in Rome because of his ancestry. But it is possible to belong to a society in one sense and not another. The fact that Caius Martius is a member of the community of political action, or is a Roman by common blood and descent, does not imply that he must be a member of the common culture of values, nor does the fact that he does not belong in the latter sense invalidate his belonging in the former two. This is also true of his Volscian-ness after his exile. He is clearly not a Volscian by birth, but he engages with their political structures in his time away from Rome. Hereafter, I will primarily focus on the ways in which he belongs by participating in the Roman state and the accompanying community of political action, although I will return to other types of belonging as this form comes into conflict with them.

At the beginning of the play, Caius Martius belongs in Rome in this political sense. However, his place in this community does not even survive the first scene. The introduction of the tribunes to the political structure of Rome, and Caius Martius's reaction to that change, marks the point at which he ceases to belong in Rome in this way. He does not cease to be a citizen, or stop caring about the political functioning of Rome – at least not until the total breakdown when he is banished from it – but the introduction of the tribunes, along with his reaction to that introduction, destroys his ability to act within the Roman political structure. At this moment, he no longer belongs in Rome because he can no longer function in it politically.

It is this loss of belonging that brings about Caius Martius's downfall and ultimate death. The first half of the play, until his banishment from Rome, exposes and comments on that loss and its impact on him. The second half, after his departure, focuses on his search for belonging elsewhere and his inability to achieve it anywhere. Ultimately that search can only end in his death, as it had threatened to do in Rome. When we read *Coriolanus* with attention to this emphasis on the tribunes and Caius Martius's reaction to them, we find that Shakespeare has woven out of Caius Martius's inability to adapt to a changing political structure a play that is a meditation on what it means to have lost a world. The play depicts the tragedy of his search in the present for a belonging that was only available in the past.

Unlike the other versions of the Coriolanus story extant in the period, Shakespeare never shows us Caius Martius before the change in the state. He passes over Martius's youth, except in retrospective speeches. Instead, *Coriolanus* begins with a riot. Specifically, the play begins *mid*-riot. The leaders of the crowd are engaged in debate about their demands by Menenius, who attempts to calm them. Caius Martius interrupts their discussion, insulting the plebeians in the process, to deliver the news that a similar riot on the other side of town has already been resolved by giving the plebeians 'five tribunes to defend their vulgar wisdoms, / Of their own choice' (1.1.210–11). On this news, along with the almost simultaneous report of a new war against the Volsces, the crowd disperses and Caius Martius and the senators go to plan the war.

What this means is that the first scene of the play reports precisely that change in political structure to which Caius Martius will not be able to adapt. Interestingly, this action occurs offstage, and Caius Martius himself brings the news onstage with him. Because of this, we never see Caius Martius in the old Rome where he belongs. By the time he enters, the change has already happened; he merely reports it. He begins his part in the play by announcing the terms of his own destruction, and the fact that he is the messenger focuses our attention not only on the political ramifications of the change but on his own personal relationship to it.

The significance of this moment has not been lost on critics of Shakespeare's play. But these critics have not read this development in the context of the contemporary Renaissance English understanding of the tribunes in the Coriolanus story that I explored above. Instead, their responses fall into two major groups – those who directly identify the tribunes with the people, as a single force,[20] and those who treat this moment as only as an inflection point in the long-term trajectory of Roman history.[21] There is overlap between these groups as well: Paul Cantor, for instance, identifies a 'division of the city into patrician and plebeian parties' in which the plebeians wield their power 'through their tribunes', thus conflating people and tribunes, but also identifies the main thrust of the play as showing 'an aristocracy on its way to becoming a democracy' and declining in virtue as it does.[22] Both of these responses miss something important about the establishment of the tribunate: the tribunes stand as a third party to both the patricians and the plebeians, and the change in Rome, while it may have long-term effects, has an immediate impact in the world of the play.

First, I would suggest that to see the tribunes as merely representatives of the plebeians is to re-enact the error made by Caius Martius and his fellow patricians. They believe that the tribunes they have allowed to be established are merely the new faces of the plebeians with whom they dealt before. But the tribunes have their own interests and their own agenda, which do not always match that of the plebeians. In this I agree with Alexander Leggatt's scepticism about the value of the tribunes to the people.[23] Like Leggatt, I believe that the new tribunes alter something about how the people and Caius Martius interact: that for them 'Coriolanus is simply the enemy', and that they use the people in order to triumph over him.[24] Caius Martius, in turn, 'is committed to an idea of how the state should be run', and thus conceives of politics differently than the tribunes do.[25] But whereas for Leggatt this difference means that the enmity between the tribunes and Caius Martius is a one-sided hatred, in the context of the Coriolanus story explored above I see it as mutual: the tribunes and Caius Martius each view the other as the fundamental enemy.

We can see this difference of interests between the people and their tribunes most clearly in the first scene of the second act, in which the tribunes plot to thwart Caius Martius's desire to be consul. In their plotting they reveal the distance between their own position and the plebeians' interests. They are aware that in public they 'must suggest the people in what hatred / He still hath held them' and emphasize 'his soaring insolence' (2.1.239–40, 248). In other words, his disdain for the people is their primary theme when manipulating the plebeians. In their own minds, however, they are primarily concerned with the fear that their 'office may, during his power, go sleep' (2.1.217). They want to retain the power of their office, and see blocking Caius Martius as key to maintaining that power. However, they do not plan to use the argument about their office to convince the people to follow them: evidently, a straightforward argument in favour of their office would not work (unlike in Plutarch, where that is exactly the argument the tribunes make). While it might seem to us that eliminating the tribunes would be a concern for the plebeians as well as the tribunes, no plebeian ever mentions such a concern, and the only semi-private conversations that the plebeians have after the institution of the tribunes are about Martius's attitudes towards the plebeians themselves, not towards the tribunes (2.3.1–45, 81–2). The people certainly share many interests and opinions with the tribunes, but this discussion shows that a gap has emerged between what the tribunes think and what they are willing to tell the citizens. They develop their plan to discuss Caius Martius's insolence and hatred rather than his desire to end their power precisely because the plebeians do not share their same priorities. Caius Martius's dispute with the tribunes is not the same as his conflict with the people, and that difference has consequences.

This leads to the second common critical error regarding the tribunes: imagining that their institution has little to no immediate effect on Rome, but only serves as the start of a slow change of social values that will lead to the decline of the Republic. This position has the obvious problem that the greatest heights of the Roman Republic happened after this change. To take this position literally would be to claim that the Republic was in decline for almost its entire existence, given that the kings were overthrown during Caius Martius's lifetime. But beyond that, I argue that to take this position is also to ignore the tribunes' near-immediate impact on Caius Martius's situation. To see this impact, we must turn to the moment of his election as consul, and examine both how it came about and how it fell apart.

The strangest fact about Caius Martius's unrealized consulship is that even though he throws a fit when he does not receive it, he does not actually seem to want to acquire it. Most obviously, he does not want to have to do what becoming consul traditionally requires: to 'speak to the people', to 'put on the gown, stand naked, and entreat them, / For my wounds' sake, to give their suffrage' (2.2.133, 136–7). He begs that he might 'o'erleap that custom', for 'it is a part / That I shall blush in acting' (2.2.135, 143–4). It pains him to have to go through with this ritual submission to the approval of the people.

His distaste for the ritual has been much discussed in the critical literature but, I suggest, it has been largely misunderstood. The scenes in which Caius Martius expresses unwillingness to beg for the people's votes, and the following scene in which he does so, have consistently been read as showing his unwillingness to submit to the people in any way, and his refusal to engage in any kind of subtle, indirect or political act.[26] I think it is more accurate to suggest, with Manfred Pfister and Jennifer Low, that this moment is not about an inherent resistance to being political, but about the physical and emotional discomfort of performing and of being seen.[27] In other words, Caius Martius is not unwilling to act politically in a general sense; he is unwilling to act out this one particular action because of what it specifically demands of him.

Looking at the details of the scene with the political elements of the historicism of setting in mind bears this out. While he is uncomfortable with the details of how he must present himself, Caius Martius still pushes through that discomfort in order to enact a political strategy of his own. When he initially expresses his unwillingness to go through these forms to become consul, he is told (by the tribunes, among others) that he has no other choice. If he wishes to receive the office, 'the people / Must have their voices; neither will they bate / One jot of ceremony' and he must 'go fit you to the custom' (2.2.138–40, 141). He must ask the people – the plebeians – for their voices, and he must do so in the 'customary gown' (2.3.85). There is no other way to be consul.

And so he does it. He goes out in the gown and begs for votes. But he does not do so in the way that consuls have done in the past. Instead, he develops a strategy to avoid that part of the requirement that troubles him: the humiliating (to him) nature of the submission to the people. This strategy relies on his knowledge of the political system in which he believes he is acting. Caius Martius knows the 'ceremony' required of him: he must speak to the plebeians, in a simple gown, and once he does that, they will confirm him as consul. As the Third Citizen says while the plebeians are waiting for Caius Martius to come to them, 'we have the power in ourselves' to deny him the consulship, 'but it is a power that we have no power to do. For, if he show us his wounds and tell us his deeds, we are to put our tongues into those wounds to speak for them. So if he tells us his noble deeds, we must also tell him our noble acceptance of them' (2.3.4–9). The 'power' of refusing him is 'a power that we have no power to do' because there is a long-standing, well-defined system in place here, one that long precedes the tribunes and one with which Caius Martius is familiar. A potential consul who has served Rome will show his wounds, name his deeds and ask for the plebeians' voices, and in return for his showing, naming and asking, they will give those voices to him. If the conditions are met, there is no room for the plebeians to exercise their 'power'.

Caius Martius intends to use this system to his own advantage. Unlike Cominius, who will later aggressively claim the status of one who 'can show for Rome / Her enemies' marks upon me' as a position of political authority (3.3.109–10), Caius Martius will do the absolute minimum to pass the plebeians' inspection while showing them as little respect as possible. He will not show his wounds publicly or show deference to the people. Instead, he treats them with ridicule, turning the phrase 'your voices', which represents their role in the system, into a mocking refrain: 'Your voices? For your voices I have fought; / Watch'd for your voices; for your voices bear / Of wounds two dozen odd; battles thrice six / I have seen and heard of; for your voices have / Done many things, some less, some more. / Your voices? Indeed I would be consul' (2.3.124–9). This cannot be meant sincerely, since Caius Martius has already expressed his disgust with this sort of rhetoric to the patricians, disdaining the idea that he should 'brag unto them "Thus I did, and thus", / Show them th'unaching scars which I should hide, / As if I had receiv'd them for the hire / Of their breath only!' (2.2.146–9). Rather, this is mockery. As the Third Citizen will later complain, 'he flouted us downright' (2.3.157). But at the same time, we should not lose track of what Martius has, technically, done here. He has named his deeds. He has requested votes. He is in the customary gown. As such, even though it is intended as mockery, it is also technically sufficient lip service to the obligations set upon him, satisfying the minimum requirements of the ritual of state.

Notably his repeated naming of his deeds and the people's knowledge of them allows him to skate by the public showing of his wounds that is supposed to signify his submission to the people for inspection. His wounds are publicly known, but never publicly shown. The wounds he has 'to show you' will only 'be yours in private', but their existence has been made so public that the citizens miss this fact as they give their voices (2.3.76). By playing on the public awareness that his deeds brought many wounds, Caius

Martius is able to avoid the humiliating (to him) act of showing them and having them seen, while still gaining the people's voices. The plebeians do his work for him, telling him that 'you have received many wounds for your country', and thus reaffirming the reality of the wounds he never shows (2.3.104–5). As long as he adopts the right posture and tells the people the minimum that they need to hear, their minds fill in the gaps in his submission for him.

And it works. We must be careful not to assume Caius Martius's strategy is a total failure simply because he does not become consul. It is true that he is far from beloved. Before he even comes onstage in the first scene, the First Citizen tells us that 'he hath faults, with surplus, to tire in repetition' (1.1.41). However, the plebeians seem willing, despite his attitudes and unpopularity, to let him pass as consul because he observed the minimum required forms. They might grumble that 'he us'd us scornfully' when asking for their voices, but they cannot deny that 'he has our voices' (2.3.160, 153). At this point, Caius Martius has received the voices required to be elected consul. As he himself will later complain when the election is revoked, he has been 'passed for consul with full voice' (3.3.57). In this moment, his minimal conformity to the requirements has worked.

This moment is a Shakespearean addition to the story, as Lisa Starks-Estes has pointed out.[28] In the Roman sources, there is no hint that Caius Martius is unwilling to show his wounds in order to be consul. I agree with Starks-Estes, following Low, that this is a matter of his discomfort with being exposed and penetrated by the eyes of those watching.[29] However, I suggest that it is also a moment that highlights the fine line between Caius Martius's political savvy relative to the plebeians alone, as in the older political structure, and his inability to function in the same political space after the tribunes' intervention. It is, after all, the tribunes who elicit in the plebeians that awareness that 'no man saw' his injuries at all (2.3.162), which prompts their willingness to reverse his election.

Thus, in this moment the play confirms for us that Caius Martius did belong in the old Rome in the political sense to some degree. He is uncomfortable performing for the people, but he is capable of functioning. He could fulfill the requirements of the (old) political system sufficiently to achieve his ends. His discomfort shows that he may not fully belong to the Roman society of culture and values, but his ability to overcome the barrier of having to gain the people's 'voices' proves that he did once, in fact, belong to the community of political action. He has acted effectively in the sphere of politics as they operated before the introduction of the tribunes, and even found a way to bend the rules slightly in his own favour.

But while his efforts would have been successful in the old system, they are not in the new. He failed to account for the presence of the tribunes, who undo his victory starting with the observation that his wounds went unseen. Much like King John struggles to accept the importance of the unanimity of his lords, Caius Martius is unable to think through the implications of his actions in the new context of the tribunate. After the plebeians are shown how Caius Martius has successfully manipulated them, the tribunes move the people to change their voice and 'pass[] him unelected' (2.3.196). They then organize the spectacle which will 'revoke / Your ignorant election' (2.3.215–16). By separating the people's interactions with Martius from the tribunes' later rhetorical triumph, Shakespeare demonstrates that Martius's political troubles come specifically from his inability to predict or counter the tribunes' actions, rather than from any inability to act politically more generally.

Of course, it is not merely Caius Martius but the entire patrician society that has failed to account for the tribunes properly, though ultimately the rest of them adapt to the new situation. Menenius has already told Caius Martius that 'the tribunes / Endue you with the people's voice' (2.3.136–7). Here Menenius is making explicit the (incorrect) assumption that he and Caius Martius share, that once the people have given their voices, the tribunes, as representatives of the people, will simply confirm that fact to the senate. But this does not happen. Like Martius, Menenius is making the mistake of thinking that the plebeians and the tribunes are one, and that the voices of the plebeians *must* be confirmed by the tribunes. However, as we have seen, far from confirming their vote and rubber-stamping the plebeians' already expressed opinion, the tribunes instead exercise their own agency, turning the plebeians against Caius Martius to save their own power. This is the moment that they have been waiting for, and they seize it.

This mistake mirrors Brutus's error in allowing Marc Antony to speak at Caesar's funeral. Like Brutus, Caius Martius and the patricians think they know how politics works, but have made a fundamental error in assessing who matters in that system and how. And like Antony, the tribunes take that opportunity to influence the plebeians behind their backs. The ensuing scenes, in which Caius Martius is rejected by the plebeians, are carefully directed by the tribunes. Before the plebeians are even allowed onstage, the tribunes incite Martius by telling him that he will not be consul. Martius responds with the lengthy rant about 'shall' that we have already examined above. The tribunes seize this moment to move from denying Martius the consulship to condemning him to death, calling Martius a 'traitorous innovator' and a 'foe to th'public weal' (3.1.175, 176). Martius then seizes Sicinius and threatens to 'shake thy bones / Out of thy garments' (3.1.179–80). It is at this moment that the plebeians enter.

The moment is expertly stage-managed to convey the message the tribunes wish to send: that Caius Martius is out of control and must be stopped. They tell the people that Caius Martius wishes 'to take from you all your power', and that 'Marcius would have all from you', but do not explain precisely what that entails (3.1.182, 195). In fact, they conspicuously refrain from saying that Caius Martius wishes to remove the tribunes. Instead, they vaguely refer to the people's own power and 'liberties' (3.1.194), and call for his death. The plebeians are never permitted to hear precisely what Caius Martius had proposed. Instead they are driven into a frenzy by the tribunes; they riot and must be 'beat in' to protect Caius Martius from being torn apart (3.1.230 s.d.).

When Martius is brought to trial, he is once again provoked into anger. Here, it is the repetition of the accusation of treachery that incites him. In this scene, the plebeians are onstage throughout; however, their participation has been curtailed by the tribunes, who have directed them through the aediles merely to echo the tribunes: 'if I say fine, cry "Fine," if death, cry "Death"' (3.3.16). The tribunes' will rules here, not the plebeians'. And so it proves: the plebeians enact the tribunes' desires, ultimately calling for Caius Martius's banishment.

The tribunes' intervention represents the disappearance of the Rome Caius Martius lived for, the Rome he grew up in and the political system in which he belonged. That was the Rome in which his manipulations of the election would have worked, and therefore the Rome in which he could have become consul without truly having had to submit to the plebeians. It was the Rome in which all that mattered were his deeds and his self. And that Rome is gone. In the moment in which the tribunes are able to undo his election,

Martius realizes that their establishment, and the structural change that it represented, has undone him as well.

Unsurprisingly, this is the moment when Caius Martius lashes out at the tribunes and calls for the abolition of their office. But he does not merely demand the destruction of the tribunes at some unspecified point in the future. He insists that the tribunes must be removed 'at once' (3.1.156). He represents the change brought on by the introduction of the tribunes as an already occurring degradation: 'you are plebeians, / If they be senators, and they are no less', 'it makes the consuls base', and 'we debase / The nature of our seats' by tolerating them (3.1.102–3, 109, 136–7). The threat is immediate because the damage it will do has already occurred and must be reversed. The 'better hour' in which he hopes to see the patricians 'throw their [the tribunes'] power i'th'dust', is the present hour, which is in his mind a better one than the riot crisis in which the tribunes were created (3.1.169, 171). Martius represents the danger as threatening the entire state, as well as his entire social class, but ultimately his counterattack is a reaction to his own realization that he himself can no longer belong in a Rome where the tribunes have power. From this we can see that Shakespeare does not, as Worden would have it, 'substitute[] psychological for constitutional perception',[30] but rather unites the two. Caius Martius is making both a statement about the dangers of constitutional reform in Rome and about his own personal needs. The combination is what makes this moment particularly potent.

In this context, when Caius Martius finally exits Rome on the defiant line 'there is a world elsewhere' (3.3.134), he is truly seeking another world: a world, like his old Rome, in which he can belong to the community of political action. I argue that he does not conceive of himself as leaving all society entirely, becoming a 'Man without a City' or stepping 'outside state and family'.[31] He only intends to leave the present Roman society. Tellingly, as he imagines the future he will carve out for himself outside of Rome, he tells his mother that she will 'hear from me still, and never of me aught / But what is like me formerly' (4.1.52–3). He looks to recreate the past in his future: not making a new world, but finding another world that already exists and matches his past. He faces not inward, but backward and outward; he does not desire to create a new, solitary Caius Martius but to recreate the former one in a different place.

It is no surprise, then, that in the search for a political community in which he can belong he turns to the only other society available: the Volscians. And he finds a place among them, at least at first. He comes offering to 'fight / Against my cankered country', in order 'to do thee service', and he is welcomed (4.5.92–3, 103). He is brought to the 'friendly senators' – note the lack of tribunes – and offered 'th'one half of my [Aufidius's] commission' (4.5.134, 140). He is 'set at the upper end o'th'table', and the senators 'stand bald before him' (4.5.195–6, 197). He has been given not only a job to do – the destruction of Rome – but a particular place in the political structure of the Volscian state. He is now co-commander with Aufidius, who has been 'cut i'th'middle' and become 'but one half of what he was yesterday' (4.5.200, 201). And notably, the position did not have to be begged: it was given 'by the entreaty and grant of the whole table' of senators, with nary a plebeian or tribune to be heard (4.5.202). He is now in the position among the Volscians that he believed was his right among the Romans.

This is an episode that is noticeably different in Shakespeare than in the other versions of the story. Both Plutarch and Livy have Caius Martius go to the Volscians, and live among them with the equivalent of Aufidius, but neither has any reference to 'senators' feasting Caius Martius. Plutarch says merely that Aufidius 'entertained him in the honourablest manner he could', while Livy explains that 'the Volcians at his comming received him courteouslie'.[32] Indeed, both authors omit any reference to the political organization of the Volscians beyond military organization. Likewise, the 1578 translation of Appian reports merely that Martius 'fled to the Volscians'.[33] Only Shakespeare provides us with a more fully realized Volscian political structure in which Caius Martius can find 'senators', and in which he can enjoy the absence of tribunes. If we attend to the significance of the tribunes in Rome, this more elaborated Volscian political structure is notable because it parallels Rome – but without the tribunes.

Caius Martius believes he has found his 'world elsewhere' among the Volscians. But his place in this community of political action is conditional: he can only occupy it if he leads them to destroy Rome. This he immediately endeavours to do. His campaign of destruction runs even to the gates of Rome.

When his army is camped before Rome's walls, Caius Martius's integration into the Volscian political community is at its height.

When Menenius comes to Martius to try to beg for Rome, he is spurned by the camp watch, who repeatedly refer to Martius as 'our general' (5.2.7, 50–1, 107). This casual designation of him as 'ours' is the sign that Caius Martius has found a place where he belongs. It is a belonging he has embraced, refusing to bear the name 'Coriolanus', with its reminder of his defeat of the Volscians at Corioles, intending instead to 'forge[] himself a name o'th'fire / Of burning Rome' (5.1.14–15). Interestingly, this would presumably have made him Caius Martius Romanus, a strange addition to our listing of ways in which a character can be 'Roman', if one only present as a momentary possibility.

But ultimately, the condition required to belong in the Volscian community of political action is too much for Caius Martius. He sends away Menenius and Cominius when they come to him, but he cannot bear to send away his family. Their prayers and entreaties he cannot reject unheard, and as he listens, he relents. He spares Rome, and does not destroy it as he had promised.

In sparing Rome, he knowingly pays the cost of never belonging anywhere. In that moment, he tells his mother 'you have won a happy victory for Rome / But for your son, believe it, O, believe it, / Most dangerously you have with him prevailed, / If not most mortal to him' (5.3.186–9). He can already see his place among the Volscians slipping away, as he fails to achieve the condition upon which his membership in their society was based, and as the disappointment and anger of the Volscians at his betrayal overwhelm his now-diminished importance to them. But he must, as he says, 'let it come' (5.3.189). He cannot destroy Rome to belong among the Volscians, even if it means his own alienation and death.

Why not? Because while Caius Martius does not belong to Rome politically anymore, he still belongs to it as part of his family. The fantasy that 'wife, mother, child, I know not' cannot be sustained beyond the moment he sees them in the flesh (5.2.81). They are not 'the state nor private friends' he rejected (5.3.18); they are his kin. It is a question of 'blood', not of politics or culture (5.3.24). This is the fact he has tried to put out of sight and therefore out of mind: he cannot 'stand / As if a man were author to himself / And knew no other kin', because the claim of 'my flesh' acts on a different level from the political exile he has embraced (5.3.35–7, 42).

He tries desperately to keep the two spheres separate, to welcome his mother, wife and child while hearing 'nought from Rome'

(5.3.93). But his mother will not let him. She reminds him of the 'mother, wife and child' who will watch 'the son, the husband and the father' destroy all they hold dear (5.3.101, 102). She tells him that he will have to trample 'thy mother's womb / That brought thee to this world' in order to destroy Rome (5.3.124–5). Her final thrust is to disclaim her own part in him: 'this fellow had a Volscian to his mother, / His wife is in Corioles and his child / Like him by chance' (5.3.178–80). The emphasis is not on his part in Roman culture or the Roman state, but in his family. Rome is 'his country' not because he belongs to it, but because they do, and he belongs to them (5.3.103).

This is a different kind of belonging, the belonging of 'common blood and descent' that we referred to earlier. This kind of tie frequently has a 'different center of gravity' from the political and cultural bonds we have been discussing.[34] In fact, Caius Martius had not originally seen his political expulsion as breaking this connection. He still identifies himself as 'your son' to his mother after his exile, and still expects that 'while I remain above the ground you shall / Hear from me still' (4.1.31, 51–2). It is only the awareness that this bond will come in direct conflict with his commitments to the Volscians that leads him to the fantasy, expressed above, that the tie has somehow broken, and that fantasy is dispelled when he actually interacts with his family. He may not be the sort of Roman who is a functioning member of the Roman political state any longer, but he will never cease to be a Roman born. His wife, mother and child are physical reminders of this.

Caius Martius cannot deny the fact that blood and kinship still connect him to Rome. He tries to balance his place in the Volscian community of political action against his blood ties to Rome, first by the fantasy that the latter no longer exist, then by begging his mother to 'remember ... the thing I have forsworn to grant' and not ask him to spare Rome, and finally by silence (5.3.79–80). But ultimately he cannot maintain both his promise to destroy Rome and his family connections. His family's appeal reaches him, as others could not, because he belongs to them in a different way than he had belonged in Rome. He finds he cannot destroy Rome over his mother's body, although he could have done (and offered to do) so over that of Menenius, his closest non-familial friend.

The different quality of this relationship forces Martius to confront the overlapping communities of belonging that are pulling him in different directions. Only Martius's family could make him choose Rome over the Volsces. Volumnia confronts Martius with the impossibility of simultaneously fulfilling both his promise to destroy Rome as part of the Volscian community of political action and his obligations as a member of his Roman familial community of common blood and descent. If he destroys Rome, his mother must cease to be his mother. This is, of course, impossible. His weeping 'O, mother, mother!' is the expression of his recognition of that impossibility (5.3.182).

Yet if he cannot destroy Rome, neither can he return to it. He can no longer belong to that community of political action, and so tells Aufidius 'I'll not to Rome; I'll back with you' (5.3.198). Even in the moment when his place among the Volscians starts sliding away, that is still the only place he has. He tries to broker a 'convenient peace' between the two states, one 'with no less honour to the [Volscians] / Than shame to th'Romans' (5.3.191, 5.6.80–1). By negotiating a treaty, he tests whether he can actually function in the Volscian political system despite his failure to destroy Rome. The establishment of a treaty is a political act, by which he hopes to preserve his place among the Volscians.

But this hope fails him when the compromise does not work. When Aufidius and Martius arrive among the Volscian leaders, the first enquiries about him are for 'our general', even from the 'Conspirators of Aufidius's faction' (5.6.9, 8 s.d.). Caius Martius has returned 'splitting the air with noise', as in a triumph, to announce the peace (5.6.51). He tries to brave out the danger, and presents to the Volscian lords the treaty 'subscrib'd by th'consuls and patricians, / Together with the seal o'th'Senate' (5.6.82–3). Even here he cannot bring himself to acknowledge the presence of the tribunes in the Roman state. But his attempt is too late. Aufidius has already sent to and spoken to the lords about Martius's failure and seized control of the moment. He brands Martius with the same term the tribunes used: 'traitor' (5.6.85). Appropriately, this is a term that directly identifies someone who has failed and betrayed a specific community of law and political action, and is now viewed as an enemy.

After being accused of treason, Martius lives for only forty-five more lines. In that period, we are treated to an eerily compressed echo of the third act. Once again his attempt to act politically fails. Once again the people are stirred up against him. Once again the lords try to calm the situation. Once again he offends those whose good favour he should be begging. This time he brags of his victory against 'your Volscians in Corioles' to those same Volscians, thus reminding them of the name he had earlier refused to acknowledge as a sign of unity with them (5.6.116). And once again the mob has its way with him: this time to his death and not his banishment.

Yet this death is neither unexpected nor unwelcome in context. Caius Martius already knew that giving in to his mother's entreaties might prove 'most mortal to him', and accepted it (5.3.189). In the brief moment between the accusation of treachery and his death among the Volscians, he baits the crowd, inviting them to 'cut me to pieces, Volsces men and lads, / Stain all your edges on me' (5.6.112–13). Crucially, he says this before the people, or even the conspirators, have actually cried for his death, which first happens at lines 120–3. This is an important moment to mark in any production: the point at which Martius asks for death before anyone even offers it to him.

Caius Martius's dare to the Volscians may be bravado, but it contains truth. It may be this premature demand for death, and not Caius Martius's other faults, that represents the 'impatience' that the Volscian lords take note of when they say, after his death, that 'his own impatience / Takes from Aufidius a great part of blame' (5.6.146–7). Aufidius may be the proximate cause of Caius Martius's death, but he is not the ultimate cause. After Caius Martius found himself in the same relation to the Volscians as he was to Rome – unable to participate adequately in the community of political action and therefore branded a traitor – he was not only willing to die, he brought it upon himself. Having failed in Rome and among the Volsces, he had nowhere left to live.

Caius Martius's death is a release. It is a release from the knowledge that there is no community of political action in which he belongs. Unlike King John, whose death comes when he is in tune with his political structure and thus memorializes his success, Caius Martius dies in the moment of his failure. He cannot live in Rome because the Rome he thought he knew is gone. He is equally unable, however, to destroy the new Rome in order to belong amongst the Volscians. This is the sense in which Caius Martius's fate was sealed the moment the tribunes were established. Their presence changed the Roman political structure, leaving nowhere for Caius Martius to belong. His death is merely the confirmation of that fact, the proof that he cannot live with the Volscians any more than he could live in the new Rome. If Caius Martius is a 'martyr to [Rome's] survival', as Patrick Gray has suggested, then he is one only in the sense that he is a martyr to his continued familial ties and their conflict with his political position.[35] Although he suspected he was going to die when he saved Rome, he does not die for Rome. His death is a result of his own failures of belonging, caused ultimately by the tribunes' existence rather than by Rome's survival. By ending his life, the Volscians have not sacrificed him for Rome. Rather, they have done him a personal favour, one he asked for: they have stopped his futile search in the present for a society in which he could belong, a society that only existed in the past.

As with *Julius Caesar*, *Coriolanus* is thus rooted in a particular Rome in a particular moment, and the characters' reactions to it: in this case Caius Martius's inability to accept the creation of the tribunes. The early Republican Rome of the play 'haunted the political unconscious' in early modern England, in Pfister's phrase, and the historical narratives surrounding both Caius Martius and the tribunes were consistent throughout the period.[36] As such, *Coriolanus*, like *Julius Caesar*, presented a relatively straightforward challenge for Shakespeare's political imagination compared with *King John* or *Macbeth* because the 'shared cultural memory' from which he and his contemporaries might draw, to borrow Hutchings's phrase, was largely in agreement with itself about the setting.[37] In the next section, we will remain in Europe but move forward in time, encountering a different aspect of Shakespeare's dramatic technique as we see the playwright adapting the same political structure – that of Renaissance Venice with its dukes – in different directions in *Merchant of Venice* and *Othello*.

PART THREE

Contemporary Europe: The Venetian republic

6

The Merchant of Venice and the weak dukes of Venice

Shakespeare did not limit himself to writing about the past. His plays are set all across his contemporary Europe as well. These plays show a similar set of interests as those we have examined already: a serious involvement with the political structure of each setting and how it affects the action of each play. And just as Shakespeare's interest in politics in the settings was not limited to the past, his treatment of republican forms of government in particular was hardly restricted to the Roman plays we have just encountered. Though England and most of its fellow nations were monarchies, there was a republic in early modern Europe almost as familiar as, and far more recent than, Rome: Venice. Shakespeare set two of his plays in Venice – *The Merchant of Venice* and *Othello* – and in both cases he introduced elements of the Venetian political structure that were absent from his sources.[1] Over the next two chapters I will examine how Shakespeare took advantage of the same contemporary understandings of the Venetian political system to craft the two plays in very different ways. Yet strikingly, his primary addition is the same in both plays: the introduction, in an extended scene, of the Duke of Venice.[2]

Why does Shakespeare add these dukes? I argue that he did so in order to engage with the most common understanding of the Venetian state circulating in early modern England. In this view, the duke was a respected figurehead within otherwise republican Venice, possessing a distinctive mixture of weak formal authority and great personal influence. Both of Shakespeare's Dukes occupy this odd position, and each is forced to operate within its constraints.

The two plays thus address the same political structure, but in opposing ways. *Merchant of Venice* emphasizes the weakness of the duke's formal role in the state, while *Othello*, which I will treat later, focuses on his ability to wield power through investigation, questioning and collaborative leadership. In both cases, this interpretation of the dukes' position changes our understanding not only of the Dukes themselves but also of the scenes in which they appear, the arc of their plays as a whole, and the more central characters with whom they interact: Shylock, Portia and Othello. In the case of *Merchant of Venice*, examining the Duke in this way allows us to see new details of how Shylock's case threatens Venice itself and how Portia saves Venice from that threat, going beyond the common commercially focused reading of the play to reveal the constitutional dangers that Shylock's case presents.

Before examining *Merchant*, however, we should familiarize ourselves with what the Renaissance English thought of the duke of Venice. The short answer is that they thought very little of him, although they thought *about* him frequently. The Venetian government was of great interest to English readers and audiences in the period. This was particularly true in the context of politics, since Venice's own *relazioni*, or 'relations', about foreign governments were the gold standard for the analysis of contemporary political structures.[3] Just as Venice was known to examine its neighbours, others examined Venice and what they saw there was unlike anything else in Europe, particularly because of the unique position of the Venetian head of state.

Venice was the epitome of Fortescue's 'politic' state, run by the aristocracy, and so most early modern English sources agreed that the duke of Venice's power was shockingly small. He ranked higher than his nobles individually, but below them collectively.[4] Some described him as a total non-entity, often called a 'cipher'.[5] Others pointed out his impressive household and estate, but observed that this was all for show, a matter of grace and dignity but not authority.[6] When they did consider his authority, they found it extremely limited.[7] Some went so far as to describe him as a slave or servant of the state, doing its work without any power of his own.[8]

The reason for this weakness was most explicitly conveyed by the work of Gasparo Contarini, whose *Commonwealth and Government of Venice* circulated influentially in England in Latin, Italian and French before being translated into English in 1599 by

Lewis Lewkenor.⁹ Contarini stressed that the duke's powers were restricted in order to protect the 'liberty of the commonwealth'.¹⁰ The weakness of the duke was necessary to Venice's freedom and to avoid the potential for tyranny.¹¹ Contarini's opinion that the duke's weakness and Venice's liberty were connected was widely shared, and the city's uniquely free and politic government was seen as one of its great national advantages.¹²

It is important to note that the English did not merely think the duke of Venice was weak: they thought the Venetians preferred him that way. William Thomas's influential *History of Italy* emphasized that 'some of the Uenetians theim selfes' referred to the duke as a slave,¹³ while Lewkenor's introduction to his translation of Contarini invited readers to marvel at the Venetian author's own description of a duke 'wholly subjected to the lawes'.¹⁴ Thus the perspective that saw the duke as a weak magistrate, explicitly reined in by the Venetian law in order to preserve the liberty of the state, was coded for Renaissance English readers and audiences as the opinion of Venice's own political and social elite and not just of English onlookers.

But accounts of the duke's position were not limited to an emphasis on his structural lack of power. There was also an awareness of the various forms of what we would now call 'soft power' – power exercised through relationships and negotiation rather than through command – available to the duke, if he chose to wield them. Intriguingly, this awareness was most explicitly expressed in Thomas and Contarini, the two most influential of the writers on the subject. Thomas believed that the duke possessed the right to be heard and to cast a vote in any decision.¹⁵ This was a privilege unique to the duke, as was the right to sit upon certain councils ex officio.¹⁶

Contarini was even more specific in describing this aspect of the duke's office. He too noted that the duke could join any vote or judicial decision, but to this he added several points of additional authority.¹⁷ According to Contarini, the duke could pass cases upwards to the councils of state and recommend punishments for offences.¹⁸ He particularly had not just the right but the duty to bring any man who abused or misused his authority for punishment by the council.¹⁹ In short, while the formal power of the duke to run the state was minimal, he had extensive power to make his voice heard, to join with other magistrates in declaring sentences and to bring forward for judgement by others those whom he thought were undermining the safety or justice of the state.

I argue that Shakespeare shared this understanding of Venice's political structure. I do not necessarily suggest that Shakespeare was intimately familiar with Contarini, nor even with Thomas, although both texts were circulating in various forms in England at the time.[20] Rather, I suggest that the overarching concern with the duke's weakness (and his limited but specific strength) that I have identified above is active in and around the trial scene in *Merchant*. Scholars of the play have missed this political and structural element of the trial because this aspect of the Venetian state is no longer familiar to us, choosing instead to focus on the play's commercial elements related to foreigners. However, I argue that the political–structural angle plays a major role in the scene, particularly in the Duke's limited ability to act, Portia's and Shylock's legal arguments, and the fates of both Shylock and Antonio.

In the act leading up to the trial scene in *Merchant*, we are told of a Duke who cannot save Antonio because of his lack of authority under the law. When Solanio reassures Antonio that 'the duke / Will never grant this forfeiture [of his bond to Shylock] to hold', Antonio tells him sadly that 'the Duke cannot deny the course of law' (3.3.24–5, 26).[21] The reason Antonio gives for this incapacity is that 'the commodity that strangers have / With us in Venice, if it be denied, / Will much impeach the justice of the state' (3.3.27–9). This reasoning presents a Venetian government tied closely to commercial and geopolitical interests and focuses the issue of Shylock's claim on the legitimacy of the legal system, or 'the justice of the state'. Many critics have adopted Antonio's logic as their explanation for the Duke's unwillingness to block Shylock's suit.[22] Holderness, most notably, refers to it as a 'judicial and commercial manifesto for Venice'.[23] This analysis assumes that the limitations on the Duke arise from the commercial and geopolitical demands on the Venetian state, and from the idea that voiding the contract between Shylock and Antonio would harm Venetian trade by endangering their reputation for justice.

We should not discount the importance of trade and justice towards foreigners in Venice. The commercial life of Venice has an important role to play in *Merchant of Venice*, and Antonio's statements about 'commodity' and 'justice' help to explain the interaction between that commercial life and the trial that results from the contract between Antonio and Shylock.[24] Certainly, Venice in the play is a city reliant on trade, and would wish to avoid a reputation for breaking contracts made with non-citizens.

However, just as it would be a mistake to ignore the commercial reading of the play, to focus only on this kind of externally directed 'commodity' and 'justice' would involve missing the significance of the restrictions on the duke *within* the Venetian system, as other parts of the play make clear. Those restrictions did not result from geopolitical and commercial calculation but from an internal Venetian desire to minimize monarchical powers in their government. This was intimately related to Venetian fears of tyranny. The entire purpose of the Venetian system was to protect the 'liberty of the commonwealth', and the weakness of the duke was to prevent him specifically from threatening that liberty.[25] It was this 'true libertie and freedom' that was seen as the key to Venetian greatness.[26] The restrictions on the duke were thus how Venice was protected from any internal threat to that liberty.[27] Any duke usurping a power he did not possess under the Venetian system of government, such as the power to dismiss Shylock's suit against Antonio, would be guilty of taking the first steps towards tyranny and the destruction not simply of Venetian 'justice' and 'commodity' but of Venetian 'freedom' as well.

Unlike Antonio, Shylock makes this threat to Venetian liberty, and not commodity, the foundation of his own arguments for the enforcement of his bond. In Act Three, Scene Two, Salerio reports to Bassanio that Shylock 'plies the Duke at morning and at night, / And doth impeach the freedom of the state / If they deny him justice' (3.2.276–8). Some critics have read Shylock's 'freedom of the state' as a reformulation of Antonio's 'justice of the state', suggesting that this too must be a commercial argument.[28] For Lupton in particular, Shylock's 'constitutional position' is ultimately the 'same point' that Antonio made in his prison speech.[29] Likewise, Holderness marks this reference to 'the Venetian constitution', but only in relation to matters of 'race and economics'.[30] Yet I suggest that given the importance of Venetian 'libertie and freedom' to Contarini, Thomas and other commentators on Venice, the constitutional argument is different from the commercial one. While Antonio 'links constitutionalism and capitalism', as Lupton puts it,[31] Shylock's constitutionalism is about not commercial but civic freedom. Shylock's arguments here rely, as they will in the trial scene, on a different conception of what lies behind the Duke's inability to cancel the debt: the role of the duke's weakness in the Venetian political structure, and the importance of that political structure to the Venetians with whom he is arguing.

I suggest that Holderness and Lupton miss this element because while they are interested in a historicized reading of Venice, that historicism lacks the careful attention to political structure in particular of the historicism of setting. Holderness even cites William Thomas's interest in Venetian liberty and the avoidance of tyranny, but applies it only to commercial issues and the status of foreigners.[32] His primary reference to the duke's position is to his ceremonial marriage to the sea and its role in maritime trade, not to his political or judicial function.[33] This means that he misses the distinction between Shylock's and Antonio's arguments, because he is looking only for issues of race and economics, even through the language of politics and constitutional law. This leads him, as her focus on Antonio's earlier speech leads Lupton, to underestimate the full nature of the threat to Venice's constitutional order represented by Shylock's argument. I would suggest also that it undersells the degree to which Shylock understands Venice: he embraces far more of the 'common values of Venetian civilization' than Holderness gives him credit for,[34] because he is capable of conjuring up this threat from the Venetian's own greatest worries about their constitution.

Antonio's first speech to the Duke at his trial supports the idea that this threat is at work in Shylock's favour. Here he admits that 'your grace hath ta'en great pains to qualify / His [Shylock's] rigorous course, but since he stands obdurate / [...]no lawful means can carry me / Out of his envy's reach' (4.1.7–10). In this speech we can recognize the limited power of the duke as described above. He can only entreat Shylock. If Shylock will not be moved, the Duke has 'no lawful means' to save Antonio, a phrasing that suggests not a sense of weighing commodity and benefit but an actual legal–constitutional bar to action.

Seen in this light, the Duke's focus on mercy in his next speech to Shylock, and Shylock's response, flow naturally from the Duke's need to use soft power only. The law leaves the issue of mercy at Antonio's trial in Shylock's hands, and the Duke can do nothing but tell him 'we all expect a gentle answer' (4.1.34). Shylock, in turn, throws the restrictions imposed by the Venetian system of government back into the Duke's face when he declares that 'if you deny it [his right to his bond], let the danger light / Upon your charter and your city's freedom' (4.1.38–9). The 'charter' of Venice would consist of the legal documents establishing the freedoms and rights of the city and its citizens, and by extension the limits placed on the governmental power over those citizens.[35] Shylock's position is that any action on the Duke's part to disallow the bond would overstep the limitations placed on him by that charter, and thereby call into question not only the charter itself but the 'city's freedom' guaranteed by that charter.

This statement accords with how the English conceived of the Venetian state structure, and it echoes Shylock's earlier reported emphasis on the 'freedom of the state'. Shylock's next claim that 'if you deny me, fie upon your law; / There is no force in the decrees of Venice' should be interpreted in the same way (4.1.101–2). The decrees of Venice of which he speaks are not only the laws that enforce contracts but also the decrees of law that bind the duke and restrict his power. Again, the assertion is personally addressed to the Duke and his potential abuse of power, with 'if you deny me' echoing the 'if you deny it' of his previous point. Shylock's concern is for the enforcement of his bond; the concern about the freedom of Venice belongs to the Venetians to whom he is speaking. But because of the importance that Venice was known to place on its liberty and on the structural weakness of its dukes, his argument gains substantial power from this appeal to the fundamental structure of the state. As with Caius Martius's briefly successful attempt to gain votes from the plebeians, what matters is his audience's understanding of what he has to say and its relation to the state, not his own belief.

The Duke's minimalist response to Shylock's refusal of mercy follows this conception of the duke's power. The Duke does not declare himself capable of ruling in Antonio's favour or voiding Shylock's suit entirely. Rather, he says that 'upon my power I may dismiss this court / Unless Bellario (a learned doctor, / Whom I have sent for to determine this) / Come here to-day' (4.1.104–7). This statement reflects the contemporary English vision of a duke who is capable of joining himself to any other court at his will, and whose power therefore lies in joining with another judge's opinion, not in arbitrating by himself alone. Without the other judge, the only power left to him is to adjourn the court until another date.

In this political–structural sense, the potential proroguing of the court in Bellario's absence becomes less of a matter of the Duke's 'power' and more of a requirement, since as we have seen, he was known to lack the power to act independently.[36] We see a similar collaborative process at work in the contemporary anonymous play *A Knacke to Know an Honest Man*, in which a character appears to stand before the duke of Venice for judgement, but the duke's decision is vetted and sustained by two others.[37] In *Merchant*, Shylock cannot 'stand for judgement' before the Duke alone, and he cannot 'have it' without Bellario's presence at the Duke's side, or at any rate that of some such 'learned doctor', as Bellario is supposed to be (4.1.103, 144). This makes Shylock's demand for judgement (and Antonio's at 4.1.83), not only a demand for impartiality but also a demand that the Duke produce an actual judge who can resolve the suit. I read 'judgement' in this part of the scene as having both the sense of making a judgement and the sense of beginning the process that will lead to judgement; in the latter case, this means bringing in a judge, like Bellario, who can actually constitute a court. The Duke is fully aware of the justice of this demand, and it prompts his mention of Bellario.

In this context we can see that Bellario is not, as some scholars have argued he is, an advocate or an expert called in to help on a particularly hard trial.[38] He is integral to the performance of 'this court', because he is the judge whose presence constitutes the court, and without whom the Duke could not continue. Bellario, or by substitution Balthasar (and not the Duke), is the judge in this case precisely because there is a system of courts and judges to which the Duke can attach himself. Bellario is part of the Venetian system of law, as the English understood it, a system of courts and judges that existed outside the political hierarchy but which the duke of Venice could choose to join in judgement.

The presence of this sort of court and judge is Shakespeare's innovation. In *Il Pecorone* and the earlier stories, Portia's counterpart disguises herself as a lawyer serving as a mediator, but there is no mention of a judge, or of anyone who would hear the case if she did not, and the proceeding does not take place in a court, but an inn.[39] This change is part of Shakespeare's overall attention to the procedures of the trial scene, along with the inclusion of the Duke. He depicts a more recognizably Venetian system of law (from an English perspective) than was contained in his source, staffing it with Bellario as a judge and endowing it with the proper restrictions on the powers of the Duke.

The fact that there is a judge in this scene – and that it is Portia-as-Balthasar through Bellario, not the Duke – also counters the most common claim of historical inaccuracy applied to *Merchant of Venice*. It has become a critical commonplace to say that the Duke is somehow the sole judge in Shylock's trial, and to argue from this basis that Shakespeare knew nothing about Venetian courts.[40] But Shakespeare's Duke does not preside over this court. He is merely attached to it. The historical accuracy of Shakespeare's court lies in this distinction, which results from the duke's unique position within the Venetian political structure.

In reading Bellario as a Venetian judge, it is important to note that Padua, where he resides and where Portia-as-Balthasar claims to come from (4.1.118), was in fact a part of the Venetian state in the sixteenth century.[41] By not only inventing Bellario, but making him Paduan, Shakespeare makes an additional change to his sources in which the lady-as-lawyer claimed to come from Bologna, which was never under Venetian rule.[42] Padua, by contrast, was substantially integrated with Venetian society, especially in law. Paduan legal scholars were granted special privileges in Venice, and Paduan posts were staffed by Venetian officials.[43] By making Bellario a Paduan, therefore, Shakespeare positions him directly within the Venetian system. Padua is thus, like the Rialto or the implicit presence of the Jewish ghetto, another location intended to remind the audience of the distinctively Venetian context of the play. The court proceeding takes place in Venice so that the Duke can join himself to the decision, but Bellario, the Paduan-Venetian judge, is the one whose presence allows the court to function at all.

This explains why Portia sends to him immediately upon hearing of the trial, with the clear expectation that doing so will allow her and Nerissa to 'see [their] husbands' in Venice at the trial (3.4.58). Their arrangement to allow her to substitute for him must have already happened before the Duke reveals to the audience that it is Bellario 'whom I have sent for to determine this' (4.1.106). In order for Portia to have substituted herself for him, then, Portia must have known in advance that the Duke would send specifically to Bellario as the judge for the case. Portia has heard from Salerio that Shylock is pursuing a 'plea / Of forfeiture, of justice, and his bond' against Antonio, and she therefore knows what type of case this is

(3.2.281–2). Since Bellario is her 'cousin' (3.4.50), she would know if he would be a likely candidate to judge this trial. This knowledge is easily explained once we understand that Bellario is a Paduan (and therefore Venetian) judge, with a known area of expertise, who can be expected to be called on in this case.

Once Portia-as-Balthasar has taken Bellario's place as judge and begun the trial, we see a major shift in the speech patterns of the scene towards a greater sense of formality. We can see this both in who speaks and in how they express themselves. Before Portia arrives, most of the conversation is about Shylock's intransigence, not the case itself, and Bassanio takes a major role alongside the Duke in remonstrating with Shylock about the bond (4.1.1–117, especially 62–7). After 'Balthasar' enters, Bassanio is quiet unless spoken to, like the rest of those not directly involved,[44] and the conversation acquires the rhythms of the courtroom. In the second part of the scene, Portia, the Duke and Shylock speak about the case; Antonio speaks in answer to Portia when he 'beseech[es] the court / To give the judgement'; and Bassanio answers Portia's questions about Antonio's ability to 'discharge the money', and responds to Antonio's seeming last words (4.1.204, 238–9). There is a general shift in the scene towards the more formal attitudes of a trial, where speech is more tightly controlled. This shift reflects the difference between the period when the Duke and Bassanio are trying to convince Shylock to settle out of court and the actual trial, when Portia-as-Balthasar has arrived to serve as judge.

The same moment signals a shift in the language used about the court, and in particular about the Duke and Portia-as-Balthasar. The Duke introduces Portia as a 'young and learned doctor' and Bellario's letter calls her a 'young doctor', meaning a doctor of laws (4.1.144, 152). But thereafter she is usually addressed as a judge, or else the court as a whole is invoked. Shylock calls her a 'wise young judge', a 'worthy judge', a 'noble judge', a 'wise and upright judge' and so on (4.1.220, 232, 242, 246). Gratiano, echoing Shylock mockingly, calls her an 'upright judge', and a 'learned judge', repeatedly (4.1.308, 309, 314, 319). Antonio refers to 'the court' that he wishes to 'give the judgement', and then to 'the Duke and all the court' (4.1.239, 240, 376). This constant echoing of Portia's individual role as judge, and of 'the court' as the formal engine by which judgement is given and mercy ratified, resonates with the

English conception of the Venetian system. It is precisely because Portia herself is (pretending to be) a judge that there is a court, and it is precisely because she plays that role that the Duke can join his voice to that court. He has attached himself to Portia's court, and that court is in session from her arrival on.

But although the court is in session, the focus on mercy does not fade. Indeed, Portia's most memorable speech is spent urging Shylock to be merciful, the same theme that Bassanio and the Duke pursued before her arrival. Yet there is a distinct difference in how that mercy is presented. The earlier arguments focused on a personal mercy that drew its power from 'pity' for and 'commiseration' with Antonio (4.1.26, 29). Portia, by contrast, emphasizes instead a mercy that seems not to rely on the details of the situation before her. She speaks of 'the quality of mercy' generally, even universally, reminding Shylock that 'in the course of justice none of us / Should see salvation' (4.1.180, 195–6). Buried at the end of her beautiful speech, however, is one crucial detail that is directly applicable to the case before her: 'this strict court of Venice / Must needs give sentence 'gainst the merchant there' (4.1.199–200).

It is this detail that explains both why Portia continues the emphasis on mercy into the actual trial and why she frames that mercy differently. Portia's speech on mercy is intimately concerned with the issue of what Venice – and particularly Venetian courts and dukes – can and cannot do. It is saturated with the language of royalty. Mercy, and the repudiation of strict law that it celebrates, is 'above the sceptered sway' that belongs to 'the force of temporal power, / The attribute to awe and majesty, / Wherein doth sit the fear and dread of kings' (4.1.189, 186–8). Specifically, mercy is situated within the conscience of an individual monarch. It 'becomes / The throned monarch better than his crown', and 'is enthroned in the hearts of kings' (4.1.184–5, 190). Portia's mercy is a check on the severity of kings, as well as a prerogative power, in that it 'seasons justice' (4.1.193). Royal justice is in turn figured as 'the force of temporal power', and the 'sceptred sway' of supreme rule (4.1.186, 189); mercy within the heart of the king is the only check on the use of the royal power to administer justice. But the Venetian duke was not a king. The power that would be his in a purely monarchical state had been placed within the Venetian court system instead. Shylock can show mercy because he can individually renounce his suit, but Venice cannot show mercy because it operates in a world of corporate, rather than individual, authority. There can be no mercy in a Venetian court because there is no king to provide it.

Portia believes that there is a moral imperative towards mercy in this case. Yet at the same time, she must acknowledge that mercy has at its heart a notion of individual power, specifically the power to dispense with or alter the law, and that Venice, with its court system, must be 'strict'. Mercy is the divine prerogative of a king; Venetian justice is the legal product of a court.

Why then does Portia speak so much of mercy? I suggest that she talks about it precisely because it cannot naturally be exercised within the Venetian system. This has the seemingly perverse result that mercy is pushed outward from the state onto Shylock, to whom Portia must look to restore the mercy that has been systematically excised from the court. Many critics have noted that this has some relation to the English legal distinction between the common law and equity courts, but I think it is important to remember, as Jessica Apolloni reminds us, that 'Italian materials' remain 'at the heart' of this depiction.[45] Thus while Shakespeare 'translates' the Venetian system for an English audience, in Apolloni's term, it remains a Venetian system.[46] As such, that translation must go through the Italian context, just as we saw the issue of the succession in *King John* through the lens of the medieval context. Portia's need for mercy cannot, therefore, be satisfied simply by appealing to an equity court because Venice has no such courts; while the comparison may flatter an English audience secure in the knowledge that mercy has a place within their system, in the world of the play the only way to ease the course of harsh justice is to convince Shylock to do so.

In this speech, then, we see Portia trying to rewrite Shylock. She looks to soften him, flattering him with the connection between royalty and the mercy he could offer, while suggesting the unique power that mercy represents in Venice, where royalty is absent. She hopes to make mercy compelling to Shylock through attraction, rather than coercion, thus explaining how it can be true both that the 'the quality of mercy is not strained' (4.1.180), i.e. constrained or forced, and at the same time that Shylock's mercy is somehow unavoidable: he '*must* ... be merciful' (4.1.178) (emphasis mine). She attempts to find in Shylock's potential for mercy a solution to the absence of mercy from that Venetian system, and entice or compel him to provide that solution.

It is not surprising that this attempt fails, since Shylock is neither a Christian nor likely to see himself as a king in Venice. Instead he calls for justice and rejects Portia's pleas in favour of mercy. This forces Portia onto another tack in order to rescue Antonio and also create a space for the morally necessary category of mercy. After one more failed attempt to locate either that rescue or that mercy outside of the laws, in Shylock, she seeks them within the law, in an extremely narrow reading of the bond and ultimately in the Alien Statute.

These two moves are actually part of a single arc, which begins even before Portia tells Shylock that the bond 'doth give thee here no jot of blood' (4.1.302). Its first step, counter-intuitively, is Portia delivering Shylock his penalty, telling Antonio 'you must prepare your bosom for his knife' (4.1.241). However, it is not Antonio's preparation but Shylock's that she is interested in. She asks him first if he has scales to weigh the pound of flesh, and then, more crucially, if he will 'have by some surgeon, Shylock, on your charge, / To stop his wounds, lest he do bleed to death' (4.1.253–4). Shylock, who of all people knows that bleeding when cut is a common human frailty, is intent on seizing his penalty and does not notice the importance of this request. He dismisses her request with a curt 'is it so nominated in the bond?' (4.1.255).

At this point Portia makes her last attempt to bring Shylock's mercy into the case, answering him 'it is not so expressed, but what of that? / 'Twere good you do so much for charity' (4.1.256–7). He refuses: 'I cannot find it; 'tis not in the bond' (4.1.258). From this moment on, Shylock is doomed, caught in the remorseless logic that will result from his refusal to show even enough mercy to staunch Antonio's bleeding. What seem at the time to be Antonio's last words lengthens the process out a little, but when the scene returns to the case at hand and Shylock demands that they 'pursue sentence' (4.1.294), his fall from triumph to defeat is swift. Immediately upon granting him his pound of flesh, Portia removes the possibility of actually taking it, insisting that the law gives him no blood: 'take thou thy pound of flesh. / But in the cutting it, if thou dost shed / One drop of Christian blood, thy lands and goods / Are by the laws of Venice confiscate / Unto the state of Venice' (4.1.304–8).

This sudden refusal to allow Shylock to spill any blood at all seems to contradict Portia's suggestion a mere fifty lines before that he provide a surgeon to stop up the blood he would inevitably shed. It is crucial here to realize that this moment is yet another Shakespearean addition to this scene. In *Il Pecorone* and other extant variations of the flesh-bond story,[47] the only trick is the quibble about blood: the bond gives no blood, so the Jew cannot cut the merchant's flesh. In that situation, we might agree with the Somali man who recommended to Isak Denisen that Shylock use a hot knife to draw no blood,[48] or with Charles Fried and others who argue that if Shylock could not work around the restriction, he should be free to let the penalty go.[49] But much as the Bastard would actually have been allowed to inherit in *King John* had he not chosen otherwise, Shakespeare's legal reading here may surprise us. The quibble-only resolution is not actually present in *Merchant*. Instead of proceeding directly to the blood trick, Shakespeare has Portia ask Shylock for a doctor, explicitly suggesting that Antonio might be allowed to bleed, if that blood were staunched so that he did not 'bleed to death'. How, then, does Shakespeare's Portia save Antonio, if not merely by re-analysing the contract?

I believe that Portia's cruel ingenuity here has been glossed over too easily by both critics and performers, and that it plays a central role in Shakespeare's new ending to the scene. That ending hinges on the Alien Statute, which Portia quotes at length:

> It is enacted in the laws of Venice,
> If it be proved against an alien,
> That by direct, or indirect attempts
> He seek the life of any citizen,
> The party 'gainst the which he doth contrive,
> Shall seize one half his goods, the other half
> Comes to the privy coffer of the state,
> And the offender's life lies in the mercy
> Of the Duke only, 'gainst all other voice.
>
> (4.1.344–52)

Like Portia's suggestion that Shylock staunch Antonio's wounds, this statute is entirely Shakespeare's addition to the scene. I argue that the two additions work together to transform the earlier versions' resolution of the scene, with its emphasis on the re-reading of the bond itself, into a new one more interested in how the enforcement of the bond interacts with Venetian law and the political structure.

As her counterparts in the earlier stories do, Portia finds that 'this bond doth give thee here no jot of blood' (4.1.301). She then proceeds, as above, to declare this an illegal 'attempt' on Antonio's life. Both pieces of reasoning seem nonsensical to many legal commentators, who note that any bond which permits the cutting of flesh must permit the shedding of blood when cutting that flesh, and that any contract that includes the death of one party is invalid on the face.[50] In addition, as we have seen, Portia herself has already seemingly endorsed the possibility of Shylock cutting Antonio through her request for a surgeon. How is her legal trickery possible?

I suggest that the answer to this lies in the specific sequence of events. It is clear that when the 'merry sport' of the bond (1.3.141) is first sealed, the penalty is not equated to Antonio's death. It is hard to see Antonio signing, or any notary notarizing, a bond with an explicit murder as its penalty. Yet by the end of the scene Portia nonetheless states that 'it appears by manifest proceeding' that Shylock has made an attempt on Antonio's life (4.1.354).

When, then, does Shylock's suit become an attempt on Antonio's life? The standard scholarly and judicial answer is that it always was, and Portia and the Duke erred in not striking the bond down as unenforceable. This seems reasonable; after all, even if you heat the knife, cutting a pound of flesh from Antonio's breast, 'nearest his heart', is very likely to kill him. But the scene itself seems to resist such a reading: as Fried and Richard Strier have suggested, we must assume the bond is considered enforceable under Venetian law, or else the entire litigation is meaningless.[51] There must then be a point where the initially enforceable cutting of flesh becomes unforceable, and in doing so becomes not merely void but legally punishable as attempted murder.

I argue that this change is produced by the combination of Shylock's refusal of Portia's idea of a surgeon and his insistence on cutting Antonio. He has first admitted in open court that he will let the bleeding kill Antonio, and not take any step to stop it; immediately thereafter, he still moves to cut Antonio's breast. It is at this point that Shylock's never-realized legally permissible shedding of blood becomes legally impermissible attempted murder and thus that his very shedding of blood becomes legally impermissible as well.

Once he has admitted his desire, or at least willingness, to let Antonio bleed to death, there is no turning back. Not only can he no longer have the flesh, he can no longer reject taking the penalty. Even when he tries to leave without doing anything to Antonio, 'the law hath yet another hold' on Shylock (4.1.343). After his refusal to provide a surgeon and his express willingness to cut Antonio, the law dooms him because it punishes 'attempts', and not merely successes. It is for this reason that Portia, unlike her counterpart in the sources, tells Shylock that his shedding of 'one drop of Christian blood' is subject not just to a close reading of the bond, but to 'the laws of Venice', and in particular that if he does anything to harm Antonio his 'lands and goods / Are … confiscate' (4.1.306–7). This is the penalty laid out in the Alien Statute, although she has not yet read it out in court.

I believe this may be the only statute at play in the scene. When Portia promises Shylock that 'thyself shall see the act' that makes her ruling 'law' (4.1.310, 309), I argue, she means the Alien Statute. Because of Shylock's rejection of the surgeon, shedding blood has taken on a new meaning in this scene that it lacks in the source texts, one that brings the Alien Statute into play in the first moment that the blood would otherwise be shed. The distinction made about 'Christian blood' (4.1.306), then, is not so much the indication of a law that distinguishes between all Christians and all Jews categorically, but the marker of a law that distinguishes between the all-Christian citizenry and the Jewish alien Shylock. Because Portia has maneuvered Shylock into a position where his imminent shedding of blood constitutes an explicit threat to Antonio's life, the Alien Statute is active in the scene even before it is quoted. It governs both direct attempts to kill a citizen – like offering to cut Antonio's heart out – and indirect ones – like refusing a surgeon to prevent his death – and thus traps Shylock entirely. His push to execute the sentence against Antonio without a doctor present becomes sufficient evidence of an attempt within the harsh legal world of the play, without his putting knife to flesh. This is why his guilt is 'manifest' (4.1.354), and why Portia commands him to fall 'down, therefore, and beg mercy of the Duke' (4.1.359).

This immediate move to judgement and sentencing in a Venetian court would have been seen as typical of Venice by the English, for whom, as David McPherson has suggested, the Venetians had a reputation for justice that was swift, severe and cruel in the extreme.[52] Indeed, in capital cases, as Thomas notes, 'the partie hym selfe [was] neuer suffred to speake',[53] as Shylock is not until after his pardon. The thoughtless moment in which Shylock rejected the idea of a surgeon has doomed him, whether he takes the flesh or not, and by law it does so without his having a chance to defend himself.

The relevance of the Alien Statute to Shylock's shedding of blood helps to explain why Portia continues on to employ the Alien Statute against him even after Shylock has already abandoned his attempt to kill Antonio. Unlike the other versions of the story, in which the legal quibble of flesh vs. blood in the bond is the only factor, *Merchant of Venice* includes a larger statutory issue that cannot be avoided once the legal machinery has begun to move. This results from Shakespeare's expansion of the Venetian legal system. However, there is more than legal inevitability at play here, at least if we accept Portia's earlier position about the moral necessity of mercy. At the same time that it prevents Shylock from taking the flesh, the Alien Statute also provides a space for that mercy. This time, however, the mercy is contained within the law, not placed outside it. The statute itself gives Shylock's life to 'the mercy / Of the Duke only, 'gainst all other voice' (4.1.351–2).

The Duke immediately exercises that mercy: 'I pardon thee thy life before thou ask it' (4.1.365). But he does not overstep the bounds of the city's charter in doing so because of the statutory permission Portia has supplied. This is crucial not only because of the restrictions on the Venetian dukes that we have already explored, but also because careful attention to it answers a long line of critical reactions that have seen the Duke's pardon as a violation of Venetian political and legal structures.[54] The statute Portia has read gives him this new authority *within* the laws, not outside them. The Duke pardons Shylock because he has the legal right to, not as a general case, but under this specific statute.

Yet there remains a danger in giving the Duke this power, even under the colour of a specific statute. In the English view of the Venetian system, the city's freedom relied on the dukes being restricted by the very laws that gave them power.[55] We can hear an indication of this in Portia's earlier insistence that 'there is no power in Venice / Can alter a decree established. / 'Twill be recorded for a precedent, / And many an error by the same example / Will rush into the state' (4.1.214–18). Precedent was known to be a crucial part of the Venetian legal system in this period.[56] As such, to have initially denied Shylock's legitimate contractual claim would have required Portia and the Duke to 'wrest once the law to your authority', which 'must not be' (4.1.211, 214). In this sort of matter 'the Venetian law / Cannot impugn' Shylock, and any attempt by the Duke to stop him himself would be illegitimate (4.1.174–5). But even though the Alien Statute means that the Duke is not violating the law here, giving him discretion threatens creating dangerous precedents within the state. It is worth noting how quickly the Duke moves from pardoning Shylock's life under the statute to agreeing to 'quit the fine for one half of his goods', a right he technically does not possess (4.1.377).

At the same time, allowing the Duke this discretion gives Antonio a strange power over Shylock's fate. Because the Duke threatens to 'recant / The pardon' (4.1.387–8) if Shylock does not agree to Antonio's conditions, Antonio is able to force Shylock to accept terms that differ from the statute despite having no legal authority to do so. This moment makes it clear that while the general power of mercy that could have saved Antonio was dangerous because it would have threatened the foundational restrictions on the duke – and threatened the future of commerce – even this limited statutory grant of mercy can lead quite quickly to the abuse of discretionary power.

The danger inherent in invoking mercy, even within the realm of Venetian law, may help explain why Portia would prefer Shylock to show mercy, rather than having to rely on the Alien Statute. It also partly explains why the other Venetians continually offer Shylock so much money to drop his suit rather than risking the trial. The space opened up for the exercise of the Duke's mercy is ultimately necessary to save Antonio's life, since the Alien Statute directly references the Duke's mercy. But even though this mercy exists within the laws, it remains a threat to the limitations on the duke's power, and thus to the Venetian state as it was understood in early modern England. The danger of mercy is reduced by the Alien Statute, but not eliminated, even as it saves Antonio.

But Antonio is not the only one who appears to have been saved: the entirety of the Venetian system is saved from the terrible choice that Shylock had presented to it. Entering the trial scene, Shylock has maneuvered the Venetians into an unpalatable position in which either one of their own must die at the hands of an alien bent on revenge, or the fundamental basis of their state, the check on tyrannical monarchical power within their government, must be ignored in order to stop him. As Portia-as-Balthasar navigates her way between these two dangers, ultimately landing on the Alien Statute, she does not merely protect Antonio. She saves the entire Venetian system of government from being exposed to the danger of precedent: either the frightening precedent of allowing Shylock to kill a citizen, or the even more destructive one of perverting not only the laws of contract, but also the fundamental laws of the state to preserve his life. Like the tribunes in *Coriolanus* undoing Caius Martius's election, she finds a way around Shylock's initially successful appeal to a particular aspect of the political structure. Portia saves the merchant of Venice from his persecutor, but she also saves Venice from itself, even if she does so by opening up a space for mercy that is immediately abused in its own right.

7

Othello, soft power and the search for truth

If *Merchant of Venice* hinges on the restrictions known to be placed on the dukes of Venice, *Othello* speaks to the power they were understood to have retained despite those restrictions. Yet this difference is primarily a matter of emphasis. *Othello* acknowledges the limits that the early modern English believed were placed on the dukes, but chooses instead to emphasize the subtle forms of soft power they possessed within the Venetian system. In particular, it focuses on how the dukes could serve as a model for investigation outside of a legal setting: not standing as a judge in judgement, but bringing out the truth through informal enquiry. In that context, I argue, we can see in the Duke of *Othello* a positive version of the elements of persuasion and investigation that will reappear in tragic form later in the play. This heightens the tragedy of Othello's downfall while showing us Shakespeare's ability to craft two different versions of the Duke out of common materials.

In examining this aspect of *Othello*, we must look beyond the restrictions on the dukes that we have already encountered in discussing *Merchant of Venice*. Although the early modern English understanding of the Venetian system Shakespeare had to work with would have been similar in the two plays, the focus is different in *Othello*. The key to this difference is that *Othello* does not feature the duke in a courtroom scene. We have already seen that the early modern English believed the duke had a variety of judicial powers that relied on joining himself to other courts and councils. But he was also considered to possess a kind of consensual, semi-formal power that extended beyond the merely judicial. This power was not seen as dictatorial or tyrannical but consensual, centred on the effort to 'moderat & direct the endeuors of the rest to the cōmon good & utility of all'.[1] He was tasked with 'an especiall care to conserue the common good & the perfection of civill agreement',[2] and was intended to use his authority solely for that task. It was to this end that his voice was permitted to be heard in all deliberations, but not to be the sole voice in any.[3] He intended to watch over those in authority even as he was simultaneously watched by them.[4] It was his responsibility to work to ensure that the whole state functioned properly, and to do so not through the law and the courts, but through persuasion, discussion and observation. Such power was deemed unlikely to be abused in a tyrannical way but still permitted a good duke to do much for the peace, security and concord of the city.

Some of the power that the duke exercised in this way is easily recognizable as the kind of soft power that we have already seen in *Merchant*, such as joining with courts or participating in arguments. But his power also went beyond the kind of highly restricted legal authority on which the trial in *Merchant* hinges. The duke's role was not merely legalistic, but persuasive, drawing on the influence of his rank and his moral authority. In some ways, this duty was the entire reason that the Venetians chose to have an individual head of state. While they wished to avoid the threat of an autocratic ruler, they still needed someone with the practical authority, if not the formal power, to keep everyone else in check.[5] The soft power of the duke was a compromise between the need for someone to have the collective good in mind and the simultaneous desire to disqualify that person from abusing their supervisory power. The duke could watch the watchers, without having sufficient hard power to become a tyrant himself.

This meant that the duke's soft power took the form of persuasion, argument and discussion, not command. In this way, we can think of his power as similar to the kind of authority Malcolm wishes to wield at the end of *Macbeth*: centred on the concord of the state and sufficiently decentralized to avoid tyranny. Unlike Malcolm, however, the duke had no personal army, and the Venetian councils and senate had much more power than even the earls Malcolm creates, let alone the earlier thanes. Because of this, his power was both weaker and in a sense purer: it relied more closely on interaction with others, and it personally benefitted him less. The king might be called 'Scotland', but the duke was not equated with 'Venice'. Instead, the duke operated for the collective benefit of Venice, mediating between various power brokers within the councils and senate where hard power was concentrated.

These aspects of the duke's soft power would have been familiar to Shakespeare and his contemporaries. They are central in both Contarini and Thomas, both of whom, as we have seen, were highly influential.[6] In addition, just like the limits on the duke that we explored in the previous chapter, these strengths were also reflected in a wide range of other texts in the period, if often less precisely than the restrictions. Some of these authors explicitly cited Contarini as a source for the duke's odd form of power through affecting others.[7] Others simply showed him operating in this manner as a matter of course,[8] as we shall see Shakespeare does, or made clear that the use of this kind of authority to correct wrongs was a key component of the duke's office without making explicit why.[9] The general sense of these texts is that the duke of Venice's powers lay primarily in this kind of soft power for the purpose of 'hinder[ing] quarells and disorders of such as gouerned'.[10] To this we might add the powers noted in the previous chapter of adding a voice and casting a vote in any council, which also pointed in the direction of a duke whose powers came more from consensus than command. Similarly, *A Knacke to Know* gives us a duke who uses 'silence' to 'finde the deapth of each mans drifte' and 'discerne the truth', showing the duke's ability to sort out truths by informal means.[11] An early modern English audience would thus have been primed to expect to see a duke of Venice working closely with other Venetian nobles for the good of the city, and to see him urging and persuading them for that collective good, while remaining aware that he had 'no command' over others.[12]

It is appropriate, therefore, that the Duke in *Othello* appears in the council scene (1.3), and only in that scene. This scene, which serves as the culmination of the Venetian part of the play (and includes the command to go to Cyprus, contextualizing the part of the play set there as still Venetian), is treated by many critics as if it portrayed a legal court in session, operating formally in order to achieve justice.[13] But I agree with those who argue that the meeting shown is better understood as an emergency meeting of the Senate or a council.[14] As such, the Duke is not adjoined to a judge's court but part of the machinery of government. Therefore, this is a scene that showcases not the duke's legal position, as in *Merchant*, but his persuasive authority, such as it is. I suggest that this makes the duke's soft power even more crucial in *Othello* than it was in *Merchant*. In particular, because the scene is not a courtroom or a trial, it permits *Othello*'s Duke much more latitude of speech and action than his counterpart in *Merchant* because he is not hampered by the restrictions that would bind him in a more legally specific setting. Instead, we get to see the Duke's persuasion in action, working to bring others into accord for the benefit of Venice.

The scene begins *in media res*, with the Duke and the Senators already assembled and discussing the approaching Turkish threat. Shakespeare gives us a glimpse of the larger Venetian government here: a scene of the 'duke in council' (1.2.92, 93)[15] with the duke present and presiding, but not ruling. A portrait of a functioning political structure is compressed into the forty-eight lines before Othello and Brabantio enter, and we can recognize it as a miniature of the Venetian state Shakespeare's audience might have expected to see. The Duke consults with the Senators but neither overrides their opinions nor imposes his own will. He is clearly the first among equals, but the equality is as evident as the primacy. Even his one order – 'Write from us to him; post-post-haste, dispatch' (1.3.47) – leaves the details of the message to the author. Indeed, that 'us' is most likely a corporate, not a royal plural; the Duke has referred to himself in the singular throughout the scene (1.3.4, 10, 11) and the First Senator, whom the Duke addresses in this line, has previously used 'us' and 'we' to mean Venice or the Senate as a corporate body (1.3.20, 27, 28). The Duke's request is thus not a command to a subordinate but an urging to a colleague. Here we see Shakespeare's familiarity with the duke's institutional role as a facilitator of just this sort of meeting, as well as his expectation that his audience would immediately recognize and accept this dramatic situation.

Into this smoothly functioning, though hardly calm, council come Brabantio and Othello, with a very different issue on their minds. The Duke greets them on behalf of the group: the 'we' who 'must straight employ' Othello and 'lacked your [Brabantio's] counsel' is contrasted with the 'I' who 'did not see you', making it clear that he once again speaks for the entire council and not just himself in welcoming them (1.3.49, 52, 51). But although he welcomes them on the council's behalf, he is not the council's only voice. The First Senator speaks often, and there is even a point when the entire room speaks as one about Brabantio's accusation against Othello (1.3.74). This accusation shifts the focus of the scene away from 'the general care' and towards Brabantio's 'particular grief' (1.3.55, 56). Contrary to critical readings that would read this change as 'the Duke (Doge) and his council intervening'[16] in the dispute between Brabantio and Othello, it seems from the order of events within the scene that at this moment their dispute intervenes into the council.

But even though at this point the topic and mood of the discussion change, the Duke's role in it does not. In fact, he comes into his own in mediating between Brabantio and Othello. Yet he is an informal mediator, not a judge, fulfilling precisely the function we would expect from Contarini's account of a duke tasked with ensuring 'the perfection of civill agreement'.[17] We can see him adopt this role by looking at how he speaks: 'What in your own part can you say to this?' (1.3.75); 'Say it, Othello' (1.3.128); 'Good Brabantio, take this mangled matter at the best' (1.3.172); 'Let me speak like yourself' (1.3.200). This is the language of a man standing outside the dispute and trying to help those involved in it find common ground and truth: probing, questioning and cajoling.

It is true that Brabantio mocks the Duke's language when the latter turns to *sententiae*, the adages in rhymed couplets with which he attempts to console the angry father (1.3.203–20). But this mockery proves the intent of the Duke's words, even if they do not have the desired effect. Brabantio says the Duke is trying to 'pierce[]' his 'bruised heart' with his words (1.3.220) – that is, to break through his grief and bring him to be at peace with Othello and Desdemona's marriage. Though the Duke's words may not have succeeded in their aim, this evidence of their purpose confirms the Duke's intended role in this scene as a peacemaker.

When the scene returns to public business, the Duke continues his role as first among the equal senators in the discussion of the Turkish threat. Once again Shakespeare makes sure that orders do not come from the Duke alone. While the Duke tells Othello that 'th'affair cries haste / And speed must answer it', it is the First Senator who insists 'you must away tonight' (1.3.277–8). The closest the Duke comes to a direct command is when he tells the assembled Senate when they will meet again, but it is unclear whether this is his choice or merely a reminder of an earlier collective decision (1.3.280). Likewise, his request that Othello 'leave some officer behind' (1.3.281) to bear the commission to Cyprus is phrased as a command from the Senate as a whole, so that that officer may '*our* commission bring to you' (1.3.282) (emphasis mine). The Duke is conscientious about where authority belongs, often speaking for the Senate but never dictating to it. Between this circumspection and his treatment of the dispute about Othello's marriage, we can see in him the very image of the duke the early modern English would have been primed to expect: a man possessed of little independent authority but well versed in leadership and the techniques of soft power.

When we understand the Duke's intervention in the Senate house as an instance of this sort of positive persuasion, we can see this scene as an unrealized model for Othello's investigation of other claims throughout the play. Like Menenius's relations with the tribunes in *Coriolanus*, the Duke's intervention in the council scene shows us how the main character could address their problems, but does not, drawing our attention to their failure. In his insistence on publicly hearing from all parties and weighing their claims, the Duke serves as a point of comparison for Othello's consideration of more partial (in both senses) evidence. In particular, his treatment of 'proof' gives us a perspective on what is missing from Othello's. The Duke models for Othello three key aspects of the critical analysis of claims: he hears from all parties; he lets the parties hear each other; and he makes sure these discussions are not kept secret. While these may parallel certain aspects of a legal proceeding, they are not inherently legal processes but investigative processes that can operate, as here, outside a legal framework. Likewise, although Othello renders judgement at times, his own investigations are not truly legal proceedings in the strict sense. Thus the Duke's non-judicial interventions serve as a strong potential model for Othello's own inquiries. Yet in each case, Othello fails to follow the Duke's example, and the combination of these failures leads him to his fatal conclusion.

The Duke is insistent on hearing from more than one source. He is the one who calls for the opinions of the various parties to the situation: 'what in your own part can you [Othello] say to this' (1.3.75); 'fetch Desdemona hither' (1.3.122); 'say it, Othello' (1.3.128). He does promise that, if Desdemona has been betwitched or drugged, Brabantio may read 'the bloody book of law / … in the bitter letter / After your own sense' (1.3.68–9), but he does not quickly assume that the bewitching or drugging has actually occurred. He is unwilling to let that rest on Brabantio's word only, saying 'to vouch this is no proof' (1.3.107).

Instead, he insists on a 'more certain and overt test' than simple accusation (1.3.108). This test is not a physical or visual examination of evidence but the robust encounter of claim and counterclaim that ensues in the rest of the scene. The 'thin habits and poor likelihoods / Of modern seeming' that Brabantio has presented are not allowed to stand without Othello and Desdemona also having their say (1.3.109–10). It is on this cue about 'seeming' from the Duke that the First Senator calls for Othello to 'speak' (1.3.111). Only by contrasting and comparing perspectives can the truth be found.

This process is not kept secret or hidden. The entire conversation takes place before the whole senate. Othello and Brabantio are each present as the other speaks, and Brabantio at one point interrupts, demonstrating that both of them are actively engaged in the discussion at the same time (1.3.76). Everyone has a voice, all can hear each other, and there are independent observers, with the First Senator's occasional interventions serving as a reminder of this. This kind of open debate of matters of fact has already been modelled in public affairs by the Senate's discussion of the Turkish fleet, as Philip McGuire and Mark Matheson have pointed out,[18] with an emphasis on the 'composition in these news' and whether they should be given 'credit' (1.3.1, 2). Here, I suggest, it re-appears at a more personal level. Rather than determining the relative truth of various written reports, the Duke is weighing the passionate statements of Brabantio, Othello and Desdemona. But the process remains the same: public, open discussion in which all affected are allowed a voice.

This is the model that the play provides for rational, effective investigation into a confused or complicated situation, with the Duke as a model of informed enquiry, as was proper to the Venetian duke's role. The Duke seeks the truth, not legal evidence. The need for this kind of detailed non-judicial truth-finding arises at three other points within the play. First, Othello is called on to resolve the quarrel between Cassio and Montano; then Iago presents him with the question of Desdemona's infidelity; and finally the other characters discover Iago's deceits. In each case, the language used mirrors the Duke's in the council scene, but the first two fall short of the ideal presented there. Only in the final scene do we return to this peculiarly Venetian model for proper investigation.

The first echo of the council scene comes exactly one act later, after Cassio and Montano have come to blows. Othello enters onto a scene of chaos, and his first instinct, like the Duke's, is to ask questions – 'From whence arises this?' (2.3.165) – and to call on those present to 'speak' (2.3.174). He forms his investigation along the Duke's pattern, asking each potential witness in turn for their view: 'How comes it, Michael, you are thus forgot?' (2.3.184); 'Worthy Montano ... give me answer to it' (2.3.186, 192); 'Iago, who began't?' (2.3.213). But his investigation falters for lack of evidence when only Iago actually tells him anything: Cassio 'cannot speak', while Montano must 'spare speech, which something now offends me' (2.3.185, 195). While no one disagrees with the basic truth of what Iago says, Othello loses the opportunity to hear any exculpatory or even explanatory evidence. He therefore makes his decision on the basis of a single voice. Even though that voice was heard in public, Othello therefore still deviates from the Duke's precedent. Rather than waiting to hear from those involved themselves whenever it became possible (as the Duke did by waiting for Desdemona to arrive), Othello acts in haste. By the time Cassio has recovered enough to sue to him through Desdemona, Othello's mind has already been poisoned by Iago's later slander. By making his decision here on Iago's word alone, and not waiting for the others to be able to speak, Othello fails to meet the standard set by the Duke, and that failure sets him down the path that ultimately leads to disaster.

Othello compounds this error in judgement later by listening to Iago's accusations about Cassio and Desdemona in secret. The accusation of adultery would be difficult to hear in a fully public setting but by failing to bring in any other perspective, or ask anyone else for their thoughts, Othello exposes himself to error. In asking for proof he initially follows the Duke's insistence that 'to vouch' (1.3.107) cannot be proof, but during their tête-à-tête Iago gradually erodes away his awareness that Iago has no actual evidence. In the process, Iago also moves Othello away from placing value on debate and discussion and towards a model that prioritizes seeing, what Othello ultimately calls 'ocular proof' (3.3.363).

This is an inversion of the Duke's process. The Duke relied not on visual evidence but on the confrontation of speech against speech. His was a public, linguistic mode of proof that turned the evidence of mere vision inside out, exchanging, for instance,

Othello's outward colour for an inward one: 'your son-in-law is far more fair than black' (1.3.291). Othello himself once showed this same scepticism about visual evidence, choosing Cassio as his lieutenant over Iago even though 'his eyes had seen the proof' of Iago's soldiership (1.1.27). The play identifies this for us as the correct sceptical attitude towards visual evidence, but here Iago turns Othello away from it.

Iago starts to wean Othello away from his earlier position, and the Duke's example, by lamenting the same unreliability of visual evidence that the Duke referenced earlier: 'men should be what they seem, / Or those that be not, would they might seem none' (3.3.129–30). Yet by the end of the scene, the terms are inverted, and only sight is accepted as proof. Othello himself takes the first step, bringing sight and proof into the same sentence: 'I'll see before I doubt, when I doubt, prove' (3.3.193). Here sight and proof are linked, but still distinct; sight can create doubt, and doubt produces the need for proof. Notably, by this logic, sight cannot be proof, or else doubt, being created by sight, would prove itself. Iago seems to accept this distinction, as his 'I speak not yet of proof' is followed immediately by 'look to your wife. Observe her well with Cassio' (3.3.199–200). But by separating the sources of these terms, and negating one of them, he creates a space in which their meanings can mix, pushing aside the concept of spoken proof. Because Iago will 'not speak' of proof, it implicitly becomes Othello's 'look[ing]' and 'observ[ing]' that will provide that proof. Othello picks up on this new connection between sight and proof, urging Iago that 'if more thou dost perceive, let me know more' and asking him to 'set on thy wife to observe' (3.3.243, 244). After Othello sees Desdemona himself, he comes to a crisis, and in that crisis he unites sight and proof. He demands that Iago 'give me the ocular proof' and 'make me see't, or at the least so prove it / That the probation bear no hinge or loop / To hang a doubt on' (3.3.363, 367–9). In this final formulation sight has subsumed proof, becoming its superior; only if he cannot 'see't' would he have Iago 'prove it'.

Ironically, in this particular case, an insistence on purely visual proof might have been well-founded. Cassio and Desdemona are not lovers; had Othello refused to doubt before seeing them engage in adultery he would have been safe from Iago's blandishments. But by the time he insists on visual proof, Othello already has jealous doubts, and is already exposed to 'torture' by Iago's accusation

(3.3.371). Once he doubts, visual proof will no longer serve him because it cannot be used to *disprove* the accusation: no amount of not seeing Cassio and Desdemona abed together will convince Othello they are virtuous. Visual evidence can only convince him if the accusation is true; since it is false, visual evidence cannot satisfy him – just as visual evidence was of no use in the council scene, which was also open to disproving, rather than proving, an accusation.

But if visual evidence cannot serve Othello, because of his doubts, it also cannot directly help Iago to prove those doubts true, because the accusation is false. For this reason, at this point in the scene Iago must demur from showing Othello Desdemona's guilt visually and turn back to 'imputation and strong circumstances' instead of vision (3.3.409). He can safely do so because the earlier insistence on vision has destroyed Othello's connection to the Duke's verbal method of enquiry. With that link severed, Iago can 'vouch' whatever he likes without the fear that Othello will bring in other voices to compete with his. He launches into a dubious story – an elaborate fictional account of Cassio's dream-speech – and is able to pass it off on Othello as 'proof'. Indeed, he goes so far as to claim that 'this may help to thicken other proofs / That do demonstrate thinly', as though his fantastic story were solid evidence (3.3.432–3). Similarly, he has only to tell Othello that he saw Cassio with Desdemona's handkerchief to count it a proof 'with the other proofs' (3.3.444). This would not be effective if Othello recalled the Duke's distrust of mere vouching and demanded to hear from Cassio. But because he is no longer thinking in the Duke's terms, Othello fails to assess Iago's accusations critically, or to make them sufficiently public to allow them to be dispelled.

The same effect is at work in the next act. Although Othello observes the scene directly, Iago glosses it for him with unprovable statements about Cassio's thoughts (4.1.168). By turning Othello away from the Duke's rejection of visual evidence and elevation of proof by debate, Iago has produced a situation in which his bare assertion is proof enough, so long as it can be linked to something Othello has seen, and in which each instance of Iago asserting something about Othello's sight becomes part of a series of 'other proofs' that are never more than Iago's other assertions about additional pieces of otherwise harmless visual evidence. Since adopting this approach allows Iago to interpret Othello's sight for him, Othello is trapped in a world in which he not only relies on sight, rather than hearing, but even when he hears, he listens to only a single voice, privately. These are precisely the pitfalls that the Duke's method of investigation was designed to avoid. As in the case of the nighttime brawl, Othello fails to follow the Duke's model properly. But where his first judgement of Cassio was based on faulty, rushed application of the Duke's principles, this second failure is the result of his gradually becoming separated from those principles altogether.

Before fully succumbing to Iago and committing murder, however, Othello has three distinct opportunities to correct himself and reapply the Duke's principles. First, the emissaries from Venice arrive, bringing with them not merely a formal reminder of the duke and thus his method of enquiry (4.1.217) but also a specific example of the need for multiple witnesses and the weakness of individual verbal claims in Lodovico's statement that Othello's treatment of Desdemona 'would not be believed in Venice / Though I should swear I saw it' (4.241–2). Next, Othello himself finally questions Emilia about Desdemona, and Emilia responds that 'she is honest' (4.2.12). Then he even questions Desdemona herself, asking 'Are you not a strumpet?', and hearing her defiant answer 'No, as I am a Christian' (4.2.83, 84). Yet he ignores the Venetians, dismisses Emilia's testimony and cruelly mocks Desdemona (4.2.20–1, 90–2).

At this point, Iago has succeeded in turning Othello so far away from the Duke's model that even when he hears other voices, he can no longer listen to them. If Othello were capable of attending to his other witnesses, he would not believe Iago. But by this point, instead of comparing speech with speech and weighing them, he trusts Iago and dismisses all contrary evidence. If the Duke had acted in the same manner, Brabantio's initial accusation would have stood, and Othello would have lost Desdemona. In turn, if Othello remembered the Duke's method, he would have no reason to kill Desdemona. Her desperate, and sensible, pleas to 'send for the man, and ask him' and 'send for him hither / Let him confess the truth' echo the Duke's earlier 'fetch Desdemona hither' (5.2.50, 67–8, 1.3.122). But they fall on ears that are not merely deaf to her reason but actively corrupted with lies. Othello falsely tells her that Cassio 'hath confessed' (5.2.68). Othello has gone so far from the Duke's example that he not only refuses to send for witnesses but even supplies their part himself, inaccurately. It is hard to think of a behaviour further from the Duke's example than this.

In the aftermath of Desdemona's murder, the burden of investigation passes from Othello onto the other surviving characters, and they revive the Duke's process of investigation. Emilia uncovers the truth by making Iago and Othello 'speak' (5.2.171). Her demand that Iago speak in order to 'disprove this villain' (5.2.168) restores 'proof' to the linguistic realm rather than the visual. When she discovers that both Othello and Iago agree on Iago's role in accusing Desdemona, she in turn becomes a verbal witness for the Venetians against her husband: 'I will speak as liberal as the north' (5.2.219). Iago kills her and flees – she dies trying to bear witness, 'speaking as I think' (5.2.249) – but as he is recaptured, the Venetians take the opportunity to make him speak too, though offstage: 'this wretch hath in part confessed his villainy' (5.2.293). The unravelling of Iago's web of lies is almost complete, a result of precisely that ducal style of investigation found in the council scene: the public, open weighing of multiple perspectives and alternate versions of a story in order to arrive at the truth.

Iago seeks to foil any further efforts in this direction with his assertion that 'from this time forth I never will speak word' (5.2.301). His attempt to stymie the investigation through silence means that Gratiano's immediate response that 'torments will ope your lips' (5.2.302) should be read not merely as a threat of violence but as a promise that Iago will be forced to participate in this enquiry despite his own desires, albeit in a violent manner commensurate with the Venetian harshness we saw in *Merchant*. Iago's motives are famously difficult to ascertain throughout *Othello*, but the return of the Venetian system of investigation promises at least the attempt to find them out after the play has ended. In addition to the reported part-confession and the promise of torture, we see a third solution to the conundrum of Iago's silence in the ensuing lines, one in which Iago's hand replaces his lips in speaking for him. They have found 'a letter' that he wrote to Roderigo (5.2.305), and will use that to supply his voice. His words will be a part of the oncoming investigation by whatever means necessary.

This kind of participatory enquiry, as modelled by the Duke in the first act, is intimately related to the unique strengths and weaknesses of the ducal position as it was understood in early modern England. A Venetian duke could not afford to rely on a single voice, since his own voice was necessarily only one of many in any decision that he reached. But beyond that, reading the Duke in this way is critical to the realization that there is no trial anywhere in *Othello*; even Iago's trial will only come after the play itself is over. Considering the play through the early modern English view of the duke strengthens the play's emphasis on participation and debate, and makes it easier to see the absence of a trial. That absence in turn allows us to think beyond legal parameters and see how Othello repeatedly misses his opportunities to use the Duke's model of enquiry.

To an audience attuned to this, Othello's tragedy would be peculiarly Venetian, intimately linked to Othello's personal failure to live up to the distinctively Venetian approach of the Duke. While Othello is not in the unique political position of the Duke, the fact that the Duke was able to foil Iago's first plot in the play – using Brabantio to upset Othello's marriage – through the soft power of enquiry alone makes Othello's inability to see through the next plot despite possessing the authority of command all the more glaring. However, paradoxically, it is only because Othello is so Venetian that we can expect him to live up to the Duke's example and to realize how effective the Duke's approach is. Othello is the Moor of Venice. If Steggle is correct about early modern theatrical practice, and a title-board would have been onstage throughout the play, the audience would be continually reminded of this fact; even if not, that is still the identity the play constructs for him. As such, we expect him to act like a Venetian, which in this play means recognizing the value of the Duke's example in seeking out the truth. His failure to do so is his tragic flaw, but it is only a flaw because we acknowledge him as sufficiently Venetian in the first place.

In both *Othello* and *Merchant of Venice*, Shakespeare uses early modern English perspectives on the political structures of a contemporary European state to highlight the themes and action of the play. Both his Dukes are models of the early modern English version of the duke of Venice. By understanding them properly, we can see how their presence and role affect the thoughts, speech and action of the other characters around them, from Portia and Shylock to Iago and Othello. In *Merchant* we saw a Duke whose primary attribute was his inability: to dismiss Shylock's suit, to rule on the case without Portia, to do anything without the explicit permission of the law. When operating outside the law, the Duke is either ineffective, as when he remonstrates with Shylock, or potentially dangerous, as when he goes beyond the statute to enable Antonio's revenge on Shylock. In *Othello*, we see something quite different. The Duke is a model for productive enquiry into a difficult situation. Instead of focusing on the Duke's lack of power, the play emphasizes Othello's inability to follow the Duke's able example. The Duke is effective, efficient and powerful, almost the opposite of his counterpart in *Merchant*. Yet these two Dukes are ultimately cut from the same cloth. Each shows a different side of the prevailing early modern English conception of the weak dukes of Venice. In this we can see the mutability of a single setting, depending on the demands of the plot. Neither *Othello*'s nor *Merchant*'s Duke would come as a surprise in an early modern English theatre. By working from the same materials with a different emphasis, Shakespeare was able to craft two different but compatible visions of Venice. Armed with an awareness of the historicism of setting, we in turn can see his dramatic craft, and his political imagination, at work in both.

8

Conclusion: *Measure for Measure*, topicality and performance

Now that we have familiarized ourselves with the readings produced by the historicism of setting, I would like to turn to two major concerns about the treatment of setting that deserve specific attention. One is the question of topicality: how the plays manage to speak to their own time of composition despite being set in other times and places. The other is the question of *re*-setting, the common theatrical practice of performing Shakespeare's plays in new settings that are not the time or place implied by the text. In both cases, I suggest, we should approach these issues not by rejecting or ignoring the historicism of setting, but by working through it: by identifying exactly how the play uses its setting in order to see both how it speaks to its own time through the setting and how it might best speak to our own time with the significance of that original setting in mind.

To demonstrate what I mean by this, I will use the example of *Measure for Measure* and its Viennese setting, because the play has received substantial (and relatively recent) consideration in terms of its setting in both performance and criticism. Recent criticism has aggressively de-emphasized the importance of Renaissance Vienna to Shakespeare's work, while performances tend to re-set the play without particular reference to the original Viennese setting. I argue, however, that each of these approaches detracts from the power of the play, causing us to lose sight of the particularly Renaissance Viennese aspects of the play's portrayal of an absent duke using his very absence to consolidate religious and secular power into his own hands.

Measure for Measure is an especially appropriate case for considering issues of setting, re-setting and topicality because academic scholars have tended to downplay the significance of Renaissance Vienna to the play. Gary Taylor in particular has argued influentially that the original setting of the play was Ferrara, not Vienna, and that the received setting is the result of later revisions.[1] Even those critics, like Leah Marcus, who have acknowledged the potential importance of Vienna to the play tend to consider that the original setting is largely a stand-in for Shakespeare's London.[2]

The same de-emphasizing of the setting frequently occurs in performance, but given the inherent variability of productions, I believe a specific example will prove helpful. In March 2013, the Goodman Theatre in Chicago performed *Measure for Measure*. Personally directed by the theatre's artistic director, Robert Falls, the production was set not in Renaissance Vienna but in 1970s New York. The choice was not accidental. Brief statements in the production's programme by Falls and Neena Arndt, the production's dramaturg, explained the rationale behind the change. But while the decision was intentional, neither Falls nor Arndt saw the change as presenting any significant change to the play itself. Both emphasized the importance of the potential audience's 'familiarity' with the setting not in terms of their awareness of Renaissance Vienna but rather by suggesting that the original setting was 'obviously intended ... to reflect conditions in the London of [Shakespeare's] time' and that a new production in turn would inherently reflect the conditions of 2013 Chicago, no matter where or when it was set.[3] Arndt suggested that 'for Shakespeare, the exact time and setting were often less important' than other thematic factors, concluding that this lack of emphasis on the original place and time made Shakespeare 'not of a place, but a man for the whole globe'.[4]

I bring up this production and its treatment of setting not because I consider Falls and Arndt's approach to the setting of *Measure for Measure* unusual, but because it is so normal. Theatrical productions of all Shakespeare plays frequently adjust both the time and the place of the play according to the director's preference, so much so that the first question asked about a given production of a Shakespeare play is often 'where (or when) is it set?' The Goodman's production was a well-received example of this sort of re-setting, and I will therefore make use of it in this chapter as a stand-in for this general approach.

Because both critics and performers have argued that its setting is unimportant, I suggest that *Measure for Measure* is a useful play for examining precisely the issues I am considering here: the role of setting in performance, and the importance of the setting for topical interpretation of the play. I argue that both issues should be addressed through the historicism of setting, rather than by pushing it aside. Here that means identifying and analysing the preconceptions and assumptions about Vienna circulating in early modern England, particularly those relating to the position of the Viennese Archduke of Austria. Understanding those early modern English views of the city provides insight into major elements of the play – the Duke's disguise, the fate of Barnardine and the dramatic final scene – in ways that influence both how the play should be produced and what topical application it might have had at the time.

Despite Taylor's assertion that Vienna would have 'meant almost nothing, and absolutely nothing relevant to *Measure*' to Shakespeare's audience at the turn of the sixteenth century,[5] Vienna was well-known to the English, and had been since at least the twelfth century. Taylor's claim is based on Vienna's lack of cultural cachet in the period: its absence from poetry and the stage (*Measure for Measure* itself aside), the lack of trade between it and England, and the fact that the Holy Roman Emperor had moved his seat from it to Prague in the late sixteenth century and would not return until around the time of the Thirty Years War.[6] He suggests that the only real contemporary cultural significance of Vienna at this time was as a bulwark against the Ottoman invasion of Europe and that this threat is absent from *Measure for Measure*.[7] These factors lead him to dismiss the potential significance of a Viennese setting for the play in Shakespeare's original and thus dismiss as well the very possibility of such an initial setting, attributing the play's Vienna to a later revision by Thomas Middleton.

By focusing on cultural issues, however, Taylor ignores Vienna's political and religious distinctiveness: both in its political structure and in how that structure interacted with the denominational struggle within the city between Catholics and Protestants. While Vienna may not have been a cultural touchstone in early modern England, its political and religious situation was well understood, precisely because of two factors Taylor chooses to downplay: the Ottoman threat and the historical imprisonment of Richard I near Vienna by Leopold, Archduke of Austria.

As a result, the early modern English did have a sense of Vienna as a city, and of its political organization under the (arch)dukes of Austria. These dukes were well-attested from multiple sources, especially those concerned with Richard I: for example, the chronicler John Stow claimed in 1580 that 'Leopold, Duke of Austria' forced Richard I to help 'builde the walles aboute *Vienna,* the chiefest Cittie of *Austria*' during his captivity,[8] and other chronicles and accounts of Vienna likewise emphasized its position as the chief city of the dukes of Austria.[9] At the same time, those dukes were known to be frequently called into service in other parts of the Empire because of their political and military importance, particularly as part of the war against the Turk and the Spanish occupation of the Netherlands.[10] Finally, despite their frequent absences, the political control of the dukes of Austria over Vienna was believed to be increasing. This was especially true in religious matters, as the dukes moved from permitting the 'free exercise of two religions' (Lutheranism and Catholicism) in the city to enforcing upon non-Catholics that 'the publike exercies of their [Protestant] religion is restrailned'.[11] This was also true in more secular affairs: Vienna was once one of the free cities of the Holy Roman Empire,[12] but, as Jean Bodin had observed, a gradual consolidation of aristocratic power by the house of Austria had led to a situation in which the people of the city had 'lost their liberties'.[13] At the same time, the dukedom of Austria itself had become a massive, politically powerful title.[14] Combining these three attributes of Vienna known in the period, I suggest that, in terms of the historicism of setting, we should expect to see at the heart of *Measure for Measure* a city ruled by a duke who is frequently absent, but whose position in the political and religious life of the city is both strong and increasing.

When we look at the play, this is indeed the case. The city is ruled by a duke whose primary characteristic is his (seeming) absence from his own city. Not only that, but the play insists on a confusing multitude of potential reasons for that absence: problems in Hungary (1.2.2),[15] Poland (1.3.14), Russia (3.1.354) or Rome (3.1.355) are all possibilities, suggesting a duke who leaves the city on all kinds of foreign business frequently enough that people do not necessarily know which business has called him forth each time.

At the same time, that same duke has an 'absolute power and place here in Vienna' (1.3.13) and commands assistance at his mere word from officers of church and state alike. Most of these elements are unique to the Shakespearean version of the story, which 'strikingly enlarged the Duke's role' from that found in his sources and put him at the centre of the play.[16] In short, the political circumstances of the play are quite appropriate to Vienna, as it was understood in England in Shakespeare's time.

The implications of this political situation for *Measure for Measure* are most visible when examining the overall arc of the play. In this light, it becomes clear that *Measure for Measure* is a play about the Duke expanding his own political and religious power at the expense of all those around him. By the end of the play, Angelo is exposed and his reputation deflated; the houses of ill-repute in the suburbs of the city – outside of those walls that Richard I built – have been torn down; and Lucio, who merely spoke ill of the Duke in private, has been punished by a forced marriage. Even the trusty Provost is warned that he serves at the Duke's discretion by the latter's decision to 'discharge you of your office' (5.1.459), even if he later receives an undefined 'worthier place' (5.1.531). What is more, the entire city now knows that the Duke is watching whatever they do, even when they think he is absent, even when confessing to a priest. The Duke's apparent absence has led to a direct increase in his power over the state and its people, a curbing of their 'liberty' in exchange for his willingness to deliver them 'justice' (1.3.29): precisely the exchange he had hoped for, and precisely the exchange the Austrian dukes were believed to have achieved in Vienna over the previous century.

This expectation of an increase in the absentee Duke's power would inform the reaction not only to the Duke's machinations, but to Angelo's position as his deputy as well. If the characteristic political move of Austrian dukes was to grow their power despite their absence from the city, that expectation has significant implications for the role of the Duke's deputy. This would at first incline an audience to expect Angelo's efforts to succeed: to anticipate that the tearing down of the bawdy houses and the prosecution of Claudio will serve as the basis for a renewed degree of ducal power after the Duke returns. The Duke himself helps to stoke these expectations through his discussion with Friar Thomas near the beginning of the play (1.3.11–54).

Yet as the play moves on and it becomes clear that the Duke is in fact opposing Angelo's efforts incognito, the weight of those expectations shifts. In this Viennese context, an audience aware of Renaissance Vienna's political structure would still be looking for the Duke's power to increase, but now that expectation would work against Angelo, rather than for him. For such a Renaissance English audience seeing the play for the first time, the Viennese setting thus would have served to heighten the drama of the plot's twists and turns, leaving them wondering how the Duke would prevail: first expecting it to be through Angelo, and then against him. This is an example of how the setting can serve to reinforce reactions the audience is already having – going from thinking that Angelo may do good to wondering how Angelo will be defeated – while deepening the effect because the Viennese dukes were believed to be achieving in fact what the Duke in *Measure for Measure* achieves in fiction.

At the same time, the politically productive absenteeism of the Viennese dukes separates the Duke of *Measure for Measure* emphatically from James I of England, pulling against that strain of interpretation, both scholarly and theatrical, that sees Vienna (or indeed, all of Shakespeare's settings) as a simple metaphor for London.[17] James was emphatically not an absentee monarch. So while James had a reputation for an autocratic desire to strengthen his own power, a theme which has been well-documented in *Measure for Measure*, particularly by Dollimore,[18] the setting calls our attention to the differences between how that power was achieved and how the Duke achieves his. Both rulers may have relied on surveillance and secrecy to enhance their political standing, but the Duke does so in his apparent absence, while James was definitely present in and around London, even if his power was sometimes applied to the city only indirectly. Thus, any immediate topical application of the play's lessons about surveillance and authority would have been mediated by the known differences between how Vienna and England were governed, even if, as Dollimore and Marcus suggest, certain details of statecraft and its objects might have seemed familiar to close observers of Jacobean England.[19]

An awareness of the creeping expansion of the duke's power also helps to explain the primary foreign reference that Taylor and others cite as evidence in dating the Viennese setting to later revisions: the reference to a political situation involving the King of Hungary (1.2.1–5).[20] While it is undoubtedly true, as Taylor posits, that Vienna and Hungary were extremely topical references in the early 1620s, after the beginning of the Thirty Years War, it is wrong to assume that a reference to the connection between the two locations would have been meaningless before then. By the early 1600s, according to Sir Edwin Sandys, 'the house of *Au|stria* in *Germany*' was known to have added 'the kingdome of Bohemia with his dependāces, and of *Hungarie*' to its political sphere,[21] another instance of the duke's ever-increasing power. Intriguingly enough, according to reports current in England, this expansion came about at least partly as a result of an ecclesiastically invested archduke resigning his church office to marry a woman named Isabella.[22]

Indeed, the specific geopolitical situation Lucio describes, involving the need for a treaty between Vienna and Hungary, was present, and reported in England, in the period around when Shakespeare was writing *Measure for Measure*. The Viennese archduke Matthias was involved in a dispute with an Ottoman-backed pretender to the throne of Hungary on behalf of the Holy Roman Emperor. In 1606 the terms of the peace they had negotiated were published alongside another treaty as the 'Articles of the peace agreed vpon, between the Archduke Mathias, on the Emperours part, and the deputies of the Lord Botzkay, and of other Lords of Hungarie on the other partie'.[23] The reference here to the 'Lords' of Hungary is simply a reflection of the disputed status of the royal crown between the pretender and the Holy Roman Emperor.

The publication of this treaty provides evidence that there was a quarrel surrounding Hungary that involved the duke of Vienna around the turn of the century, not only in the 1620s, and that an awareness of this quarrel had trickled into England enough for someone to find it worthwhile to translate and publish an account of the treaty. The treaty also dovetails with our sense of the duke's increasing power, as it ultimately vested royal power in the duke during the Emperor's expected frequent absences from Hungary.[24] I do not suggest here that Shakespeare or his audience read this particular translation of this particular treaty. Rather, I argue that the translated treaty itself is evidence that there was an appetite for news about the relationship between the duke of Vienna and Hungary in the early 1600s, and that someone interested would have found connections between the two. In addition, this suggests 'Hungary' as a reference would activate the very Ottoman associations with Vienna that Taylor discounts, even without a specific reference to the Ottomans or the Turks by name. This would have worked hand in hand with increasing early modern English interest in the differences and connections between the Ottoman world and the Christian Mediterranean to make this reference if not topical at least of interest to the earlier audience for *Measure for Measure*.[25]

Whether or not we identify the Hungarian situation described in *Measure for Measure* with the quarrel preceding this particular treaty, it is also worth remembering that Lucio's mention of Hungary, for all that Taylor emphasizes its significance, is merely a rumour in the world of the play. It is as potentially false as all the other rumours about the Duke's disappearance. Therefore, there does not need to be any special topical resonance in the relationship between the duke and the king of Hungary, except the general knowledge that Hungary and Vienna were intimately connected politically, unless we also imagine that there must be pressing topical concerns motivating all the other rumours circulating in the play about the Duke's absence. Instead, I argue that all of these references serve to create the sense in the play that the Duke is frequently absent on this sort of business, but that the specific cause of this particular absence is unknown to the people and thus the subject of heated speculation. Lucio seems to be a frequent source of such rumours, as he later passes on the Russian and Roman explanations for the Duke's absence, in addition to this Hungarian one.

The reference to Hungary also points us to another foreign relationship of Vienna's in the period, one with further implications for the play: Bohemia. In addition to potentially helping explain the reference to Hungary in *Measure for Measure*, Sandys's reference to the duke's expanding power included a mention of Bohemia also falling under Viennese sway in the period. This in turn suggests we should take a close look at the condemned and stubborn Barnardine, 'a Bohemian born' (4.2.128), and reminds us that such a Bohemian would have had ample reason to live in Vienna even before the 1618 events in Bohemia that triggered the Thirty Years War (which Taylor takes as a key element in assigning the Viennese setting to Middleton's revisions in the 1620s).

In the Viennese context that I have identified here, Barnardine is an interesting case. If we read *Measure for Measure* as a story about the Duke's increasing power, his pardon of Barnardine is yet another power play. After all, as we have seen in *Merchant of Venice*, the power of pardon was a uniquely royal one. In addition, Barnardine is repeatedly established as someone who does not want to leave the prison, even as a pardoned man. His friends 'wrought reprieves for him' (4.2.133) but not a pardon, even though it was 'ever [the Duke's] manner' to either execute or release prisoners, not keep them lingering on (4.2.132). This suggests either that the murder he committed nine years before (4.2.60, 129) was so heinous that it could not be pardoned – unlikely given that he *is* pardoned at the end of the play – or that his friends did not request a full pardon. At the same time, the Provost believes he would be unwilling to depart the prison of his own accord: 'give him leave to escape hence, he would not' (4.2.145–6). He likewise refuses to leave through the judicially sanctioned method of death (though this is hardly surprising) (4.3.53–4, 57–8). His final line establishes his desire to simply be left alone in his cell: 'If you have anything to say to me, come to my ward, for thence will not I today' (4.3.60–1). Pardoning Barnardine, then, is just the sort of move that we should expect from the Duke. The move deprives Barnadine of the power to choose his own fate even as it flaunts the Duke's apparent mercy. By doing so, it turns Barnardine from 'a figure demonstrating the limits of the Duke's power' by refusing to die, as Jacques Lezra has argued he is,[26] into one demonstrating instead the *expansion* of the Duke's power via the exercise of mercy, just as we saw in *Merchant*. Paradoxically, releasing Barnardine from prison deprives him of a kind of liberty, for he 'hath evermore had the liberty of the prison' (4.2.145–6), whereas his new status in Vienna is unclear and his actions will be monitored.

Barnardine's pardon thus mirrors the larger Viennese losses of liberty throughout the play as a result of the Duke's stratagems, in that it is superficially beneficial while subtly reducing the freedom of anyone who is not the Duke. Moreover, the Bohemian Barnardine is the most likely candidate within the play for a Protestant, given the long-standing prevalence of such doctrines in that region,[27] as well as his unwillingness to let a Catholic shrive him, and he is remanded to the custody of a Catholic friar. This is not to say that Barnardine, who grew up in Vienna (4.2.128–9) and seems uninterested in any religious questions, is necessarily actively Protestant (even if he is certainly a protestant with a lower-case p against his own execution). But if we do take him as at least potentially Protestant, placing him under explicitly Catholic care would reflect yet another loss of liberty, this time of the religious freedom that Vienna was believed to have been losing alongside its political liberties.

Barnardine's desire to stay in prison is reflected, in a way, in the Goodman production's version of the character, a man who does not know how to function in society and ends up as a recidivist criminal, and who kills Isabella on the street in a brief inserted scene after the end of the play. While this treatment shows an awareness of Barnardine's prison-centric mentality, it also demonstrates the difficulties inherent in re-setting the play away from its Renaissance Viennese locale.

The addition of this moment makes the play speak directly to the pressing issue of convict recidivism in 1970s New York and 2010s Chicago.[28] But conversely, its absence from the original play should make us question how it relates to Renaissance sensibilities. While his anonymous murder nine years ago landed Barnardine in prison, there is no indication in the play that he is casually brutal, or that he is likely to re-offend, let alone in such a spectacular way. In addition, even if Barnardine wants to be in prison, we should remember that he also wants to have no one bother him. As such, another murder is perhaps the worst way to achieve his goals. The Duke is unlikely to leave the murderer of his fiancé (or even the woman who turned him down) untouched. And in a larger sense, given the play's themes centring on the Duke's exercise of power, re-offending would be unlikely to result in the same fate as before: the Duke's only remaining way to demonstrate increased control over the situation would be to actually execute Barnardine.

In other words, for Barnardine to choose this particular crime to commit would require us to go beyond his internal motivation as expressed elsewhere in the play to external theories of inherent violent recidivism. Many believe such factors to have been at work in 1970s America, but there is no indication they are so in the play's Vienna. As N. W. Bawcutt has noted, the play itself 'does not present a Viennese society riddled with evil' but merely with venal sins,[29] a society in which Barnardine's nine-year-old murder was the only serious crime mentioned before Angelo's attempted rape. We can thus see how the final scene of the Goodman *Measure for Measure*, while possibly an excellent match for the 1970s New York in which it was set, demonstrates the difference in political and social assumptions between that setting and the original Vienna of the play. In Vienna, unlike New York or Chicago, the Duke already has much greater control over issues like violent crime. By allowing the re-setting to overpower the original, this moment, the final moment the audience sees, warps the motivations that the characters demonstrate in the text to new ends.

This is not to say that an early modern Viennese setting inherently has no place for recidivism, or for murder, but rather to propose that when considering the setting – or the re-setting – of *Measure for Measure* we should attempt to ensure that our readings correspond with the world that the play itself creates: that even if a given production's 'Vienna' is not explicitly Renaissance Vienna, it should remain the play's Vienna, because the play's Vienna is the one in which all the actions and words make sense together. And this play's Vienna bears the characteristic political markings of Renaissance Vienna, as it was understood in Shakespeare's England. We should embrace this setting for what it gives to the play, not automatically abandoning it for London, Ferrara, New York or wherever. By leaning into the Viennese setting of *Measure for Measure*, we can better hear what the play itself is saying. In the case of Barnardine, this means not recasting him at the very last moment of the play as a violent recidivist but rather acknowledging simultaneously both that Barnardine prefers prison, and that he is still made subject to the Duke's power at the end via the latter's clemency and his placing of a potentially Protestant Barnardine under the surveillance of a Catholic man of the cloth.

This latter point leads us to a critical question for *Measure for Measure*: what does the play have to say about religion, when read in the context of setting? It is clear that the Vienna of *Measure for Measure* is internally Catholic. Isabella intends to become a nun, the Duke pretends to be a friar and Shakespeare garnishes each of these facts with additional detail: the religious order Isabella intends to join, the friars the Duke interacts with, the frequent mentions of confession and so on. At the same time, the Turkish threat to Christendom as a whole appears utterly absent from the play: none of the Duke's rumoured reasons for leaving the city are explicitly related to the Ottomans attacking the city itself, even if the reference to Hungary might have activated knowledge of the Ottoman threat there. Roderick Lyall has suggested that this might mean that we should see Vienna as a bastion of the counter-Reformation, with Angelo cast less as a Puritan with capital P than a lower-case puritanical Catholic moralist. This leads him to see in the final scene a Duke hewing a middle road between this 'rigorism' and the 'permissiveness' at work at the beginning of the play.[30] While this element is no doubt present in the play, I suggest that Lyall's reading gives too short shrift to the astonishing irregularity (in a Catholic context) of the Duke's not only disguising himself as a friar, but actively engaging in ecclesiastical behaviour, including taking confession. The play insists upon this as a critical element of its resolution, with the Duke deliberately orchestrating his own unmasking as the friar at the centre of the action (5.1.251–353). Yet no one seems unsettled by this revelation, except for Lucio, whose accusations against the friar to the Duke are undone by it (5.1.358). How is it that this deeply Catholic city accepts its duke impinging on holy matters?

In the context of English knowledge of Vienna that I have outlined above, I argue, this revelation would not be horrifying precisely because it would confirm what the English thought the Viennese already knew: that their dukes had increasing power over not only secular but also specifically religious aspects of their lives. They may be surprised that this power has taken the particular form it has but the mere fact of the intertwining of these two powers is not itself a problem for them. In a sense, the identification of the Duke with the friar resolves what might otherwise have been a dangerous tension in their state, one that Lucio tried to invoke in his own defence by accusing the friar of meddling in political affairs. If the Duke and friar are separate, the power of each is a threat to the other and thus to the social order. If the Duke *is* the friar, then the religious and secular powers are aligned, as they ought to be. The unmasking may still be a strange moment, but it is one that confirms, rather than challenging, the early modern English perspective on those powers' roles in Vienna. We can see this perspective reflected in an angry anti-Catholic poem of the period that describes the Duke of Austria as someone of whom "'tis hard to say, / Whether he be a Priest of holy quire, / Or souldier fierce in fight, his foes to fray',[31] that is, as someone equally involved in religious and secular disputes and poised to dominate both.

This perspective in turn implies that the Duke's position at the end of the play is not merely a compromise between earlier Catholic permissiveness and counter-Reformation rigour as Lyall suggests. Instead, it is a distinctively Viennese assertion that the Duke has authority over both secular and religious realms no matter what decision he makes in either realm, whether permissive, rigorous or somewhere in between. In this sense, I agree with Andrew Majeske's assertion that the key to the play's end lies in the Duke's assertion of raw power, though I would soften his claim that this represents an effort to 'refound the state'.[32] Rather, I argue that the Duke increases his power within the pre-existing conditions of the state identified above, including the union between religious and secular power. Vienna is still Vienna at the end of the play, but it is a Vienna in which the Duke's authority is no longer subject to question in any way: exactly what we would expect to see in a Vienna reflecting the early modern English perspectives on the duke's increasing power in the city.

This particular Vienna, in turn, would have spoken to Shakespeare's own contemporary London not because it secretly represented that London, but precisely because it represented Vienna. Perhaps it would, after all, have stoked fears of James I's surveillance and influence, by reminding its audience that Vienna had so recently lost its liberties. Certainly the union of religious and secular power in *Measure for Measure* might seem relevant to the English church, as well as to James's struggle to achieve control over the Scottish church. But it is also worth remembering while it is often identified as a problem comedy, *Measure for Measure* ends apparently happily, so perhaps the topical resonance would have been more positive, suggesting that James, like the Duke, had the power to renew and re-energize the city and the state. Whatever the ultimate implication, I suggest that *Measure for Measure* is sufficiently Viennese in itself that the parallel would be inexact, and reflect the individual's viewpoint on the political situations of both Vienna and London: perhaps it would have instead reminded some that London still had liberties that Vienna lacked, or caused them to celebrate their luck in living in a Protestant city where the dangers of a betrayed confessional were removed. This topical application of the play would have come *through* an audience's understanding of its Viennese setting, and not despite it.

More generally, in terms of topicality, I do not mean my emphasis on the importance of each play's setting to suggest that the plays only speak to their setting, and not at all to the time and place where they were and are created, produced and performed. Rather, I suggest that those topical and performative meanings exist within and through each play's engagement with its setting. Many non-Shakespearean early modern (and other) plays are, after all, set in the time and place during which and where they were written. Since it was clearly possible for early modern English dramatists to set their plays in early modern England, we should assume that plays not set in early modern England, like Shakespeare's, were set elsewhere for a reason. If they speak to the concerns of early modern England, then, they do so across the self-imposed divide between their setting and their time and place of composition. Unquestionably, they do speak across this divide. But, as we see here and as we saw with the issue of the succession in *King John*, or of equity in *Merchant of Venice*, what they have to say is still affected by how they say it which is in turn affected by the setting.

Ultimately, this approach to topicality asks us to consider how topical meaning can be expressed through the use of setting by exploring what the play has to tell us *within* the setting it has. Shakespeare's political imagination seems to have been inspired by the individual circumstances in which his plays take place. If we seek topical meaning in the work, we should expect to see it expressed through the use of the setting on its own terms rather than by ignoring the setting in favour of direct early modern English parallels. And this is precisely what we do see in Shakespeare: topical implications encoded within the actions of individual characters in their own individual circumstances, faithfully presented. In this case, if *King John* was an example of the dangers of contemplating the succession as it was figured in the medieval rather than early modern period, *Measure for Measure* stands as a depiction of royal consolidation of power over church and state, but explicitly *not* under the same conditions as in the English context.

Turning back now to the question of performance, while I suggest that the Goodman production of *Measure for Measure* let its performance setting go too far beyond the text (both in Barnardine's recidivism and potentially in other circumstances, like Angelo's use of illegal drugs in the middle of the play) let me also stress that theatre is, indeed, a living art form; that every production of a play is unique; and that each of those productions has to engage its contemporary audience. However, all too often the first step in such engagement is an automatic assumption that the setting ought to be changed, whether to a generic world or to some specific setting that is considered either more relatable for a modern audience or simply more apt for the director's vision, like the Goodman's 1970s New York. As a result, the setting is treated not as an element in the play's original meaning on its own terms, but as a movable set of signs available for dramatic repurposing as if they did not affect the play as a whole. In short, it is widely recognized that a new setting can add to a production, as in the case of the Goodman *Measure for Measure*, but rarely acknowledged that removing the old setting subtracts something as well. Re-setting is thus often treated as an unambiguous good rather than a thoughtful balancing act.

I suggest that we should cultivate the latter approach by emphasizing, as I have throughout this book, that the original setting matters. Every production will make its own choices for its own purposes, but we should treat re-setting more like how issues like cutting the text, combining parts or changing the gender of the characters are already treated: as steps that may be worth doing in the service of a production's own goals but that benefit from consideration of how they might change the overall message of the play. If re-setting a play means 'sounding Shakespeare for shared sensibilities and parallel traumas', we ought to make sure that that sounding includes the question of whether those shared parallels still ring true in the new setting.[33] This sort of attention to setting would allow actors, directors and dramaturgs to consider how to either compensate for or embrace the changes in meaning their new setting might introduce, without assuming that a change in setting is a meaning-neutral way to differentiate their production from others. This would serve as an additional tool for contemporary productions to use for their own artistic purposes, just as the original settings served as a tool for Shakespeare's own dramatic method.

What might this look like in practice? It might consist in some cases of retaining the original settings and investing work into portraying them to modern audiences in a way that stays closer to the original. But it also implies that there is value in *strategic* re-setting. In cases like the Goodman's *Measure for Measure*, more care could be taken to smooth out the rough seams where the original and production setting meet: having Barnardine violate parole, for instance, without killing Isabella. Similarly, a production of *Julius Caesar*, for instance, might look carefully at whether their chosen re-setting has a factional resonance for modern audiences that makes use of the one the original setting had for Shakespeare's contemporaries. This might mean a setting in Civil War America, for instance, or post-Saddam Iraq, rather than somewhere like Nazi Germany or generic nineteenth-century Europe. We could imagine similar efforts in regard to the other plays I have considered here: King John's England as an investment firm before the Great Recession whose CEO ignores his analysts' advice, or a nation during the recent pandemic whose leader does the same to his scientists' guidance; a post-Soviet Malcolm establishing a new order in a 'Scotland' that looks like the Baltic states; a *Coriolanus* set in the upheavals of revolutionary America and its new democratic systems; a Venice transformed into the committee-dominated EU; the Archduke of Vienna as a Wyatt Earp-style vigilante but absentee sheriff in the American West. Different cultures would, of course, have different approaches to re-setting the play; my examples are naturally best tuned to my own American context. In each case, the new setting would bear some, if not all, of the assumed relevance of the original setting, opening up the play for a new audience to see in the light of their own assumptions. By leaning into the value of the setting rather than abandoning it, a production could make the play more legible for their audience without sacrificing the creative flexibility of re-setting. Even more fantastic settings – post-apocalyptic *Macbeth*, the *Merchant of Venus* – would benefit from considering how the imagined setting interacts with the original. What elements of the original setting's meaning can be reconstituted for the audience in the new setting, and how would the changes affect the play?

Whatever approach might be adopted, it is important remember that Shakespeare's settings are not irrelevant to the plays which take place in them but can be central to their meaning. The choice to radically re-set the plays may not be as immediately arresting as other extreme choices, like the Wooster Group's 2007 *Hamlet* at the Public Theater that had actors mimic the filmed 1964 Gielgud-Burton *Hamlet* down to the movement of the camera,[34] but it may result in a final product equally distinct from the original text. Both re-setting and the less common sort of radical treatment can be justified artistically, but each deserves the careful consideration that is now usually lavished only on the latter.

However we interact with Shakespeare's plays, my central point remains a belief that Shakespeare's settings matter. Whether seeking topical meaning in Shakespeare's England or presenting the plays for modern audiences, we are best served by those approaches that acknowledge the settings and make use of them. The setting of each play constitutes the world in which the events of the play occur. Once we understand Shakespeare's own historicist approach to that setting, as filtered through his political imagination, we invariably find that such an understanding alters our readings of moments in the play that initially seemed only tangentially related to the question of setting itself, such as the quarrel between Cassius and Brutus, the nobles' insistence on Arthur's liberty or Othello's inadequate questioning of Iago. Likewise, while a given setting may be directly referenced only a few times, each setting plays a vital role in Shakespeare's construction of the play's world. If we dismiss the setting by moving too quickly to other concerns, whether those of Shakespearean England itself or those of our own time and place, we do a disservice to both the plays themselves as plays and to ourselves as readers and performers. By understanding the perspectives on each setting circulating in early modern England, we can see how the settings are fundamental to the meaning of the plays, and therefore why they should be taken seriously.

NOTES

Chapter 1

1. Peter Burke has observed that the 'ordinary educated man of about 1600' was increasingly 'aware of many ways in which the past was unlike the present'. Peter Burke, *The Renaissance Sense of the Past* (London: Edward Arnold, 1969), 48. I suggest that if this was true about the past, it was even more so about the contemporary world outside of Britain, as the British nation(s) became increasingly involved in continental European and even global politics and trade in the early modern period.
2. I take this to include *Macbeth* (Scotland), *Cymbeline* (Wales, and Britain more generally) and *King Lear* (where the boundaries between countries are less clear), all of which are typically dated to after 1603.
3. Peter Lake, *How Shakespeare Put Politics on the Stage: Power and Succession in the History Plays* (New Haven: Yale University Press, 2016), 12.
4. Jonathan Dollimore, 'Transgression and Surveillance in *Measure for Measure*', in *Political Shakespeare: Essays in Cultural Materialism*, 2nd edition, edited by Jonathan Dollimore and Alan Sinfield (Ithaca: Cornell University Press, 1994), 85.
5. John E. Alvis, 'Introductory: Shakespearean Poetry and Politics', in *Shakespeare as Political Thinker*, edited by John E. Alvis and Thomas G. West (Wilmington: ISI Books, 2000), 3.
6. Blair Worden, 'Shakespeare and Politics', in *Shakespeare and Politics*, edited by Catherine M.S. Alexander (Cambridge: Cambridge University Press, 2004), 30.
7. Patrick Gray, *Shakespeare and the Fall of the Roman Republic: Selfhood, Stoicism and Civil War* (Edinburgh: Edinburgh University Press, 2019), 19.
8. Robert Miola, *Shakespeare's Rome* (Cambridge: Cambridge University Press, 1983), 165.
9. András Kiséry, *Hamlet's Moment: Drama and Political Knowledge in Early Modern England* (Oxford: Oxford University Press, 2016), 103, 126.

10 Lorna Hutson, *Circumstantial Shakespeare* (Oxford: Oxford University Press, 2015), 1–5.
11 Dennis Austin Britton and Melissa Walter, 'Rethinking Shakespeare Source Study', in *Rethinking Shakespeare Source Study: Audiences, Authors, and Digital Technologies*, edited by Dennis Austin Britton and Melissa Walter (London: Routledge, 2018), 5–10.
12 Elizabeth E. Tavares, 'Acts of Imagination: Curating the Early Elizabethan Repertories, 1582–1594' (Ph.D. Dissertation, University of Illinois at Urbana-Champaign, 2016), 39.
13 Ibid., 72.
14 Mark Hutchings, *Turks, Repertories, and the Early Modern English Stage* (London: Palgrave Macmillan, 2017), 6.
15 Cyndia Susan Clegg, *Shakespeare's Reading Audiences: Early Modern Books and Audience Interpretation* (Cambridge: Cambridge University Press, 2017), 8, 10.
16 Lucy Munro, 'Writing a Play with Robert Daborne', in *Rethinking Theatrical Documents in Shakespeare's England*, edited by Tiffany Stern (London: Arden Shakespeare, 2020), 19.
17 Sarah Wall-Randell, 'What Is a Staged Book? Books as "Actors" in the Early Modern English Theatre', in *Rethinking Theatrical Documents in Shakespeare's England*, edited by Tiffany Stern (London: Arden Shakespeare, 2020), 132.
18 See Lake, *How Shakespeare Put Politics on the Stage*, 38–49; Anna R. Beer, *Sir Walter Ralegh and His Readers in the Seventeenth Century: Speaking to the People* (New York: St. Martin's Press, 1997), 36–7; Thomas Fulton, 'The Politics of Renaissance Historicism: Valla, Erasmus, Colet, and More', in *Rethinking Historicism from Shakespeare to Milton*, edited by Ann Baynes Coiro and Thomas Fulton (Cambridge: Cambridge University Press, 2012), 106.
19 See Lukas Erne, *Shakespeare as Literary Dramatist*, 2nd edition (Cambridge: Cambridge University Press, 2013), 50–1; Alvis, 'Introductory', 2–3; Jeremy Lopez, 'Imagining Shakespeare's Audience', in *The Oxford Handbook of Shakespearean Comedy*, edited by Heather Hirschfield (Oxford: Oxford University Press, 2018), 425.
20 These tendencies have been known for quite some time; E.A.J. Honigmann compiled a number of these references back in the 1980s, though he groups them under 'plotting' rather than 'setting'. E.A.J. Honigmann, *Shakespeare's Impact on His Contemporaries* (London: Macmillan Press, 1982), 93–5. For a more recent study of early modern marginalia surrounding Shakespeare, which also notes the focus on political concerns, see Jean-Christophe Mayer, *Shakespeare's Early Readers: A Cultural History from 1590 to 1800* (Cambridge: Cambridge University Press, 2018), 178–80.

21 Annabel Patterson, 'Political Thought and the Theater, 1580–1630', in *A Companion to Renaissance Drama*, edited by Arthur F. Kinney (Oxford: Blackwell, 2002), 28–9, 37.
22 Douglas Bruster, *Drama and the Market in the Age of Shakespeare* (Cambridge: Cambridge University Press, 1992), 10.
23 Matthew Steggle, 'Title- and Scene-Boards: The Largest, Shortest Documents', in *Rethinking Theatrical Documents in Shakespeare's England*, edited by Tiffany Stern (London: Arden Shakespeare, 2020), 123.
24 Sir Philip Sidney, *The Defence of Poesie* (London: William Ponsonby, 1595), H4r.
25 David McInnis, *Mind-Travelling and Voyage Drama in Early Modern England* (New York: Palgrave Macmillan, 2013), 38–50.
26 See Duncan Salkeld, *Shakespeare & London* (Oxford: Oxford University Press, 2018), 90; Lawrence Manley and Sally-Beth MacLean, *Lord Strange's Men and Their Plays* (New Haven: Yale University Press, 2014), 216–17 for examples of the threat of censorship in the period in practice.
27 In particular, Shakespeare avoids entirely the contemporary city comedy genre that so many of his contemporaries contributed to. Christopher Marlowe appears, like Shakespeare, to have written only plays set in other times and places, but his early death meant he only wrote six plays that we know of, more than thirty fewer than Shakespeare.

Chapter 2

1 John Fortescue, *A learned commendation of the politique lawes of Englande*, translated by Robert Mulcaster (London: Richard Tottill, 1567), 83v.
2 See Alan Cromartie, *The Constitutionalist Revolution* (Cambridge: Cambridge University Press, 2009), 23–30 for a more in-depth discussion of Fortescue, consent and counsel. See Mark Kishlansky, *A Monarchy Transformed: Britain 1603–1714* (London: The Penguin Press, 1996), 36–7 on the distinctions made between the 'mixed monarchy' of England and continental tyranny.
3 Cromartie, *The Constitutionalist Revolution*, 30 (emphasis in the original). See also Bradin Cormack, *A Power to Do Justice: Jurisdiction, English Literature, and the Rise of the Common Law, 1509–1625* (Chicago: University of Chicago Press, 2007), 349n89 on Fortescue's insistence that 'the king must first consult the representative assembly'.

4 Cromartie, *The Constitutionalist Revolution*, 104.
5 See Stephen A. Chavura, *Tudor Protestant Political Thought 1547–1603* (Leiden: Brill, 2003), 4; Norman Jones, 'Parliament and the Political Society of Elizabethan England', in *Tudor Political Culture*, edited by Dale Hoak (Cambridge: Cambridge University Press, 1995), 227.
6 The 1534 edition lists no author or publisher on the title page, but only 'The boke of Magna Carta with diuers other statutes, whose names appere in the nexte lefe folowynge, translated into Englyshe'. The first page of statutes then lists Magna Carta as 'The great Chartour made in the.ix. yere of kyng Henry the thyrd' (1). This was a longstanding tradition, dating back as late as the 1280s. Paul Brand, 'The First Century of Magna Carta: The Diffusion of Texts and Knowledge of the Charter', *William and Mary Bill of Rights Journal* 25 (2016): 449.
7 On Lambarde's primacy, see Faith Thompson, *Magna Carta: Its Role in the Making of the English Constitution, 1300–1629* (Minneapolis: University of Minnesota Press, 1948), 187. For more on Lambarde's influence, see Ralph Turner, *Magna Carta* (London: Routledge, 2003), 141 and Rebecca J. Brackmann, '"That auntient authoritie": Old English Laws in the Writings of William Lambarde', in *Renaissance Retrospections*, edited by Sarah A. Kelen (Kalamazoo: Medieval Institute Publications, 2013), 111–26. For more on the history of Magna Carta as the first statute, see Thomas Barnes, *Shaping of the Common Law: From Glanvill to Hale, 1188–1688* (Stanford: Stanford University Press, 2008), 24–5.
8 See William Rastall, *A Collection in English, of the Statutes Now in Force* (London: Society of Stationers, 1621), A3r; Fernandino Pulton, *An Abstract of All the Penall Statutes Which Be Generall, in Force and Law* (London: Christopher Barker, 1592), A3v.
9 I have consulted several versions of this exchange, both in manuscript form (in British Library Add MS 48102A and University of Chicago MS 220) and in the edition eventually printed in 1658 as *Of the Severall Opinions of Sundry Learned Antiquaries* (London: William Leake, 1658). This particular version of the quotation is drawn from British Library Add MS 48102A, 4v. The translation provided is mine. Sir John Doddridge, a jurist, and Francis Tate, a lawyer and MP, are the two authors within the manuscript who quote Tacitus, referencing *Germania* 7 and 11. Cornelius Tacitus, *Agricola, Germania, Dialogus*, Loeb Classical Library 35, edited and translated by William Peterson (Cambridge: Harvard University Press, 1970), 140, 146.
10 'Antiquitie of Parliaments', University of Chicago MS 220, 8.
11 Ibid., 8, 51.

12 For a good summary of the relationship between chroniclers, sixteenth-century legal commentators and Magna Carta, see Thompson, *Magna Carta*, 182, 187.
13 John Cowell, *The Interpreter* (Cambridge: Iohn Legate, 1607), R1v.
14 Turner, *Magna Carta*, 147.
15 Robert Snagg, *The Antiquity & Original of the Court of Chancery and Authority of the Lord Chancellor of England* (London: Henry Seile, 1654).
16 Ibid., 8.
17 Ibid., 6.
18 In the published version, Snagg's preface is pages 1–28, and the reading itself pages 29–88.
19 It is of course impossible to know how much, or how much of, Snagg's epistle would have circulated after it was first written, but certainly it was not delivered publicly as part of the education of young lawyers, as the reading was.
20 Andrew Zurcher, *Shakespeare and the Law* (London: Methuen, 2010), 191.
21 Patrick Collinson, *Elizabethan Essays* (London: The Hambledon Press, 1994), 43. For more on how early modern audiences might have seen a connection between the government of their own historical period and the earlier times portrayed in Shakespeare's plays, see Peter Herman, 'Equity and the Problem of Theseus in *A Midsummer Night's Dream*: Or, the Ancient Constitution in Ancient Athens', *Journal for Early Modern Cultural Studies* 14, no. 1 (2014): 8–9.
22 Collinson, *Elizabethan Essays*, 20.
23 Sir Thomas Smith, *De Republica Anglorum*, edited by Mary Dewar (1583; repr. Cambridge: Cambridge University Press, 1982), 76.
24 Jones, 'Parliament', 242, 230.
25 John Guy, 'The Rhetoric of Counsel in Early Modern England', in *Tudor Political Culture*, edited by Dale Hoak (Cambridge: Cambridge University Press, 1995), 294, 303.
26 Ibid., 298, with particular emphasis on the idea of the nobility as the monarch's 'natural counselors'.
27 Jones, 'Parliament', 236.
28 Steven Alford, *The Early Elizabethan Polity: William Cecil and the British Succession Crisis, 1558–1569* (Cambridge: Cambridge University Press, 1998), 7; Dale Hoak, 'Sir William Cecil, Sir Thomas Smith, and the Monarchical Republic of Tudor England', in *The Monarchical Republic of Early Modern England: Essays in Response to Patrick Collinson*, edited by John F. McDiarmid (Aldershot: Ashgate, 2007), 38–9; John F. McDiarmid, 'Common

Consent, *Latinitas*, and the "Monarchical Republic" in Mid-Tudor Humanism', in *The Monarchical Republic of Early Modern England: Essays in Response to Patrick Collinson*, edited by John F. McDiarmid (Aldershot: Ashgate, 2007), 66.
29 Alford, *Early Elizabethan*, 33, quoting Sir Francis Knollys.
30 Ibid., 75.
31 Steven Alford, *Kingship and Politics in the Reign of Edward VI* (Cambridge: Cambridge University Press, 2002), 64.
32 Alford, *Early Elizabethan*, 75, 69–70; Steven Alford, 'The Political Creed of William Cecil', in *The Monarchical Republic of Early Modern England: Essays in Response to Patrick Collinson*, edited by John F. McDiarmid (Aldershot: Ashgate, 2007), 86.
33 Variations on this question are a critical commonplace, both in literary studies (see for example Richard Wilson, 'A Scribbled Form: Shakespeare's Missing Magna Carta', *Shakespeare Quarterly* 67, no. 3 (2016): 344–70, Kenan Yerli, 'Understanding Shakespeare's King John and Magna Carta in the Light of New Historicism', *Bilgi* 20, no. 1 (2018): 241–59 and Neil Heims, *Bloom's How to Write about Shakespeare's Histories* (New York: Bloom's Literary Criticism, 2010), 82) and even in legal circles (see Barnes, *Shaping the Common Law*, 26–7).
34 See Richard J. Ross, 'The Commoning of the Common Law: The Renaissance Debate over Printing English Law, 1520–1640', *University of Pennsylvania Law Review* 146, no. 2 (1998), 410–14 for a discussion of growing legal literacy in sixteenth-century England.
35 For these criticisms, see among others Ian Ward, 'Issues of Kingship and Governance in *Richard II*, *Richard III*, and *King John*', *Shakespeare Yearbook* 8 (1997), 411; Harold Goddard, *The Meaning of Shakespeare* (Chicago: University of Chicago Press, 1951), 141; for particular examples of the critical tendency to put the Bastard in John's place at the centre of the play, see Ward, 424n36 and Julia C. Van De Water, 'The Bastard in *King John*', *Shakespeare Quarterly* 11, no. 2 (1960): 137–46.
36 See Phyllis Rackin, *Stages of History: Shakespeare's English Chronicles* (Ithaca: Cornell University Press, 1990), 183; Carole Levin, *Propaganda in the English Reformation: Heroic and Villainous Images of King John* (Lewiston, NY: The Edwin Mellen Press, 1988); and Lane Sobehrad, 'King John in History' (M.A. Thesis, Southern Methodist University, 2010).
37 I shall hereafter refer to *The Troublesome Raigne of King John* as '*The Troublesome Raigne*', and continue to reserve '*King John*' for Shakespeare's play. There is some disagreement about which play came first, although I believe the evidence is strongest for an

earlier date for *The Troublesome Raigne*. For a short bibliographic discussion of the issue of dating, see Geoffrey Bullough, *Narrative and Dramatic Sources of Shakespeare*, 8 vols. (New York: Columbia University Press, 1962–75), 4:4–5; for more detail on the significance of the differences between the texts for dating the plays, see Sidney Thomas, '"Enter a Sheriffe": Shakespeare's *King John* And *The Troublesome Raigne*', *Shakespeare Quarterly* 37, no. 1 (1986): 98–100 and Beatrice Groves, 'Memory, Composition, and the Relationship of "King John" to "The Troublesome Raigne of King John,"' *Comparative Drama* 38, no. 2/3 (2004), 280–1.
38 See Bullough, *Narrative and Dramatic Sources*, 4:9–23.
39 Levin, *Propaganda*, 201.
40 Ibid., 201–2.
41 All citations of *King John* come from William Shakespeare, *King John*, edited by Jesse M. Lander and J.J.M. Tobin, Arden 3rd Series (London: Bloomsbury, 2018) unless otherwise noted.
42 For the details of these changes see, among others, Paola Pugliatti, *Shakespeare the Historian* (Basingstoke: Macmillan, 1996), 84–8 and Edward I. Berry, *Patterns of Decay: Shakespeare's Early Histories* (Charlottesville: University Press of Virginia, 1975), 114.
43 Although my focus is not on the physical geography of the play, it is worth noting that by focusing on Angiers, a town in France then under English rule but not so in Shakespeare's time, the play re-emphasizes the historical distance between the setting and the time of composition and performance.
44 See Eugene M. Waith, '*King John* and the Drama of History', *Shakespeare Quarterly* 29, no. 2 (1978), 192 and Roy Battenhouse, '*King John*: Shakespeare's Perspective and Others', *Notre Dame English Journal* 14, no. 3 (1982), 191, among others.
45 See J.E. Neale, *Elizabeth I and Her Parliaments, 1559–1581* (London: Jonathan Cape, 1964), 110, 132–3, 140–50, 157, 174–6, 366–7; J.E. Neale, *Elizabeth I and Her Parliaments, 1584–1601* (London: Jonathan Cape, 1971), 251–66. Interestingly, most of the parliaments before 1584 included Robert Snagg himself as an MP (see Neale, *1559–1581*, 433).
46 For an account of the differences between the two scenes and their relation to the order controversy, see Edward Gieskes, '"He Is but a Bastard to the Time": Status and Service in "The Troublesome Raigne of John" and Shakespeare's "King John"', *ELH* 65, no. 4 (1998), 779–87.
47 All citations from *The Troublesome Raigne* are from 'The Troublesome Raigne of King John', in Bullough, *Narrative and Dramatic Sources*, Vol. 4, and are cited by part (I or II) and line number.
48 See E.W. Ives, 'The Genesis of the Statute of Uses', *The English Historical Review* 82, no. 325 (1967), 673, 695 on the changes to

medieval common law inheritance introduced by the Statute of Uses and modified by the Statute of Wills under Henry VIII.
49 Zurcher, *Shakespeare and the Law*, 192.
50 Ibid.
51 The excellent 2012 production of *King John* by Bard on the Beach in Vancouver, British Columbia choreographed this scene beautifully: John and Philip circled each other in the centre of the stage, clasping forearms, while Pandulph and the rest swirled around them. In such a setting John's silence and Philip's agonized indecision become intensely obvious and very moving.
52 Smith, *De Republica*, 85.
53 For a brief discussion of the significance of this change in terminology, see William Haugaard, *Elizabeth and the English Reformation: The Struggle for a Stable Settlement of Religion* (Cambridge: Cambridge University Press, 1968), 105.
54 Shakespeare, *King John*, 267n.
55 Neale, *1559–1581*, 251.
56 Alford, *Early Elizabethan*, 33, quoting Knollys.
57 See Neale, *1584–1601*, in particular 214, 388, and 437; T.E. Hartley, *Elizabeth's Parliaments: Queen, Lords and Commons 1559–1601* (Manchester: Manchester University Press, 1992), 162.
58 William Shakespeare, *Macbeth*, edited by Sandra Clark and Pamela Mason, Arden 3rd Series (London: Bloomsbury Arden, 2015), 3.1.120–2. All citations to *Macbeth* are from this edition unless otherwise noted.
59 See John of Salisbury, *Policraticus*, edited and translated by Cary J. Nederman (Cambridge: Cambridge University Press, 1990), xviii–xxi.
60 Oxford English Dictionary, 3rd edition, 2000, s.v. 'manner'
61 Smith, *De Republica*, 56.
62 Levin, *Propaganda*, 209; Ward, 'Issues of Kingship', 411; Lukas Lammers, *Shakespearean Temporalities: History on the Early Modern Stage* (New York: Routledge, 2018), 124.
63 Bullough, *Narrative and Dramatic Sources*, 4:19–20; Battenhouse, 'Shakespeare's Perspective', 192.
64 Lammers, *Shakespearean Temporalities*, 125.

Chapter 3

1 See Michael Hawkins, 'History, Politics, and *Macbeth*', in *Focus on 'Macbeth'*, edited by John Russell Brown (London: Routledge & Kegan Paul, 1982), 174; Harry Berger, 'The Early Scenes of *MacBeth*: Preface to a New Interpretation', *ELH* 47, no. 1 (1980): 5; John

Kerrigan, *Archipelagic English: Literature, History, and Politics 1603–1707* (Oxford: Oxford University Press, 2008), 102.
2   As do many productions. See Sandra Clark and Pamela Mason, Introduction to *Macbeth*, by William Shakespeare, edited by Sandra Clark and Pamela Mason, Arden 3rd Series (London: Bloomsbury, 2015), 116–21.
3   William C. Carroll, 'Historicizing Historicism', in *Shakespeare in Our Time: A Shakespeare Association of America Collection*, edited by Dympna Callaghan and Suzanne Gossett (London: Bloomsbury Arden Shakespeare, 2016), 218–19.
4   Hutson, *Circumstantial Shakespeare*, 172.
5   Jonathan Hope and Michael Whitmore, 'The Language of *Macbeth*', in *Macbeth: The State of the Play*, edited by Ann Thompson (London: Bloomsbury, 2014), 198.
6   See Bernice W. Kliman, 'Thanes in the Folio *Macbeth*', *Shakespeare Bulletin* 9, no. 1 (1991): 5–8; Oliver R. Baker, 'Duncan's Thanes and Malcolm's Earls: Name Dropping in *Macbeth*', *Notes and Queries* 56, no. 4 (2009): 591–5; and Oliver R. Baker, 'The Thanes in *Macbeth*: Fealty and Obedience in the *True Lawe of Free Monarchies*', *Shakespeare* 10 (2014), http://dx.doi.org/10.1080/17450918.2014.96 5726 for the justification for grouping these characters together. The named thanedoms also unite the physical geography of the setting with the political system.
7   William Lambarde, *A Perambulation of Kent* (London: Edmund Bollifant, 1596), 500.
8   Richard Hakluyt, *The principal nauigations, voyages, traffiques and discoueries of the English nation made by sea or ouer-land, to the remote and farthest distant quarters of the earth, at any time within the compasse of these 1600. yeres*, Vol. 2 (London: George Bishop, Ralph Newberie, and Robert Barker, 1599), 126; John Selden, *Titles of Honor* (London: William Stansby for John Helme, 1614), 268; Arthur Hopton, *A concordancy of yeares* (London: Company of Stationers, 1612), 160 [190]. Selden's and Hopton's works were published later, but summarize their findings out of several earlier texts, allowing us to see how the term had been used over time.
9   Selden, *Titles of Honor*, 285.
10 Ibid., 285–6. Selden's use of Buchanan here points us to the fact that Scottish ideas about Scotland also circulated into England in this period. On the relationship between Buchanan and *Macbeth*, see David Norbrook, '*Macbeth* and the Politics of Historiography', in *Politics of Discourse: The Literature and History of Seventeenth-Century England*, edited by Kevin Sharpe and Steven N. Zwicker (Berkeley: University of California Press, 1987), 78–116.
11 John Skene, *De Verborum Significatione* (Edinburgh: David Lindsay, 1681), I2v (first published in 1597); Cowell, *The Interpreter*, Ttt2r-v;

George Buck, *Daphnis Polystephanos* (London: G. Eld for Thomas Adams, 1605), A4r.
12 William Camden, 'Scotland', in *Britain*, trans. Philemon Holland (London: George Bishop and John Norton, 1610), 7.
13 Susan Reynolds, 'Afterthoughts on *Fiefs and Vassals*', *Haskins Society Journal* 9 (1997), 1.
14 Susan Reynolds, *Fiefs and Vassals: The Medieval Evidence Reinterpreted* (Oxford: Oxford University Press, 1994), 7.
15 Reynolds' reference for that name is a miscitation of D.B. Smith, 'Sir Thomas Craig, Feudalist', *The Scottish Historical Review* 12, no. 47 (1915): 271–302. Reynolds cites it as 'Sir Thomas Smith, Feudalist'.
16 John Selden, *Iani Anglorum facies altera Memoriâ nempè à primulâ Henrici II. adusq[ue] abitionem quod occurrit prophanum Anglo-Britanniae ius resipiens succincto diegematikos connexum filo* (London: Thomas Snodham, 1610); for Lambarde, see n7, above.
17 Graham Holderness, Nick Potter and John Turner, *Shakespeare: The Play of History* (Houndsmills: Macmillan Press, 1988), 86–7; see also Kenneth Muir, introduction to William Shakespeare, *Macbeth*, edited by Kenneth Muir, Arden 2nd Series (London: Methuen & Co., 1951), xvi–xxvi.
18 Leslie Dodd, 'Historical Introduction', in Thomas Craig of Riccarton, *Jus Feudale Tribus Libris Comprehensum*, translated, edited and annotated by Leslie Dodd (Edinburgh: Stair Society, 2017), xxxi–xxxv.
19 Ibid., xxxiv, xxxv. Dodd also suggests that delay in actual printing may reflect an unusually wide circulation in manuscript, which would explain the lack of urgency in the face of frequent petitions that it should be printed. Ibid., xxxv–xxxvi.
20 Sebastiaan Verweij, *The Literary Culture of Early Modern Scotland: Manuscript Production and Transmission, 1560–1625* (Oxford: Oxford University Press, 2016), 110.
21 British Library Stowe MS 385.
22 Priscilla Bawcutt, 'Crossing the Border: Scottish Poetry and English Readers in the Sixteenth Century', in *The Rose and the Thistle: Essays on the Culture of Late Medieval and Renaissance Scotland*, edited by Sally Mapstone and Juliette Wood (Phantassie: Tuckwell Press, 1998), 68. For more on the nature of the cross-border manuscript exchange, see Verweij, *Literary Culture*, 248–55. For a specific example of manuscript exchange around this time, see Sebastiaan Verweij, '"Booke, Go thy Ways": The Publication, Reading, and Reception of James VI / I's Early Poetic Works', *Huntington Library Quarterly* 77, no. 2 (2014), 111–31.
23 Thomas Craig of Riccarton, *Jus Feudale Tribus Libris Comprehensum*, Book 1, translated, edited and annotated by Leslie Dodd (Edinburgh: Stair Society, 2017), 329. Where possible, I have used this most

recent, if still incomplete, edition of Craig's text. I will cite page numbers parenthetically when citing this translation of Craig, or cite it as 'Craig'.

24 Thomas Craig, *The Jus Feudale*, translated by James Avon Clyde (Edinburgh: William Hodge & Company, 1934), 513. Where necessary, as here, I cite the older translation because Dodd has not yet translated the second and third books of the *Jus Feudale*.

25 John Monipennie, *Certeine Matters Concerning the Realme of Scotland, Composed Together* (London: A. Hatfield for John Blasket[?], 1603), C3; Thomas Milles, *A Catalogue of the Kings of Scotland* (London: William Iaggard, 1610), 4.

26 Raphael Holinshed, *Chronicles of England, Scotland, and Ireland* (1587; The Holinshed Project, 2009), 5:176, http://www.english.ox.ac.uk/Holinshed/texts.php?text1=1587_1263; Peter Heyleyn, *Mikrokosmos A Little Description of the Great World. Augmented and Reuised* (Oxford: John Lichfield and William Turner, 1625), 509.

27 Selden, *Titles of Honor*, 286. It is intriguing to note that Selden found space for all three definitions of thane in a single work.

28 Ibid., 239.

29 Skene, *De verborum*, I2v.

30 *The Actis and Constitutiounis of the Realme of Scotland* (n.p.: Ed. Henrison, 1566), 156r.

31 Kerrigan, *Archipelagic English*, 105; Norbrook, 'Politics of Historiography', 110.

32 Holinshed, *Chronicles*, 5:170; Hector Boece, *Heir beginnis the hystory and croniklis of Scotland* (Edinburgh: Thomas Davidson, 1540), 171. For a more complete discussion of potential sources for the Scottish history in *Macbeth*, see Henry N. Paul, *The Royal Play of Macbeth: When, Why, and How It Was Written by Shakespeare* (New York: Macmillan Company, 1950), 204–25.

33 On the transition between hereditary and non-hereditary titles, see Craig, 105; Jean Bodin, *The six bookes of a common-weale*, trans. Richard Knolles (London: G. Bishop, 1606), 482; Jean de Serres, *A general inuentorie of the history of France from the beginning of that monarchie, vnto the treatie of Veruins, in the year 1598*, trans. Edward Grimeston (London: George Eld, 1607), 104; Cowell, *The Interpreter*, Aa1r-v; Selden, *Titles of Honor*, 202, 229.

34 Maurice Hunt, 'Duncan, Macbeth, and the Thane of Cawdor', *Studies in the Humanities* 28, no. 1–2 (2001), 7.

35 Craig, *The Jus Feudale*, trans. Clyde, 374. Cowell also uses the term 'improper' for these kinds of holdings, see Cowell, *The Interpreter*, Bb1r.

36 See Craig, *The Jus Feudale*, trans. Clyde, 374.

37 Buck, *Daphnis Polystephanos*, A4r.
38 See Holinshed, *Chronicles*, 5:168; Boece, *Hystory*, 171.
39 John Leslie, *De origine, moribus & rebus gestis Scotorum libri decem* (1578; repr., London: Robert Boulter, 1677), 195.
40 Selden, *Titles of Honor*, 267, 285.
41 Craig, *The Jus Feudale*, trans. Clyde, 1039.
42 Ibid., 591.
43 Ibid., 589.
44 *Macbeth*, 5.3.28n.; Oxford English Dictionary, 3rd edition, 2007, s.v. 'purgative' A1, which dates this meaning back to the fourteenth century.
45 Craig, *The Jus Feudale*, trans. Clyde, 653.
46 William Lambarde, *A Perambulation of Kent* (London: Ralph Newbery, 1576), 366.
47 Lambarde, *A perambulation* (1596), 501.
48 Giovanni Botero, *The trauellers breuiat*, trans. I.R. (London: Edmond Bollifant for John Jaggard, 1601), 125.
49 Ibid.
50 Craig, 327; Cowell, *The Interpreter*, Aa4r-v.
51 Botero, *Traveller's Breviat*, 125.
52 Rebecca Lemon, 'Sovereignty and Treason in *Macbeth*', in '*Macbeth*': *New Critical Essays*, edited by Nick Moschovakis (London: Routledge, 2008), 80; Hawkins, 'History', 187.
53 Sharon O'Dair, 'Conduct (Un)becoming or, Playing the Warrior in *Macbeth*', in *Shakespeare and Moral Agency*, edited by Michael D. Bristol (London: Continuum, 2010), 74.
54 Hutson, *Circumstantial Shakespeare*, 1–3.
55 Ibid., 45.
56 Ibid., 112, 118. It is fair to note, however, that Hutson examines 'where' in particular relation to *Two Gentlemen of Verona*, one of Shakespeare's plays with the least clear sense of what political state is intended.
57 Ibid., 152.
58 Ibid., 154.
59 Ibid., 156.
60 Ibid., 172.
61 See Holinshed, *Chronicles*, 5:176; Boece, *Hystory*, 178–9; George Buchanan, *The History of Scotland*, Vol. 1, trans. James Aikman (Glasgow: Blackie Fullarton & Co. and Archibald Fullarton & Co., 1827), 337; John Leslie, *The Historie of Scotland*, trans. James Dalrymple, edited by E.G. Cody (Edinburgh: Scottish Text Society, 1888), 309; William Stewart, *The Buik of the Croniclis of Scotland*, edited by William B. Turnbull (London: Longman, Brown, Green, Longmans, and Roberts, 1858), line 40646.

62 Boece, *Hystory*, D2v.
63 Holinshed, *Chronicles*, 4:22.
64 Buchanan, *History*, 337.
65 See Coppélia Kahn, *Man's Estate: Masculine Identity in Shakespeare* (Berkeley: University of California Press, 1981), 175–93, esp. 178–80; Julie Barmazel, '"The Servant to Defect": Macbeth, Impotence, and the Body Politic', in *'Macbeth': New Critical Essays*, edited by Nick Moschovakis (New York: Routledge, 2008), 118–31.
66 See Richard Strier, *The Unrepentant Renaissance: From Petrarch to Shakespeare to Milton* (Chicago: University of Chicago Press, 2011), 133–8; Janet Adelman, *Suffocating Mothers: Fantasies of Maternal Origin in Shakespeare's Plays, 'Hamlet' to 'The Tempest'* (New York: Routledge, 1992), 131–2.
67 William T. Liston, '"Male and Female He Created Them": Sex and Gender in "Macbeth"', *College Literature* 16 (1989), 238.
68 See Kerrigan, *Archipelagic English*, 110–11.
69 Holinshed, *Chronicles*, 5:175.
70 In fact, Craig, though acknowledging the difficulty in dating Scottish feudalism in detail, traced it back to the time between the reigns of Malcolm II and Malcolm III, which includes the reign of Macbeth (Craig, 163–7).
71 William Camden, *Remaines of a greater worke, concerning Britaine, the inhabitants thereof, their languages, names, surnames, empreses, wise speeches, poësies, and epitaphes* (London: G. E. for Simon Waterson, 1605), 50.
72 Cowell, *The Interpreter*, Aa1r.
73 John Speed, *The Theatre of the Empire of Great Britaine* (London: John Sudbury and Georg Humble, 1612), 4.
74 Holinshed, *Chronicles,* 5:165–7, 178.
75 Margaret Downs-Gamble, '"To th' Crack of Doom": Sovereign Imagination as Anamorphosis in Shakespeare's "Show of Kings"', in *Celtic Shakespeare: The Bard and the Borderers*, edited by Willy Maley and Rory Loughnane (Farnham: Ashgate, 2013), 161n16.
76 Holinshed, *Chronicles*, 5:172.
77 Lammers, *Shakespearean Temporalities*, 178, 179; Hutson, *Circumstantial Shakespeare*, 166.
78 Boece, *Hystory*, 173v; Holinshed, *Chronicles*, 5:171.
79 See Boece, *Hystory*, 173v–174r; Holinshed, *Chronicles*, 5:171–2.
80 Holinshed, *Chronicles*, 5:172.
81 Boece, *Hystory*, 173v.
82 Holinshed, *Chronicles*, 5:171.
83 Ibid.
84 Paul, *Royal Play*, 198.

85 Holinshed, *Chronicles*, 5:150.
86 Ibid., 5:171.
87 Ibid., 5:150.
88 Ryan Davidson, 'The Malleable Macbeth: Understanding the Evolving Image of an Obscure Medieval King' (M.A. Thesis, University of Guelph, 2008), 54.
89 This is Holinshed's spelling; Boece spells it Lugtak, and Buchanan Luthlac.
90 Holinshed, *Chronicles*, 5:176.
91 This is particularly true if we follow the old critical position which suggests that Macbeth himself might be the third murderer who shows up unexpectedly at the death of Banquo (see Theodore Halbert Wilson, 'The Third Murderer', *The English Journal* 18, no. 5 (1929), 419.
92 See Holinshed, *Chronicles*, 5:176; Boece, *Hystory*, 178r.
93 Ibid.; Buchanan, *History*, 337.
94 Holinshed, *Chronicles*, 5:176.

Chapter 4

1 Lucius Cornelius Sulla was often referred to as 'Sylla' or 'Silla' in the early modern period; I will refer to him as Sulla except where quoting.
2 Vivian Thomas, *Shakespeare's Roman Worlds* (London: Routledge, 1989), 2; Geoffrey Bullough, *Narrative and Dramatic Sources of Shakespeare*, 8 vols. (New York: Columbia University Press, 1962–75), 5:4.
3 For the commonalities between these *Lives*, see Christopher Pelling, 'Plutarch's Method of Work in the Roman Lives', *The Journal of Hellenistic Studies* 99 (1979): 75, 83. The references for the various lives within the 1579 Thomas North translation of Plutarch are as follows: *Caius Marius*, 451–79; *Sulla*, 499–525; *Marcus Crassus*, 600–22; *Pompey*, 678–718; *Julius Caesar*, 763–96; *Marcus Tullius Cicero*, 912–37; *Marcus Antonius*, 970–1010; *Marcus Brutus*, 1055–80. Plutarch, *The Lives of the Noble Grecians and Romanes*, trans. Thomas North (London: Thomas Vatroullier and John Wright, 1579). Hereafter cited as 'North', although in the following section I will refer to the various *Lives* by citing North, the page number, and the name of the relevant life in parentheses.
4 See North, 501 (*Marius*), 506, 522 (*Sylla*), 604 (*Crassus*), 685 (*Pompey*), 765 (*Caesar*), 972 (*Antony*), 1056 (*Brutus*).

5   North, 763 (*Caesar*).
6   North, 519 (*Sylla*), 604 (*Crassus*).
7   North, 790, 794 (*Caesar*).
8   North, 917 (*Cicero*).
9   North, 918 (*Cicero*).
10 Livy, *The Romane Historie*, trans. Philemon Holland (London: Adam Islip, 1600), 1248, 1250, 1252, 1257, 1259. Hereafter cited as 'Holland, *Livius*'.
11 Suetonius, *The historie of tvvelve Caesars emperours of Rome*, trans. Philemon Holland (London: H. Lownes and G. Snowdon for Matthew Lownes, 1606). Hereafter this text will be cited as 'Holland, *Suetonius*', G4v, 15.
12 Cornelius Tacitus, *The annales of Cornelius Tacitus. The description of Germanie*, trans. Richard Grenewey (London: Arn. Hatfield for Bonham and Iohn Norton, 1598), 1.
13 Appian, *An auncient historie and exquisite chronicle of the Romanes warres, both ciuile and foren*, trans. W.B. (London: Henrie Bynniman, 1578), 158. In addition, as G.K. Hunter has noted, the translator, 'W.B.', altered the order of the text, focusing the reader's attention on the civil wars and their destructive nature. G.K. Hunter, 'A Roman Thought: Renaissance Attitudes to History Exemplified in Shakespeare and Jonson', in *Shakespeare and History*, edited by Stephen Orgel and Sean Keilen (New York: Garland Publishing, Inc., 1999), 198.
14 Eutropius, *A briefe chronicle*, trans. Nicolas Havvard (London: Thomas Marshe, 1564), 53, 68.
15 Lucan, *Lucans first booke translated line for line*, trans. Christopher Marlowe (London: P. Short and Walter Burre, 1600), 27.
16 *The Consent of Time* and *The First Part of the Dial of Days* in 1590, *The Stratagems of Jerusalem* in 1602, *The Practice of Policy* in 1604, and *The Tragicomedy of Serpents* in 1607.
17 Lodowick Lloyd, *The Practice of Policy* (London: Simon Stafford, 1604), 35.
18 Lodowick Lloyd, *The stratagems of Ierusalem* (London: Thomas Creede, 1602), 263.
19 William Fulbecke, *An historicall collection of the continuall factions, tumults, and massacres of the Romans and Italians during the space of one hundred and twentie yeares next before the peaceable empire of Augustus Caesar* (London: William Ponsonby, 1601).
20 Freyja Cox-Jensen, 'Ancient Histories of Rome in Sixteenth-Century England: A Reconsideration of Their Printing and Circulation', *Huntington Library Quarterly* 83, no. 3 (2020), 422–5.

21 See Richard Rainolde, *A chronicle of all the noble emperours of the Romaines from Iulius Caesar, orderly to this moste victorious Emperour Maximilian, that now gouerneth, with the great warres of Iulius Caesar, [and] Pompeius Magnus* (London: Thomas Marshe, 1571), A1v, ff; Thomas Churchyard, *A generall rehearsall of warres, called Churchyardes choise* (London: Edward White, 1579), D2v; E. L., *Romes monarchie, entituled the globe of renowmed glorie* (London: The Widow Orrin for Matthew Lawe, 1596), G1vff.
22 See Clement Edmondes, *Obseruations vpon the fiue first bookes of Caesars commentaries* (London: Peter Short, 1600), 123; Augustine, *Of the citie of God vvith the learned comments of Io. Lod. Viues*, trans. I.H. (London: George Eld, 1610), 36.
23 See William Cornwallis, *Essayes* (London: Edmund Mattes, 1600), Cc3r–v; Thomas Digges, *Foure paradoxes, or politique discourses* (London: H. Lownes for Clement Knight, 1604), 71; Robert Persons, *A conference about the next succession to the crowne of Ingland diuided into tvvo partes* ([Antwerp?]: R. Doleman, 1595), 20. For more on Persons's view of this period as distressed by faction, see Paulina Kewes, 'Translations of State: Ancient Rome and Late Elizabethan Political Thought', *Huntington Library Quarterly* 83, no. 3 (2020), 480, 484.
24 See W. Averell, *A dyall for dainty darlings, rockt in the cradle of securitie* (London: Thomas Hackette, 1584), B4v; Pierre de la Primaudaye, *The French academie*, trans. T.B. (London: Edmund Bollifant for G. Bishop and Ralph Newbery, 1586), 217, 342, 709; Innocent Gentillet, *A discourse vpon the meanes of vvel governing and maintaining in good peace, a kingdome, or other principalitie*, trans. Simon Patericke (London: Adam Islip, 1602), 154.
25 Churchyard, *Churchyard's Choice*, D2v; Gentillet, *Discourse*, 154.
26 D. Alan Orr, 'Civic Catholicism, Military Humanism, and the Decline of Justice in Thomas Lodge's *The Wovnds of Ciuill War*', *Huntington Library Quarterly* 83, no. 1 (2020), 51.
27 Cox-Jensen, 'Ancient Histories', 436–7.
28 Colin Burrow, *Shakespeare and Classical Antiquity* (Oxford: Oxford University Press, 2013), 216.
29 Ibid., 222.
30 All citations from the play are from William Shakespeare, *Julius Caesar*, edited by David Daniell, Arden 3rd Series (Walton-on-Thames: Thomas Nelson and Sons Ltd, 1998).
31 Jan H. Blits, *Rome and the Spirit of Caesar: Shakespeare's* Julius Caesar (Lanham: Lexington Books, 2015), 32.
32 See among others Stella Achilleos, 'Friendship and Good Counsel: The Discourses of Friendship and Parrhesia in Francis Bacon's *The Essayes*

or *Counsels, Civill and Morall'*, in *Friendship in the Middle Ages and Early Modern Age: Explorations of a Fundamental Ethical Discourse*, edited by Albrecht Classen and Marilyn Sandidge (Berlin: De Gruyter, 2010), 648; Laurie Shannon, *Sovereign Amity: Figures of Friendship in Shakespearean Contexts* (Chicago: University of Chicago Press, 2002), 3; Tom MacFaul, *Male Friendship in Shakespeare and His Contemporaries* (Cambridge: Cambridge University Press, 2007), 1.
33 Andrew Hadfield, *Shakespeare and Republicanism* (Cambridge: Cambridge University Press, 2005), 170.
34 MacFaul, *Male Friendship*, 116. For analysis of why *amicitia* more commonly has a broader meaning, see among others P. A. Brunt, *The Fall of the Roman Republic* (Oxford: Clarendon Press, 1988), 351–81, 443–502; David Konstan, *Friendship in the Classical World* (Cambridge: Cambridge University Press, 1997), 122–48.
35 William Shakespeare, *Titus Andronicus*, edited by Jonathan Bate, Arden 3rd Series (London: Routledge, 1995), 1.1.9, 18, 56, 218. Unlike *Julius Caesar*, however, *Titus Andronicus* also uses 'friend' in its more affective meaning.
36 North, 778, 786, 1059.
37 Ibid., 795. Lepidus similarly appears seemingly out of nowhere in Act Four of *Julius Caesar* as well.
38 Hadfield, *Shakespeare and Republicanism*, 171.
39 Shakespeare, of course, re-uses this idea to devastating effect in *King Lear*.
40 Ernest Schanzer, *The Problem Plays of Shakespeare* (London: Routledge & Kegan Paul, 1963), 29; Michael Platt, *Rome and Romans According to Shakespeare* (Salzburg: Institut Für Englische Sprache Und Literatur, 1976), 197; Thomas, *Shakespeare's Roman Worlds*, 86.
41 North, 791.
42 Ibid.
43 Ibid., 792.
44 Platt, *Rome and Romans*, 203; Hugh Grady, 'Moral Agency and Its Problems in *Julius Caesar*: Political Power, Choice, and History', in *Shakespeare and Moral Agency*, edited by Michael D. Bristol (London: Continuum, 2010), 22; Brower, *Hero & Saint*, 229.
45 Worden, 'Shakespeare and Politics', 30.
46 North, 977–8, 1067.
47 North, 978.
48 Platt, *Rome and Romans*, 187.
49 North, 786.
50 Ibid., 786, 790.
51 Ibid., 1079–80.

52 Tavares, 'Acts of Imagination', 77.
53 Stuart Gillespie, 'The Availability of the Classics: Readers, Writers, Translation, Performance', in *The Oxford History of Classical Reception in English Literature, Volume 2 (1558–1660)*, edited by Patrick Cheney and Philip Hardie (Oxford: Oxford University Press, 2015), 64.

Chapter 5

1 I will hereafter, except in quotations, use 'Caius Martius' to refer to the man and 'Coriolanus' to refer to the story as a whole.
2 North, 240; Holland, *Livius*, 65.
3 North, 246.
4 Holland, *Livius*, 66.
5 North, 248.
6 Holland, *Livius*, 67.
7 Livy, *Ab Urbe Condita*, edited by Robert Seymour Conway and Charles Flamstead Walters (Oxford: Clarendon Press, 1946), II.34.8–9. Translations from this edition's Latin are my own. In order to distinguish versions of Livy more easily in this section, I will cite from Holland's translation in parentheses.
8 Livy, II.35.3.
9 Ibid., II.35.2.
10 Cox-Jensen, 'Ancient Histories', 424–5.
11 Lloyd, *The Consent of Time*, 496, 497; Appian, *Auncient History*, 1; Thomas Lanquet et al., *An Epitome of Chronicles* (London: Thomas Marsh, 1559), 46; William Painter, *The Palace of Pleasure* (London: Henry Denham, 1566), 9v–10v.
12 Digges, *Four Paradoxes*, 104–5; Alexander Sylvain, *The Orator*, trans. Lazarus Pyott (London: Adam Islip, 1596), 34, 35.
13 Nicolas Barnaud, *Le reveille-matin des Francois, et de leurs voisins* (Edinburgh: Iaques Iames, 1574), 124.
14 All quotations from the play come from William Shakespeare, *Coriolanus*, edited by Peter Holland, Arden 3rd Series (London: Bloomsbury, 2013).
15 North, 246; Holland, *Livius*, 67.
16 Manfred Pfister, 'Acting the Roman: *Coriolanus*', in *Identity, Otherness and Empire in Shakespeare's Rome*, edited by Maria del Sapio Garbero (Farnham: Ashgate, 2009), 42.
17 I am indebted for this terminology to Len Scales's work on German identity in the long fourteenth century. I do not suggest here that

Coriolanus draws on medieval German concepts of identity, but rather that the play demonstrates a similarly categorizable set of competing allegiances for Caius Martius to navigate – and that we should not reinvent the wheel when looking for ways to categorize them. Len Scales, *The Shaping of German Identity: Authority and Crisis, 1245–1414* (Cambridge: Cambridge University Press, 2012), 518.
18 Ibid.
19 Ibid., 12.
20 See for example Paul Cantor, *Shakespeare's Rome: Republic and Empire* (Ithaca, NY: Cornell University Press, 1976), 13; Clifford Chalmers Huffman, '*Coriolanus*' in Context (Cranbury, NJ: Associated University Presses, Inc., 1971), 179; Oliver Arnold, *The Third Citizen: Shakespeare's Theater and the Early Modern House of Commons* (Baltimore: Johns Hopkins University Press, 2007), 192–204.
21 See among others Cantor, *Shakespeare's Rome*, 13, 50–1, 80; Jan H. Blits, *Spirit, Soul, and City: Shakespeare's* Coriolanus (Lanham: Lexington Books, 2005), 26.
22 Cantor, *Shakespeare's Rome*, 65, 70, 80.
23 Alexander Leggatt, *Shakespeare's Political Drama: The History Plays and the Roman Plays* (London: Routledge, 1988), 197–8.
24 Ibid., 197.
25 Ibid., 202.
26 Warren Chernaik, *The Myth of Rome in Shakespeare and His Contemporaries* (Cambridge: Cambridge University Press, 2011), 191; Thomas, *Shakespeare's Roman Worlds*, 161, 174; Huffman, '*Coriolanus*' in Context, 188; Blits, *Spirit, Soul, and City*, 104; Cantor, *Shakespeare's Rome*, 90; Thomas P. Anderson, *Shakespeare's Fugitive Politics* (Edinburgh: Edinburgh University Press, 2016), 48.
27 Pfister, 'Acting', 41–2; Jennifer Low, '"Bodied Forth": Spectator, Stage, and Actor in Early Modern Theater', *Comparative Drama* 39, no. 1 (2005): 19.
28 Lisa S. Starks-Estes, 'Virtus, Vulnerability, and the Emblazoned Male Body in Shakespeare's *Coriolanus*', in *Violent Masculinities: Male Aggression in Early Modern Texts and Culture*, edited by Jennifer Feather and Catherine E. Thomas (New York: Palgrave Macmillan, 2013), 91.
29 Ibid., 92.
30 Worden, 'Shakespeare and Politics', 32.
31 Cantor, *Shakespeare's Rome*, 99; Reuben A. Brower, *Hero & Saint: Shakespeare and the Graeco-Roman Heroic Tradition* (New York: Oxford University Press, 1971), 366; for a similar take, see also Miola, *Shakespeare's Rome*, 192.

32 North, 250; Holland, *Livius*, 67.
33 Appianus, *Auncient History*, 1.
34 Scales, *German Identity*, 11.
35 Gray, *Shakespeare and the Fall of the Roman Republic*, 16.
36 Pfister, 'Acting', 35.
37 Hutchings, *Turks*, 6.

Chapter 6

1 For sources, see 'Translation from the First Story of the Fourth Day of Ser Giovanni, *Il Pecorone*', in William Shakespeare, *Merchant of Venice*, edited by John Russell Brown, Arden 2nd Series (London: Arden, 1955, rpt. 2003), 140–53; 'Cinthio and Minor Sources', in William Shakespeare, *Othello*, edited by E.A.J. Honigmann, Arden 3rd Series (London: Arden, 1997, rpt. 2004), 368–87; Bullough, *Narrative and Dramatic Sources*, 1:445–514, esp. 446–54 and 7:193–268, esp. 200.
2 Although it is now standard to use the Italian 'doge' for this office and its holder, I will use 'duke' throughout as this was the favoured term in early modern England, and 'Duke' for the Shakespearean characters.
3 Kiséry, *Hamlet's Moment*, 106–7.
4 John Rainolds, *The summe of the conference betwene Iohn Rainoldes and Iohn Hart touching the head and the faith of the Church* (London: George Bishop, 1584), 665.
5 Charles Merbury, *A briefe discourse of royall monarchie* (London: Thomas Vautrollier, 1581), 40; Thomas Floyd, *The picture of a perfit common wealth* (London: Simon Stafford, 1600), 13.
6 William Thomas, *The historie of Italie* (London: TB, 1549), 77; Regius, *Aristotles politiques* (London: Adam Islip, 1598), 223.
7 Persons, *A Conference*, 11, 13; *The riddles of Heraclitus and Democritus* (London: Arn. Hatfield for Iohn Norton, 1598), *1r; Jean de Hainault, *The estate of the Church*, trans. Simon Patrike (London: Thomas Creede, 1602), 297; George Abbot, *A briefe description of the whole worlde* (London: T. Iudson for John Browne, 1599), A4v.
8 *The riddles of Heraclitus and Democritus*, *1r; Thomas, *Historie*, 77.
9 For Contarini's importance to English perspectives on Venice, see J.G.A. Pocock, *The Machiavellian Moment* (Princeton: Princeton University Press, 1975), 320; Andrew Hadfield, 'Shakespeare and Republican Venice', in *Visions of Venice in Shakespeare*, edited by Laura Tosi and Shaul Bassi (London: Ashgate, 2011), 67–82; and

Peter G. Platt, '"The Meruailouse Site": Shakespeare, Venice, and Paradoxical Stages', *Renaissance Quarterly* 54 (2001): 121–54, especially 132–4. For early modern English access to the text, see Hadfield, *Shakespeare and Republicanism*, 43, 79. For the various translations of Contarini and their availability, see Carole Levin and John Watkins, *Shakespeare's Foreign Worlds: National and Transnational Identities in the Elizabethan Age* (Ithaca: Cornell University Press, 2009), 117.

10 Gasparo Contarini, *The Common-wealth and Gouvernment of Venice*, trans. Lewis Lewkenor (1599. Rpt. Amsterdam: Theatrum Orbis Terrarum, 1969), 78. At 81, it is 'the liberty of our commonwealth', though the sentiment remains the same.
11 Ibid., 40, 78, 82.
12 Hadfield, 'Shakespeare and Republican Venice', 70.
13 Thomas, *Historie*, 77. For Thomas's influence on English views of Venice, see Hadfield, 'Shakespeare and Republican Venice', 68.
14 Contarini, *Common-wealth*, A2v.
15 Thomas, *Historie*, 77.
16 Ibid., 77–8.
17 Contarini, *Common-wealth*, 41–2.
18 Ibid., 41.
19 Ibid.
20 Thomas's work was printed in 1549; Lewkenor's translation of Contarini was likely published too late for Shakespeare or his audience to have read it before *Merchant of Venice* was written, but Contarini's original work was published before Thomas's, and had appeared in multiple foreign editions, some of which circulated in England (see n9).
21 All citations from the play are from William Shakespeare, *The Merchant of Venice*, edited by John Drakakis, Arden 3rd Series (London: Arden, 2010), except as otherwise noted.
22 See Daniel J. Kornstein, *Kill All the Lawyers?: Shakespeare's Legal Appeal* (Princeton: Princeton University Press, 1994), 74; Craig Bernthal, *The Trial of Man: Christianity and Judgement in the World of Shakespeare* (Wilmington, DE: ISI Books, 2003), 113; Peter J. Alscher, '"I Would Be Friends with You…" Staging Directions for a Balanced Resolution to "The Merchant of Venice" Trial Scene', *Cardozo Studies in Law and Literature* 5, no. 1 (1993): 6; Julia Reinhard Lupton, *Citizen-Saints: Shakespeare and Political Theology* (Chicago: University of Chicago Press, 2005), 88.
23 Graham Holderness, *Shakespeare and Venice* (Farnham: Ashgate, 2010), 76.
24 As Charles Fried has noted, there is some question as to whom the parties are to the initial contract – in particular, whether Bassanio

has any legal involvement in the contract, or whether it is simply between Antonio and Shylock, with the former giving Bassanio the resultant money. Charles Fried, 'Opinion of Fried, J., Concurring in the Judgement', in *Shakespeare and the Law: A Conversation among Disciplines and Professions*, edited by Bradin Cormack, Martha C. Nussbaum, and Richard Strier (Chicago: University of Chicago Press, 2013), 158.
25 Contarini, *Common-wealth*, 78, 81.
26 Ibid., 40.
27 Regius, *Aristotles politiques*, 295.
28 Thomas C. Biello, 'Accomplished with What She Lacks: Law, Equity, and Portia's Con', in *The Law in Shakespeare*, edited by Constance Jordan and Karen Cunningham (Houndmills: Palgrave Macmillan, 2007), 123; William Shakespeare, 'The Comical History of the Merchant of Venice, or Otherwise Called the Jew of Venice', in *The Norton Shakespeare Based on the Oxford Edition*, edited by Stephen Greenblatt et al. (New York: W.W. Norton, 1997), 1123, n2.
29 Lupton, *Citizen-Saints*, 88.
30 Holderness, *Shakespeare and Venice*, 79.
31 Lupton, *Citizen-Saints*, 88.
32 Holderness, *Shakespeare and Venice*, 26.
33 Ibid., 61.
34 Ibid., 81.
35 *Oxford English Dictionary*, 2nd edition, 1989, s.v. 'charter'. Venice was known to have such 'charters of their common weale'. Francesco Guiccardini, *The historie of Guicciardin*, trans. Geffray Fenton (London: Thomas Vautroullier, 1579), 415. Samuel Lewkenor, brother of Lewis, writes of the Venetians having been originally granted their peculiar rights by Charlemagne, in a form analogous to the granting of a charter, though he does not mention a particular document. Samuel Lewkenor, *A discourse not altogether vnprofitable, nor vnpleasant for such as are desirous to know the situation and customes of forraine cities without trauelling to see them* (London: I.W. for Humfrey Hooper, 1600), 30v.
36 Contarini, *Common-wealth*, 42. Interestingly, this section of Contarini was quoted (in a slightly different though anonymous translation) in a text published in England in 1598, the year before Lewkenor's translation came out, suggesting that this element of Contarini's text in particular circulated in England even without a full translation. Regius, *Aristotles politiques*, 171.
37 *A pleasant conceited comedie, called, A knacke to know an honest man* (London: for Cuthbert Burby, 1596), B1r–B2v.

38 For this claim, see among many others Mark Edwin Andrews, *Law versus Equity in 'The Merchant of Venice': A Legalization of Act IV, Scene I With Foreword, Judicial Precedents, and Notes* (Boulder: University of Colorado Press, 1965), 5; Fried, 'Opinion of Fried, J.', 156. See also Richard Posner, 'Law and Commerce in *The Merchant of Venice*', in *Shakespeare and the Law: A Conversation among Disciplines and Professions*, edited by Bradin Cormack, Martha C. Nussbaum and Richard Strier (Chicago: University of Chicago Press, 2013), 148–9.

39 *Il Pecorone*, 149.

40 Roberta Mullini, 'Streets, Squares, and Courts: Venice as a Stage in Shakespeare and Ben Jonson', in *Shakespeare's Italy: Functions of Italian Locations in Renaissance Drama*, edited by Michele Marrapodi et al. (Manchester: Manchester University Press, 1993), 164; Jack D'Amico, *Shakespeare and Italy* (Gainesville: University Press of Florida, 2001), 105; Murray J. Levith, *Shakespeare's Italian Settings and Plays* (Basingstoke: Macmillan, 1989), 26.

41 Thomas, *Historie*, 76; Guiccardini, *Historie*, 445. For more on the integration between the two cities, and English knowledge of it, see Levin and Watkins, *Shakespeare's Foreign Worlds*, 131; David C. McPherson, *Shakespeare, Jonson, and the Myth of Venice* (Newark: University of Delaware, 1990), 58; James S. Grugg, 'When Myths Lose Power: Four Decades of Venetian Historiography', *The Journal of Modern History* 58 (1986): 75.

42 See *Il Pecorone*, 150.

43 Hakluyt, *Principal Navigations*, 2:151; Robert Dallington, *The View of Fraunce* (London: Symon Stafford, 1604), D4v.

44 As previously noted, the case is Shylock against Antonio ('the merchant' against 'the Jew' in Portia's words [4.1.170]) and Bassanio is neither plaintiff nor defendant.

45 Jessica Apolloni, 'Law and Literature in Comparative Perspectives: Tracing Shylock's Case from Italian *novelle* to American Courtrooms', *Forum Italicum* 53, no. 2 (2019): 354. Apolloni summarizes the critical consensus about common law and equity at 356–7.

46 Ibid., 356, 357.

47 Although *Il Pecorone* appears to be the primary source for *Merchant*, Geoffrey Bullough has noted the flesh-bond narrative and the blood-flesh quibble in a wide variety of sources dating from the twelfth century on. None but *Merchant* include the offer to staunch the blood or the subsequent turn to Venetian (or any other) law. Bullough, *Narrative and Dramatic Sources*, 1:446–54.

48 See Daniel A. Farber, 'Legal Formalism and the Red-Hot Knife', *The University of Chicago Law Review* 66, no. 3 (1999): 597.

49 Fried, 'Opinion of Fried, J.', 162.

50 See Posner, 'Law and Commerce', 149; Richard Strier, 'Shakespeare and Legal Systems: The Better, The Worse (but Not Vice Versa)', in *Shakespeare and the Law: A Conversation among Disciplines and Professions*, edited by Bradin Cormack, Martha C. Nussbaum, and Richard Strier (Chicago: University of Chicago Press, 2013), 191, 198.
51 See Fried, 'Opinion of Fried, J.', 157; Strier, 'Shakespeare and Legal Systems', 190–1.
52 McPherson, *Myth of Venice*, 37.
53 Thomas, *Historie*, 81.
54 See most significantly John W. Draper, 'Shakespeare and the Duke of Venice', *The Journal of English and Germanic Philology* 46, no. 1 (1947): 77–8; Hadfield, 'Shakespeare and Republican Venice', 77; and Lupton, *Citizen-Saints*, 88.
55 Contarini, *Commonwealth*, 40.
56 Laura Ikins Stern, 'Politics and Law in Renaissance Florence and Venice', *The American Journal of Legal History* 46, no. 2 (2004): 221. It was this aspect of Venetian law that Samuel Lewkenor placed at the heart of the Venetian charter issued by Charlemagne. Lewkenor, *Discourse*, 30v.

Chapter 7

1 Contarini, *Commonwealth*, 39.
2 Ibid., 38.
3 Thomas, *Historie*, 77–8; Contarini, *Common-wealth*, 41–2.
4 Contarini, *Commonwealth*, 41.
5 Ibid., 40.
6 The publication of Lewkenor's 1599 translation would only have increased Contarini's circulation in the period between the writing of the two plays.
7 Bodin, *Six Books*, 192; Regius, *Aristotles politiques*, 172.
8 See, for example, Painter, *The Palace of Pleasure*, 283ff. where the Duke operates outside the law (but not illegally) by employing poor youths to seek out the truth for him.
9 William Fulwood, *The enimie of idlenesse* (London: Henry Bynneman, 1568), 84–5; Guiccardini, *Historie*, 265.
10 de Hainault, *Estate of the Church,* 208.
11 *A pleasant conceited comedie*, B2r.
12 Bodin, *Six Books*, 192.
13 Hadfield, 'Shakespeare and Republican Venice', 78; Levith, *Shakespeare's Italian Settings*, 33.

14 Mullini, 'Streets, Squares, and Courts', 165; Pamela K. Jensen, '"This Is Venice": Politics in Shakespeare's *Othello*', in *Shakespeare's Political Pageant: Essays in Politics & Literature*, edited by Joseph Alulis and Vickie Sullivan (Lanham: Rowman & Littlefield Publishers, 1996), 158; Richard McAdams, 'Vengeance, Complicity, and Criminal Law in *Othello*', in *Shakespeare and the Law: A Conversation among Disciplines and Professions*, edited by Bradin Cormack, Martha C. Nussbaum, and Richard Strier (Chicago: University of Chicago Press, 2013), 124; Strier, 'Shakespeare and Legal Systems', 200.

15 I take this to be a reference to the situation as we see it in 1.3, with the Duke joining the council rather than ruling it. There is also a reference to 'the Senate' having sent for Othello (1.2.46). The best way to square these different references, I believe, is to treat this as a meeting of an unspecified one of the Venetian councils, which were in turn composed of senators. This could also explain the earlier, somewhat strange, reference to the 'consuls, raised and met' (1.2.41) – members of a small, elite council could well be referred to in this way. All citations to *Othello*, unless otherwise noted, come from William Shakespeare, *Othello*, edited by E.A.J. Honigmann, Arden 3rd Series (London: Arden, 1997, rpt. 2004).

16 Hadfield, 'Shakespeare and Republican Venice', 79.

17 Contarini, *Common-wealth*, 29.

18 Philip C. McGuire, '*Othello* as an "Assay of Reason"', *Shakespeare Quarterly* 24, no. 2 (1973): 199–200; Mark Matheson, 'Venetian Culture and the Politics of *Othello*', *Shakespeare Survey* 48 (1995): 128.

Chapter 8

1 Gary Taylor, 'Shakespeare's Mediterranean *Measure for Measure*', in *Shakespeare and the Mediterranean: The Selected Proceedings of the International Shakespeare Association World Congress Valencia, 2001–1*, edited by Tom Clayton, Susan Brock, and Vicente Forés (Newark: University of Delaware Press, 2004), 250–5.

2 Leah Marcus, *Puzzling Shakespeare: Local Reading and Its Discontents* (Berkeley: University of California Press, 1988), 165. Marcus's treatment of Vienna as Vienna is primarily concerned with the question of what it would mean for London to turn into Vienna. It is worth noting that when Marcus's lengthy section on *Measure for Measure* was excerpted by Richard Wheeler for the volume *Critical Essays on Shakespeare's* Measure for Measure, he reprinted only the material specific to London, not her thoughts on the significance of the Viennese setting as Vienna itself. See Leah Marcus, 'London', in

Critical Essays on Shakespeare's Measure for Measure, edited by Richard Wheeler (Boston: G. K. Hall & Co., 1999), 56–78.
3   Robert Falls, 'Why Measure for Measure', *Shakespeare's 'Measure for Measure' Directed by Robert Falls*. Playbill, March 2013.
4   Neena Arndt, 'Time, Place, and Measure for Measure', *Shakespeare's 'Measure for Measure' Directed by Robert Falls*. Playbill, March 2013.
5   Taylor, 'Shakespeare's Mediterranean', 246. This assertion is echoed by his collaborator John Jowett in the introduction to *Measure for Measure* in the co-edited complete works of Middleton: 'the play's setting in Vienna ... would have had little special relevance in 1603–4'. John Jowett, 'Measure for Measure: A Genetic Text', in *Thomas Middleton: The Collected Works*, edited by Gary Taylor and John Lavagnino (Oxford: Clarendon Press, 2007), 1544.
6   Taylor, 'Shakespeare's Mediterranean', 244–6.
7   Ibid., 245.
8   John Stow, *The chronicles of England from Brute vnto this present yeare of Christ. 1580* (London: Ralphe Newberie, at the assignment of Henrie Bynneman, 1580), 122–3.
9   de Serres, *General Inventory*, 156; Abraham Ortelius, *An epitome of Ortelius his Theater of the vvorld* (London: Iohn Norton, 1601), 51v; Lewkenor, *Discourse*, 18v, 20v.
10 John Polemon, *All the famous battels that haue bene fought in our age throughout the worlde, as well by sea as lande* (London: Henrye Bynneman & Francis Coldock, 1578), 207; Johannes Sleidanus, *A famouse cronicle of oure time, called Sleidanes Commentaries*, translated by Ihon Daus (London: Ihon Daie, for Nicholas Englande, 1560), 466v; Jean François Le Petit, *The Low-country common wealth contayninge an exact description of the eight vnited Prouinces*, translated by Edward Grimeston (London: George Eld, 1609), 14, 19, 22; Emmanuel van Metereen, *A true discourse historicall, of the succeeding gouernours in the Netherlands, and the ciuill warres there begun in the yeere 1565*, translated by Thomas Churchyard and Richard Robinson (London: Matthew Lownes, 1602), 1.
11 Friedrich III, *A Christian confession of the late moste noble and mightie prince, Friderich of that name the third, Count Palatine by [ye] Rhein, one of the electours of the holy Empire, and Duke in Bauire* (London: Christopher Barkar, 1577), F4v.
12 Lewkenor, *Discourse*, 20v; Luis de Granada, *A Memoriall of a Christian life*, translated by W.S. (London: Michaell Sparke, 1586), 523.
13 Bodin, *Six Books*, 616. While Bodin was of course French, his influence on English understandings of European politics in this period should not be underestimated. Daniel Woolf, 'From Hystories

to the Historical: Five Transitions in Thinking about the Past, 1500–1700', *Huntington Library Quarterly* 68, no. 1/2 (2005): 61.
14 Botero, *Traveller's Breviat*, 67; François de la Noue, *The politicke and militarie discourses of the Lord de La Nouue*, translated by Edward Aggas (London: Thomas Orwin, 1587), 252.
15 All citations of *Measure for Measure* are from William Shakespeare, *Measure for Measure*, edited by A.R. Braunmuller and Robert N. Watson, Arden 3rd Series (London: Bloomsbury, 2020).
16 N.W. Bawcutt, introduction to William Shakespeare, *Measure for Measure*, Oxford's World Classics, edited by N.W. Bawcutt (Oxford: Oxford University Press, 1991), 53.
17 Roderick Lyall, '"Here in Vienna": The Setting of *Measure for Measure* and the Political Semiology of Shakespeare's Europe', in *Shakespeare and European Politics*, edited by Dirk Delabatista, Paul Franzen and Jozef De Vos (Newark: University of Delaware Press, 2008), 84; Marcus, *Puzzling*, 162–84; more broadly, see Peter Whitfield, 'Mapping Shakespeare's World', in *The Cambridge Guide to the Worlds of Shakespeare*, edited by Bruce R. Smith (Cambridge: Cambridge University Press, 2016), 11.
18 Dollimore, 'Transgression', 81.
19 Marcus, *Puzzling*, 179–82, Dollimore, 'Transgression', 76–7, 81.
20 Taylor, 'Shakespeare's Mediterranean', 247–8; Jowett, 'Measure for Measure', 1544–5; Richard Wilson, 'As Mice by Lions. Political Theology and *Measure for Measure*', *Shakespeare* 11, no. 2 (2015): 173.
21 Edwin Sandys, *A relation of the state of religion and with what hopes and pollicies it hath beene framed, and is maintained in the severall states of these westerne parts of the world.* (London: Simon Waterson, 1605), E3r.
22 *Newes from diuers countries as, from Spaine, Antwerpe, Collin, Venice, Rome, the Turke, and the prince Doria: and how the archduke of Austria is intended to resigne his cardinall hat through his marrying with the king of Spaines daughter* (London: Valentine Sims, 1597), 4, 7. Admittedly, the Archduke was a real cardinal and not a pretend friar, but the 'king of Spaines daughter' was indeed Isabella. The marriage took place in 1599. de Hainault, *Estate of the Church*, 708.
23 *Articles of the peace agreed vpon, between the Archduke Mathias, on the Emperours part, and the deputies of the Lord Botzkay, and of other Lords of Hungarie on the other partie In like manner, the articles, and conditions of truce, set downe betweene the Emperour and the great Turke, for 15. yeares* (London: Nathaniel Butter, 1607), 1. The situation surrounding this treaty is in many ways similar

to that surrounding the 1621 treaty that Jowett emphasizes as a potential topical reference in the Middleton complete works. Jowett, 'Measure for Measure', 1545. 'Lord Botzkay' was the regent for the pretender, who was a minor.

24 *Articles of the Peace*, 3.
25 For more on early modern English knowledge of the Ottoman Mediterranean, see Tavares, 'Acts of Imagination', 58n116; Hutchings, *Turks*, 23–38.
26 Jacques Lezra, 'Pirating Reading: The Appearance of History in *Measure for Measure*', *ELH* 56, no. 2 (1989): 255.
27 As early as 1560 an English translation of Johannes Sleidanus's *Commentaries* noted that Martin Luther was initially called a 'Bohemer' for his objections to the Catholic faith because of the lingering legacy of Jan Hus. Sleidanus, *Commentaries*, 26r.
28 Recidivism, the tendency of released prisoners to revert to criminal behaviour, became a major subject of sociological and legal study in the United States beginning in the 1970s. Michael Reisig et al., 'The Effect of Racial Inequality on Black Male Recividism', *Justice Quarterly* 24 (2007): 409; John F. Wallerstedt, *Returning to Prison*, Bureau of Justice Statistics Special Report (1984).
29 Bawcutt, 'Introduction', 25.
30 Lyall, 'Here in Vienna', 74–89.
31 Francis Herring, *Popish Pietie*, translated by A.P. (London: William Jones, 1610). Although this poem, which links Catholic villainy to the Gunpowder Plot, postdates *Measure for Measure*, it serves to demonstrate both that the perspective on the Viennese dukes that I have proposed here extended beyond *Measure* itself and that it did so before Taylor's proposed date for Middleton's revisions. In addition, since the duke of Austria who married the Infanta at the turn of the sixteenth century did in fact initially hold ecclesiastical office, the dual element in the dukedom identified so clearly here was also present before the play was written.
32 Andrew Majeske, 'Equity's Absence: The Extremity of Claudio's Prosecution and Barnardine's Pardon in Shakespeare's *Measure for Measure*', *Law and Literature* 21, no. 2 (2009): 169.
33 Julia Reinhard Lupton, 'Periodic Shakespeare', in *Early Modern Histories of Time: The Periodizations of Sixteenth- and Seventeenth-Century England*, edited by Kristen Poole and Owen Williams (Philadelphia: University of Pennsylvania Press, 2019), 200.
34 For a fuller account of the production, see Sarah Werner, 'Two Hamlets: Wooster Group and Synetic Theater', *Shakespeare Quarterly* 59, no. 3 (2008): 323–9.

WORKS CITED

Abbot, George. *A briefe description of the whole worlde*. London: T. Iudson for John Browne, 1599.

Achilleos, Stella. 'Friendship and Good Counsel: The Discourses of Friendship and Parrhesia in Francis Bacon's The Essayes or Counsels, Civill and Morall'. In *Friendship in the Middle Ages and Early Modern Age: Explorations of a Fundamental Ethical Discourse*, edited by Albrecht Classen and Marilyn Sandidge, 643–74. Berlin: De Gruyter, 2010.

The actis and constitutiounis of the Realme of Scotland maid in Parliamentis haldin be the rycht excellent, hie and mychtie Princeis Kingis Iames the First, Secund, thrid, Feird, Fyft, and in tyme of Marie now Quene of Scottis. N.p.: Ed. Henrison, 1566.

Adelman, Janet. *Suffocating Mothers: Fantasies of Maternal Origin in Shakespeare's Plays, 'Hamlet' to 'The Tempest'*. New York: Routledge, 1992.

Alford, Steven. *The Early Elizabethan Polity: William Cecil and the British Succession Crisis, 1558–1569*. Cambridge: Cambridge University Press, 1998.

Alford, Steven. *Kingship and Politics in the Reign of Edward VI*. Cambridge: Cambridge University Press, 2002.

Alford, Steven. 'The Political Creed of William Cecil'. In *The Monarchical Republic of Early Modern England: Essays in Response to Patrick Collinson*, edited by John F. McDiarmid, 75–90. Aldershot: Ashgate, 2007.

Alscher, Peter J. '"I Would Be Friends with You…" Staging Directions for a Balanced Resolution to "The Merchant of Venice" Trial Scene'. *Cardozo Studies in Law and Literature* 5, no. 1 (1993): 1–33.

Alvis, John E. 'Introductory: Shakespearean Poetry and Politics'. In *Shakespeare as Political Thinker*, edited by John E. Alvis and Thomas G. West, 1–28. Wilmington, DE: ISI Books, 2000.

Anderson, Thomas P. *Shakespeare's Fugitive Politics*, Edinburgh: Edinburgh University Press, 2016.

Andrews, Mark Edwin. *Law versus Equity in 'The Merchant of Venice': A Legalization of Act IV, Scene I with Foreword, Judicial Precedents, and Notes*. Boulder: University of Colorado Press, 1965.

Apolloni, Jessica. 'Law and Literature in Comparative Perspectives: Tracing Shylock's Case from Italian *novelle* to American Courtrooms'. *Forum Italicum* 53, no. 2 (2019): 350–62.

Appian. *An auncient historie and exquisite chronicle of the Romanes warres, both ciuile and foren*. Translated by W.B. London: Henrie Bynniman, 1578.

Arndt, Neena. 'Time, Place, and Measure for Measure'. *Shakespeare's 'Measure for Measure' Directed by Robert Falls*. Playbill, March 2013.

Arnold, Oliver. *The Third Citizen: Shakespeare's Theater and the Early Modern House of Commons*. Baltimore: Johns Hopkins University Press, 2007.

Articles of the peace agreed vpon, between the Archduke Mathias, on the Emperours part, and the deputies of the Lord Botzkay, and of other Lords of Hungarie on the other partie In like manner, the articles, and conditions of truce, set downe beweene the Emperour and the great Turke, for 15. yeares. London: Nathaniel Butter, 1607.

Augustine. *Of the citie of God vvith the learned comments of Io. Lod. Viues*. Translated by I.H. London: George Eld, 1610.

Averell, W. *A dyall for dainty darlings, rockt in the cradle of securitie*. London: Thomas Hackette, 1584.

Baker, Oliver R. 'Duncan's Thanes and Malcolm's Earls: Name Dropping in *Macbeth*'. *Notes and Queries* 56, no. 4 (2009): 591–5.

Baker, Oliver R. 'The Thanes in *Macbeth*: Fealty and Obedience in the *True Lawe of Free Monarchies*'. *Shakespeare* 10 (2014). http://dx.doi.org/10.1080/17450918.2014.965726.

Barmazel, Julie. '"The Servant to Defect": Macbeth, Impotence, and the Body Politic'. In *'Macbeth': New Critical Essays*, edited by Nick Moschovakis, 118–31. New York: Routledge, 2008.

Barnaud, Nicolas. *Le reveille-matin des Francois, et de leurs voisins*. Edinburgh: Iaques Iames, 1574.

Barnes, Thomas. *Shaping of the Common Law: From Glanvill to Hale, 1188–1688*. Stanford: Stanford University Press, 2008.

Battenhouse, Roy. '*King John*: Shakespeare's Perspective and Others'. *Notre Dame English Journal* 14, no. 3 (1982): 191–215.

Bawcutt, N.W. 'Introduction'. In William Shakespeare. *Measure for Measure*. Oxford's World Classics, edited by N.W. Bawcutt. Oxford: Oxford University Press, 1991.

Bawcutt, Priscilla. 'Crossing the Border: Scottish Poetry and English Readers in the Sixteenth Century'. In *The Rose and the Thistle: Essays on the Culture of Late Medieval and Renaissance Scotland*, edited by Sally Mapstone and Juliette Wood, 59–76. Phantassie: Tuckwell Press, 1998.

Beer, Anna R. *Sir Walter Ralegh and His Readers in the Seventeenth Century: Speaking to the People*. New York: St. Martin's Press, 1997.

Berger, Harry. 'The Early Scenes of *MacBeth*: Preface to a New Interpretation'. *ELH* 47, no. 1 (1980): 1–31.
Bernthal, Craig. *The Trial of Man: Christianity and Judgement in the World of Shakespeare*. Wilmington, DE: ISI Books, 2003.
Berry, Edward I. *Patterns of Decay: Shakespeare's Early Histories*. Charlottesville: University Press of Virginia, 1975.
Biello, Thomas C. 'Accomplished with What She Lacks: Law, Equity, and Portia's Con'. In *The Law in Shakespeare*, edited by Constance Jordan and Karen Cunningham, 109–26. Houndmills: Palgrave Macmillan, 2007.
Blits, Jan H. *Rome and the Spirit of Caesar: Shakespeare's* Julius Caesar. Lanham: Lexington Books, 2015.
Blits, Jan H. *Spirit, Soul, and City: Shakespeare's* Coriolanus. Lanham: Lexington Books, 2005.
Bodin, Jean. *The six bookes of a common-weale*. Translated by Richard Knolles. London: G. Bishop, 1606.
Boece, Hector. *Heir beginnis the hystory and croniklis of Scotland*. Edinburgh: Thomas Davidson, 1540.
The boke of Magna Carta with diuers other statutes. London: Robert Redman, 1534.
Botero, Giovanni. *The trauellers breuiat*. Translated by I.R. London: Edmond Bollifant for John Jaggard, 1601.
Brackmann, Rebecca J. '"That Auntient Authoritie": Old English Laws in the Writings of William Lambarde'. In *Renaissance Retrospections*, edited by Sarah A. Kelen, 111–26. Kalamazoo: Medieval Institute Publications, 2013.
Brand, Paul. 'The First Century of Magna Carta: The Diffusion of Texts and Knowledge of the Charter'. *William and Mary Bill of Rights Journal* 25 (2016): 437–53.
British Library Additional MS 48102A. British Library, London.
British Library Stowe MS 385. British Library, London.
Britton, Dennis Austin and Melissa Walter. 'Rethinking Shakespeare Source Study'. In *Rethinking Shakespeare Source Study: Audiences, Authors, and Digital Technologies*, edited by Dennis Austin Britton and Melissa Walter, 1–16. London: Routledge, 2018.
Brower, Reuben A. *Hero & Saint: Shakespeare and the Graeco-Roman Heroic Tradition*. New York: Oxford University Press, 1971.
Brunt, P. A. *The Fall of the Roman Republic*. Oxford: Clarendon Press, 1988.
Bruster, Douglas. *Drama and the Market in the Age of Shakespeare*. Cambridge: Cambridge University Press, 1992.
Buchanan, George. *The History of Scotland*. Translated by James Aikman. Glasgow: Blackie Fullarton & Co. and Archibald Fullarton & Co., 1827.
Buck, George. *Daphnis polystephanos*. London: G. Eld for Thomas Adams, 1605.

Bullough, Geoffrey. *Narrative and Dramatic Sources of Shakespeare*. 8 vols. New York: Columbia University Press, 1962–75.

Burke, Peter. *The Renaissance Sense of the Past*. London: Edward Arnold, 1969.

Burrow, Colin. *Shakespeare and Classical Antiquity*. Oxford: Oxford University Press, 2013.

Camden, William. *Remaines of a greater worke, concerning Britaine, the inhabitants thereof, their languages, names, surnames, empreses, wise speeches, poësies, and epitaphes*. London: G. E. for Simon Waterson, 1605.

Camden, William. 'Scotland'. *Britain*. Translated by Philemon Holland. London: George Bishop and John Norton, 1610.

Cantor, Paul. *Shakespeare's Rome: Republic and Empire*. Ithaca, NY: Cornell University Press, 1976.

Carroll, William C. 'Historicizing Historicism'. In *Shakespeare in Our Time: A Shakespeare Association of America Collection*, edited by Dympna Callaghan and Suzanne Gossett, 211–19. London: Bloomsbury Arden Shakespeare, 2016.

Chavura, Stephen A. *Tudor Protestant Political Thought 1547–1603*. Leiden: Brill, 2003.

Chernaik, Warren. *The Myth of Rome in Shakespeare and His Contemporaries*. Cambridge: Cambridge University Press, 2011.

Churchyard, Thomas. *A generall rehearsall of warres, called Churchyardes choise*. London: Edward White, 1579.

Clegg, Cyndia Susan. *Shakespeare's Reading Audiences: Early Modern Books and Audience Interpretation*. Cambridge: Cambridge University Press, 2017.

Collinson, Patrick. *Elizabethan Essays*. London: The Hambledon Press, 1994.

Contarini, Gasparo. *The Common-wealth and Gouvernment of Venice*. Translated by Lewis Lewkenor. Amsterdam: Theatrum Orbis Terrarum, 1969. First published 1599 by John Windet.

Cormack, Bradin. *A Power to Do Justice: Jurisdiction, English Literature, and the Rise of the Common Law, 1509–1625*. Chicago: University of Chicago Press, 2007.

Cornwallis, William. *Essayes*. London: Edmund Mattes, 1600.

Cowell, John. *The Interpreter*. Cambridge: Iohn Legate, 1607.

Cox-Jensen, Freyja. 'Ancient Histories of Rome in Sixteenth-Century England: A Reconsideration of Their Printing and Circulation'. *Huntington Library Quarterly* 83, no. 3 (2020): 415–40.

Craig, Thomas. *Jus Feudale Tribus Libris Comprehensum*. Translated, edited and annotated by Leslie Dodd. Edinburgh: Stair Society, 2017.

Craig, Thomas. *The Jus Feudale*. Translated by James Avon Clyde. Edinburgh: William Hodge & Company, 1934.

Cromartie, Alan. *The Constitutionalist Revolution.* Cambridge: Cambridge University Press, 2009.

Dallington, Robert. *The View of Fraunce.* London: Symon Stafford, 1604.

D'Amico, Jack. *Shakespeare and Italy.* Gainesville: University Press of Florida, 2001.

Davidson, Ryan. 'The Malleable Macbeth: Understanding the Evolving Image of an Obscure Medieval King'. M.A. Thesis, University of Guelph, 2008.

Digges, Thomas. *Foure paradoxes, or politique discourses.* London: H. Lownes for Clement Knight, 1604.

Dollimore, Jonathan. 'Transgression and Surveillance in *Measure for Measure*'. In *Political Shakespeare: Essays in Cultural Materialism*, 2nd edition, edited by Jonathan Dollimore and Alan Sinfield, 72–87. Ithaca: Cornell University Press, 1994.

Downs-Gamble, Margaret. '"To th' Crack of Doom": Sovereign Imagination as Anamorphosis in Shakespeare's "show of kings"'. In *Celtic Shakespeare: The Bard and the Borderers*, edited by Willy Maley and Rory Loughnane, 157–68. Farnham: Ashgate, 2013.

Draper, John W. 'Shakespeare and the Duke of Venice', *The Journal of English and Germanic Philology* 46, no. 1 (1947): 75–81.

Edmondes, Clement. *Obseruations vpon the fiue first bookes of Caesars commentaries setting fourth the practise of the art military in the time of the Roman Empire.* London: Peter Short, 1600.

E.L. *Romes monarchie, entituled the globe of renowmed glorie.* London: The Widow Orrin for Matthew Lawe, 1596.

Erne, Lukas. *Shakespeare as Literary Dramatist*, 2nd edition. Cambridge: Cambridge University Press, 2013.

Eutropius. *A briefe chronicle.* Translated by Nicolas Havvard. London: Thomas Marshe, 1564.

Falls, Robert. 'Why Measure for Measure'. *Shakespeare's 'Measure for Measure' Directed by Robert Falls.* Playbill, March 2013.

Farber, Daniel A. 'Legal Formalism and the Red-Hot Knife'. *The University of Chicago Law Review* 66, no. 3 (1999): 597–606.

Floyd, Thomas. *The Picture of a Perfit Common Wealth.* London: Simon Stafford, 1600.

Fortescue, John. *A Learned Commendation of the politique lawes of Englande.* Translated by Robert Mulcaster. London: Richard Tottill, 1567.

Fried, Charles. 'Opinion of Fried, J., Concurring in the Judgement'. In *Shakespeare and the Law: A Conversation among Disciplines and Professions*, edited by Bradin Cormack, Martha C. Nussbaum, and Richard Strier, 156–63. Chicago: University of Chicago Press, 2013.

Friedrich III. *A Christian Confession of the Late Moste Noble and Mightie Prince, Friderich of that Name the Third, Count Palatine by [ye] Rhein, one of the Electours of the Holy Empire, and Duke in Bauire.* London: Christopher Barkar, 1577.

Fulbecke, William. *An historicall collection of the continuall factions, tumults, and massacres of the Romans and Italians during the space of one hundred and twentie yeares next before the peaceable empire of Augustus Caesar*. London: William Ponsonby, 1601.

Fulton, Thomas. 'The Politics of Renaissance Historicism: Valla, Erasmus, Colet, and More'. In *Rethinking Historicism from Shakespeare to Milton*, edited by Ann Baynes Coiro and Thomas Fulton, 87–112. Cambridge: Cambridge University Press, 2012.

Fulwood, William. *The enimie of idlenesse*. London: Henry Bynneman, 1568.

Gentillet, Innocent. *A discourse vpon the meanes of vvel governing and maintaining in good peace, a kingdome, or other principalitie*. Translated by Simon Patericke. London: Adam Islip, 1602.

Gieskes, Edward. '"He Is but a Bastard to the Time": Status and Service in "The Troublesome Raigne of John" and Shakespeare's "King John"'. *ELH* 65, no. 4 (1998): 779–98.

Gillespie, Stuart. 'The Availability of the Classics: Readers, Writers, Translation, Performance'. In *The Oxford History of Classical Reception in English Literature, Volume 2 (1580–1660)*, edited by Patrick Cheney and Philip Hardie, 57–73. Oxford: Oxford University Press, 2015.

Goddard, Harold. *The Meaning of Shakespeare*. Chicago: University of Chicago Press, 1951.

Grady, Hugh. 'Moral Agency and Its Problems in *Julius Caesar*: Political Power, Choice, and History'. In *Shakespeare and Moral Agency*, edited by Michael D. Bristol, 15–28. London: Continuum, 2010.

de Granada, Luis. *A Memoriall of a Christian life*. Translated by W.S. London: Michaell Sparke, 1586.

Gray, Patrick. *Shakespeare and the Fall of the Roman Republic: Selfhood, Stoicism and Civil War*. Edinburgh: Edinburgh University Press, 2019.

Groves, Beatrice. 'Memory, Composition, and the Relationship of "King John" to "The Troublesome Raigne of King John"'. *Comparative Drama* 38, no. 2/3 (2004): 277–90.

Grugg, James S. 'When Myths Lose Power: Four Decades of Venetian Historiography'. *The Journal of Modern History* 58 (1986): 43–94.

Guicciardini, Francesco. *The historie of Guicciardin*. Translated by Geffray Fenton. London: Thomas Vautroullier, 1579.

Guy, John. 'The Rhetoric of Counsel in Early Modern England'. In *Tudor Political Culture*, edited by Dale Hoak, 292–310. Cambridge: Cambridge University Press, 1995.

Hadfield, Andrew. 'Shakespeare and Republican Venice'. In *Visions of Venice in Shakespeare*, edited by Laura Tosi and Shaul Bassi, 67–82. London: Ashgate, 2011.

Hadfield, Andrew. *Shakespeare and Republicanism*. Cambridge: Cambridge University Press, 2005.

de Hainault, Jean. *The Estate of the Church with the Discourse of Times*. Translated by Simon Patrike. London: Thomas Creede, 1602.

Hakluyt, Richard. *The principal nauigations, voyages, traffiques and discoueries of the English nation made by sea or ouer-land, to the remote and farthest distant quarters of the earth, at any time within the compasse of these 1600. yeres*. London: George Bishop, Ralph Newberie, and Robert Barker, 1599.

Hartley, T.E. *Elizabeth's Parliaments: Queen, Lords and Commons 1559–1601*. Manchester: Manchester University Press, 1992.

Haugaard, William. *Elizabeth and the English Reformation: The Struggle for a Stable Settlement of Religion*. Cambridge: Cambridge University Press, 1968.

Hawkins, Michael. 'History, Politics, and *Macbeth*'. In *Focus on 'Macbeth'*, edited by John Russell Brown, 155–88. London: Routledge & Kegan Paul, 1982.

Heims, Neil. *Bloom's How to Write About Shakespeare's Histories*. New York: Bloom's Literary Criticism, 2010.

Herman, Peter. 'Equity and the Problem of Theseus in *A Midsummer Night's Dream*: Or, the Ancient Constitution in Ancient Athens'. *Journal for Early Modern Cultural Studies* 14, no. 1 (2014): 4–31.

Herring, Francis. *Popish pietie*. Translated by A.P. London: William Jones, 1610.

Heyleyn, Peter. *Mikrokosmos: A Little Description of the Great World. Augmented and Reuised*. Oxford: John Lichfield and William Turner, 1625.

Hoak, Dale. 'Sir William Cecil, Sir Thomas Smith, and the Monarchical Republic of Tudor England'. In *The Monarchical Republic of Early Modern England: Essays in Response to Patrick Collinson*, edited by John F. McDiarmid, 37–54. Aldershot: Ashgate, 2007.

Holderness, Graham. *Shakespeare and Venice*. Farnham: Ashgate, 2010.

Holderness, Graham, Nick Potter and John Turner. *Shakespeare: The Play of History*. Houndsmills: Macmillan Press, 1988.

Holinshed, Raphael. *Chronicles of England, Scotland, and Ireland*. 1587; The Holinshed Project, 2009. http://www.english.ox.ac.uk/holinshed/.

Honigmann, E.A.J. *Shakespeare's Impact on His Contemporaries*. London: Macmillan Press, 1982.

Hope, Jonathan and Michael Whitmore. 'The Language of *Macbeth*'. In *Macbeth: The State of the Play*, edited by Ann Thompson, 183–210. London: Bloomsbury, 2014.

Hopton, Arthur. *A concordancy of yeares*. London: Company of Stationers, 1612.

Huffman, Clifford Chalmers. *'Coriolanus' in Context*. Cranbury, NJ: Associated University Presses, Inc., 1971.

Hunt, Maurice. 'Duncan, Macbeth, and the Thane of Cawdor'. *Studies in the Humanities* 28, no. 1–2 (2001): 1–30.

Hunter, G.K. 'A Roman Thought: Renaissance Attitudes to History Exemplified in Shakespeare and Jonson'. In *Shakespeare and History*, edited by Stephen Orgel and Sean Keilen. New York: Garland Publishing, Inc., 1999.

Hutchings, Mark. *Turks, Repertories, and the Early Modern English Stage*. London: Palgrave Macmillan, 2017.

Hutson, Lorna. *Circumstantial Shakespeare*. Oxford: Oxford University Press, 2015.

Ikins Stern, Laura. 'Politics and Law in Renaissance Florence and Venice'. *The American Journal of Legal History* 46, no. 2 (2004): 209–34.

Ives, E.W. 'The Genesis of the Statute of Uses'. *The English Historical Review* 82, no. 325 (1967): 673–97.

Jensen, Pamela K. '"This Is Venice": Politics in Shakespeare's *Othello*'. In *Shakespeare's Political Pageant: Essays in Politics & Literature*, edited by Joseph Alulis and Vickie Sullivan, 155–88. Lanham, MD: Rowman & Littlefield Publishers, 1996.

John of Salisbury. *Policraticus*. Edited and translated by Cary J. Nederman. Cambridge: Cambridge University Press, 1990.

Jones, Norman. 'Parliament and the Political Society of Elizabethan England'. In *Tudor Political Culture*, edited by Dale Hoak, 226–42. Cambridge: Cambridge University Press, 1995.

Jowett, John. 'Measure for Measure: A Genetic Text'. In *Thomas Middleton: The Collected Works*, edited by Gary Taylor and John Lavagnino, 1542–85. Oxford: Clarendon Press, 2007.

Kahn, Coppélia. *Man's Estate: Masculine Identity in Shakespeare*. Berkeley: University of California Press, 1981.

Kerrigan, John. *Archipelagic English: Literature, History, and Politics 1603–1707*. Oxford: Oxford University Press, 2008.

Kewes, Paulina. 'Translations of State: Ancient Rome and Late Elizabethan Political Thought'. *Huntington Library Quarterly* 83, no. 3 (2020): 468–98.

Kiséry, András. *Hamlet's Moment: Drama and Political Knowledge in Early Modern England*. Oxford: Oxford University Press, 2016.

Kishlansky, Mark. *A Monarchy Transformed: Britain 1603–1714*. London: The Penguin Press, 1996.

Kliman, Bernice W. 'Thanes in the Folio *Macbeth*'. *Shakespeare Bulletin* 9, no. 1 (1991): 5–8.

Konstan, David. *Friendship in the Classical World*. Cambridge: Cambridge University Press, 1997.

Kornstein, Daniel J. *Kill All the Lawyers?: Shakespeare's Legal Appeal*. Princeton: Princeton University Press, 1994.

Lake, Peter. *How Shakespeare Put Politics on the Stage: Power and Succession in the History Plays*. New Haven: Yale University Press, 2016.

Lambarde, William. *A Perambulation of Kent*. London: Ralph Newbery, 1576.

Lambarde, William. *A Perambulation of Kent*. London: Edmund Bollifant, 1596.
Lammers, Lukas. *Shakespearean Temporalities: History on the Early Modern Stage*. New York: Routledge, 2018.
Lanquet, Thomas et al. *An Epitome of Chronicles*. London: Thomas Marsh, 1559.
de La Primaudaye, Pierre. *The French Academie*. Translated by T.B. London: Edmund Bollifant for G. Bishop and Ralph Newbery, 1586.
Le Petit, Jean François. *The Low-country Common Wealth Contayninge an Exact Description of the Eight Vnited Prouince*. Translated by Edward Grimeston. London: George Eld, 1609.
Leggatt, Alexander. *Shakespeare's Political Drama: The History Plays and the Roman Plays*. London: Routledge, 1988.
Lemon, Rebecca. 'Sovereignty and Treason in *Macbeth*'. In '*Macbeth*': *New Critical Essays*, edited by Nick Moschovakis, 73–87. London: Routledge, 2008.
Leslie, John. *De origine, moribus & rebus gestis Scotorum libri decem*. 1578. Reprint, London: Robert Boulter, 1677.
Leslie, John. *The Historie of Scotland*. Translated by James Dalrymple. Edited by E.G. Cody. Edinburgh: Scottish Text Society, 1888.
Levin, Carole. *Propaganda in the English Reformation: Heroic and Villainous Images of King John*. Lewiston, NY: The Edwin Mellen Press, 1988.
Levin, Carole and John Watkins. *Shakespeare's Foreign Worlds: National and Transnational Identities in the Elizabethan Age*. Ithaca: Cornell University, 2009.
Levith, Murray J. *Shakespeare's Italian Settings and Plays*. Basingstoke: Macmillan, 1989.
Lewkenor, Samuel. *A discourse not altogether vnprofitable, nor vnpleasant for such as are desirous to know the situation and customes of forraine cities without trauelling to see them*. London: I.W. for Humfrey Hooper, 1600.
Lezra, Jacques. 'Pirating Reading: The Appearance of History in *Measure for Measure*'. *ELH* 56, no. 2 (1989): 255–92.
Liston, William T. '"Male and Female He Created Them": Sex and Gender in "Macbeth"'. *College Literature* 16, no. 3 (1989): 232–9.
Livy. *Ab Urbe Condita*. Edited by Robert Seymour Conway and Charles Flamstead Walters. Oxford: Clarendon Press, 1946.
Livy. *The Romane Historie*. Translated by Philemon Holland. London: Adam Islip, 1600.
Lloyd, Lodowick. *The Consent of Time*. London: George Bishop and Ralph Nevvberie, 1590.
Lloyd, Lodowick. *The first part of the diall of daies*. London: Roger Ward, 1590.

Lloyd, Lodowick. *The Practice of Policy*. London: Simon Stafford, 1604.
Lloyd, Lodowick. *The stratagems of Ierusalem*. London: Thomas Creede, 1602.
Lloyd, Lodowick. *The tragicocomedie of serpents*. London: Thomas Purfoot and Arthur Johnson, 1607.
Lopez, Jeremy. 'Imagining Shakespeare's Audience'. In *The Oxford Handbook of Shakespearean Comedy*, edited by Heather Hirschfield, 411–25. Oxford: Oxford University Press, 2018.
Low, Jennifer. '"Bodied Forth": Spectator, Stage, and the Actor in the Early Modern Theater'. *Comparative Drama* 39, no. 1 (2005): 1–29.
Lucan. *Lucans first booke translated line for line*. Translated by Christopher Marlowe. London: P. Short and Walter Burre, 1600.
Lupton, Julia Reinhard. *Citizen-Saints: Shakespeare and Political Theology*. Chicago: University of Chicago Press, 2005.
Lupton, Julia Reinhard. 'Periodic Shakespeare'. In *Early Modern Histories of Time: The Periodizations of Sixteenth- and Seventeenth-Century England*, edited by Kristen Poole and Owen Williams, 198–214. Philadelphia: University of Pennsylvania Press, 2019.
Lyall, Roderick. '"Here in Vienna": The Setting of *Measure for Measure* and the Political Semiology of Shakespeare's Europe'. In *Shakespeare and European Politics*, edited by Dirk Delabatista, Paul Franzen, and Jozef De Vos, 74–89. Newark: University of Delaware Press, 2008.
MacFaul, Tom. *Male Friendship in Shakespeare and His Contemporaries*. Cambridge: Cambridge University Press, 2007.
Majeske, Andrew. 'Equity's Absence: The Extremity of Claudio's Prosecution and Barnardine's Pardon in Shakespeare's *Measure for Measure*'. *Law and Literature* 21, no. 2 (2009): 169–84.
Manley, Lawrence and Sally-Beth MacLean. *Lord Strange's Men and Their Plays*. New Haven: Yale University Press, 2014.
Marcus, Leah. 'London'. In *Critical Essays on Shakespeare's* Measure for Measure, edited by Richard Wheeler, 56–78. Boston: G. K. Hall & Co., 1999.
Marcus, Leah. *Puzzling Shakespeare: Local Reading and Its Discontents*. Berkeley: University of California Press, 1988.
Matheson, Mark. 'Venetian Culture and the Politics of *Othello*'. *Shakespeare Survey* 48 (1995): 123–33.
Mayer, Jean-Christophe. *Shakespeare's Early Readers: A Cultural History from 1590 to 1800*. Cambridge: Cambridge University Press, 2018.
McAdams, Richard. 'Vengeance, Complicity, and Criminal Law in *Othello*'. In *Shakespeare and the Law: A Conversation among Disciplines and Professions*, edited by Bradin Cormack, Martha C. Nussbaum, and Richard Strier, 121–43. Chicago: University of Chicago Press, 2013.

McDiarmid, John F. 'Common Consent, *Latinitas*, and the "Monarchical Republic" in Mid-Tudor Humanism'. In *The Monarchical Republic of Early Modern England: Essays in Response to Patrick Collinson*, edited by John F. McDiarmid, 55–74. Aldershot: Ashgate, 2007.

McGuire, Philip C. '*Othello* as an "Assay of Reason"'. *Shakespeare Quarterly* 24, no. 2 (1973): 198–209.

McInnis,David. *Mind-Travelling and Voyage Drama in Early Modern England*. New York: Palgrave Macmillan, 2013.

McPherson, David C. *Shakespeare, Jonson, and the Myth of Venice*. Newark: University of Delaware, 1990.

Merbury, Charles. *A briefe discourse of royall monarchie*. London: Thomas Vautrollier, 1581.

Milles, Thomas. *A catalogue of the kings of Scotland Together with their seuerall armes, wiues, and issue*. London: 1610.

Miola, Robert. *Shakespeare's Rome*. Cambridge: Cambridge University Press, 1983.

Monipennie, John. *Certeine matters concerning the realme of Scotland, composed together*. London: A. Hatfield for John Blasket[?], 1603.

Mullini, Roberta. 'Streets, Squares, and Courts: Venice as a Stage in Shakespeare and Ben Jonson'. In *Shakespeare's Italy: Functions of Italian Locations in Renaissance Drama*, edited by Michele Marrapodi et al. 158–70. Manchester: Manchester University Press, 1993.

Munro, Lucy. 'Writing a Play with Robert Daborne'. In *Rethinking Theatrical Documents in Shakespeare's England*, edited by Tiffany Stern, 17–32. London: Arden Shakespeare, 2020.

Neale, J.E. *Elizabeth I and Her Parliaments, 1559–1581*. London: Jonathan Cape, 1964.

Neale, J.E. *Elizabeth I and Her Parliaments, 1584–1601*. London: Jonathan Cape, 1971.

Newes from diuers countries as, from Spaine, Antwerpe, Collin, Venice, Rome, the Turke, and the prince Doria: And how the arch-duke of Austria is intended to resigne his cardinall hat through his marrying with the king of Spaines daughter. London: Valentine Sims, 1597.

Norbrook, David. '*Macbeth* and the Politics of Historiography'. In *Politics of Discourse: The Literature and History of Seventeenth-Century England*, edited by Kevin Sharpe and Steven N. Zwicker, 78–116. Berkeley: University of California Press, 1987.

de la Noue, François. *The politicke and militarie discourses*. Translated by Edward Aggas. London: Thomas Orwin, 1587.

O'Dair, Sharon. 'Conduct (Un)becoming or, Playing the Warrior in *Macbeth*'. In *Shakespeare and Moral Agency*, edited by Michael D. Bristol, 71–85. London: Continuum, 2010.

Of the Severall Opinions of Sundry Learned Antiquaries. London: William Leake, 1658.

Orr, D. Alan. 'Civic Catholicism, Military Humanism, and the Decline of Justice in Thomas Lodge's *The Wovnds of Ciuill War*'. *Huntington Library Quarterly* 83, no. 1 (2020): 33–60.

Ortelius, Abraham. *An Epitome of Ortelius his Theater of the Vvorld*. London: Iohn Norton, 1601.

Painter, William. *The Palace of Pleasure*. London: John Kingston and Henry Denham, 1566.

Patterson, Annabel. 'Political Thought and the Theater, 1580–1630'. In *A Companion to Renaissance Drama*, edited by Arthur F. Kinney, 25–39. Oxford: Blackwell, 2002.

Paul, Henry N. *The Royal Play of Macbeth: When, Why, and How It Was Written by Shakespeare*. New York: Macmillan Company, 1950.

Pelling, Christopher. 'Plutarch's Method of Work in the Roman Lives'. *The Journal of Hellenistic Studies* 99 (1979): 74–96.

Persons, Robert. *A conference about the next succession to the crowne of Ingland diuided into tvvo partes*. Antwerp: R. Doleman, 1595.

Pfister, Manfred. 'Acting the Roman: *Coriolanus*'. In *Identity, Otherness and Empire in Shakespeare's Rome*, edited by Maria del Sapio Garbero, 35–47. Farnham: Ashgate, 2009.

Platt, Michael. *Rome and Romans According to Shakespeare*. Salzburg: Institut Für Englische Sprache Und Literatur, 1976.

Platt, Peter G. '"The Meruailouse Site": Shakespeare, Venice, and Paradoxical Stages'. *Renaissance Quarterly* 54, no. 1 (2001): 121–54.

A pleasant conceited comedie, called, A knacke to know an honest man. London: for Cuthbert Burby, 1596.

Plutarch. *The Lives of the Noble Grecians and Romanes*. Translated by Thomas North. London: Thomas Vatroullier and John Wright, 1579.

Pocock, J.G.A. *The Machiavellian Moment*. Princeton: Princeton University Press, 1975.

Polemon, John. *All the Famous Battels that haue bene Fought in Our Age Throughout the Worlde, as well by Sea as Lande*. London: Henrye Bynneman & Francis Coldock, 1578.

Posner, Richard. 'Law and Commerce in *The Merchant of Venice*'. In *Shakespeare and the Law: A Conversation among Disciplines and Professions*, edited by Bradin Cormack et al., 147–55. Chicago: University of Chicago Press, 2013.

Pugliatti, Paola. *Shakespeare the Historian*. Basingstoke: Macmillan, 1996.

Pulton, Fernandino. *An abstract of all the Penall Statutes which be generall, in force and law*. London: Christopher Barker, 1592.

Rackin, Phyllis. *Stages of History: Shakespeare's English Chronicles*. Ithaca: Cornell University Press, 1990.

Rainolde, Richard. *A chronicle of all the noble emperours of the Romaines from Iulius Caesar, orderly to this moste victorious Emperour*

Maximilian, that now gouerneth, with the great warres of Iulius Caesar, [and] Pompeius Magnus. London: Thomas Marshe, 1571.

Rainolds, John. *The summe of the conference betwene Iohn Rainoldes and Iohn Hart touching the head and the faith of the Church*. London: George Bishop, 1584.

Rastall, William. *A Collection in English, of the Statutes Now in Force*. London: Society of Stationers, 1621.

Regius. *Aristotles politiques*. London: Adam Islip, 1598.

Reisig, Michael et al. 'The Effect of Racial Inequality on Black Male Recividism'. *Justice Quarterly* 24 (2007): 408–34.

Reynolds, Susan. 'Afterthoughts on *Fiefs and Vassals*'. *Haskins Society Journal* 9 (1997): 1–16.

Reynolds, Susan. *Fiefs and Vassals: The Medieval Evidence Reinterpreted*. Oxford: Oxford University Press, 1994.

Ross, Richard J. 'The Commoning of the Common Law: The Renaissance Debate over Printing English Law, 1520–1640'. *University of Pennsylvania Law Review* 146, no. 2 (1998): 323–461.

Salkeld, Duncan. *Shakespeare & London*. Oxford: Oxford University Press, 2018.

Sandys, Edwin. *A relation of the state of religion and with what hopes and pollicies it hath beene framed, and is maintained in the severall states of these westerne parts of the world*. London: Simon Waterson, 1605.

Scales, Len. *The Shaping of German Identity: Authority and Crisis, 1245–1414*. Cambridge: Cambridge University Press, 2012.

Schanzer, Ernest. *The Problem Plays of Shakespeare*. London: Routledge & Kegan Paul, 1963.

Selden, John. *Iani Anglorum facies altera Memoriâ nempè à primulâ Henrici II. adusq[ue] abitionem quod occurrit prophanum Anglo-Britanniae ius resipiens succincto diegematikos connexum filo*. London: Thomas Snodham, 1610.

Selden, John. *Titles of Honor*. London: William Stansby for John Helme, 1614.

de Serres, Jean. *A general inuentorie of the history of France from the beginning of that monarchie, vnto the treatie of Veruins, in the year 1598*. Translated by Edward Grimeston. London: George Eld, 1607.

Shakespeare, William. *Coriolanus*. Edited by Peter Holland. Arden 3rd Series. London: Bloomsbury, 2013.

Shakespeare, William. 'The Comical History of the Merchant of Venice, or Otherwise Called the Jew of Venice'. In *The Norton Shakespeare Based on the Oxford Edition*, edited by Stephen Greenblatt et al., 1081–145. New York: W.W. Norton, 1997.

Shakespeare, William. *Julius Caesar*. Edited by David Daniell. Arden 3rd Series. Walton-on-Thames: Thomas Nelson and Sons Ltd, 1998.

Shakespeare, William. *King John*. Edited by Jesse M. Lander and J.J.M. Tobin. Arden 3rd Series. London: Bloomsbury, 2018.
Shakespeare, William. *Macbeth*. Edited by Kenneth Muir. Arden 2nd Series. London: Methuen & Co., 1951.
Shakespeare, William. *Macbeth*. Edited by Sandra Clark and Pamela Mason. Arden 3rd Series. London: Bloomsbury, 2015.
Shakespeare, William. *Measure for Measure*. Edited by A.R. Braunmuller and Robert N. Watson. Arden 3rd Series. London: Bloomsbury, 2020.
Shakespeare, William. *Othello*. Edited by E.A.J. Honigmann. Arden 3rd Series. London: Arden, 1997. Reprinted 2004.
Shakespeare, William. *The Merchant of Venice*. Edited by John Drakakis. Arden 3rd Series. London: Arden, 2010.
Shakespeare, William. *The Merchant of Venice*. Edited by John Russell Brown. Arden 2nd Series. London: Arden, 1955. Reprinted 2003.
Shakespeare, William. *Titus Andronicus*. Edited by Jonathan Bate. Arden 3rd Series. London: Routledge, 1995.
Shannon, Laurie. *Sovereign Amity: Figures of Friendship in Shakespearean Contexts*. Chicago: University of Chicago Press, 2002.
Sidney, Sir Philip. *The Defence of Poesie*. London: William Ponsonby, 1595.
Skene, John. *De verborum significatione*. Edinburgh: David Lindsay, 1681.
Sleidanus, Johannes. *A famouse cronicle of oure time, called Sleidanes Commentaries*. Translated by Ihon Daus. London: Ihon Daie, 1560.
Smith, D.B. 'Sir Thomas Craig, Feudalist'. *The Scottish Historical Review* 12, no. 47 (1915): 271–302.
Smith, Sir Thomas. *De Republica Anglorum*. Edited by Mary Dewar. 1583. Repr. Cambridge: Cambridge University Press, 1982.
Snagg, Robert. *The Antiquity & Original of the Court of Chancery and Authority of the Lord Chancellor of England*. London: Henry Seile, 1654.
Sobehrad, Lane. 'King John in History'. M.A. Thesis, Southern Methodist University, 2010.
Speed, John. *The Theatre of the Empire of Great Britaine*. London: John Sudbury and Georg Humble, 1612.
Starks-Estes, Lisa S. 'Virtus, Vulnerability, and the Emblazoned Male Body in Shakespeare's *Coriolanus*'. In *Violent Masculinities: Male Aggression in Early Modern Texts and Culture*, edited by Jennifer Feather and Catherine E. Thomas, 85–108. New York: Palgrave Macmillan, 2013.
Steggle, Matthew. 'Title- and Scene-Boards: The Largest, Shortest Documents'. In *Rethinking Theatrical Documents in Shakespeare's England*, edited by Tiffany Stern, 111–27. London: The Arden Shakespeare, 2020.

Stewart, William. *The Buik of the Croniclis of Scotland*. Edited by William B. Turnbull. London: Longman, Brown, Green, Longmans, and Roberts, 1858.
Stow, John. *The Chronicles of England from Brute Vnto this Present Yeare of Christ*. 1580. London: Ralphe Newberie, at the assignment of Henrie Bynneman, 1580.
Strier, Richard. 'Shakespeare and Legal Systems: The Better, The Worse (but Not Vice Versa)'. In *Shakespeare and the Law: A Conversation among Disciplines and Professions*, edited by Bradin Cormack, Martha C. Nussbaum, and Richard Strier, 174–200. Chicago: University of Chicago Press, 2013.
Strier, Richard. *The Unrepentant Renaissance: From Petrarch to Shakespeare to Milton*. Chicago: University of Chicago Press, 2011.
Suetonius, *The historie of tvvelve Caesars emperours of Rome*. Translated by Philemon Holland. London: H. Lownes and G. Snowdon for Matthew Lownes, 1606.
Sylvain, Alexander. *The Orator*. Translated by Lazarus Pyott. London: Adam Islip, 1596.
Tacitus, Cornelius. *Agricola, Germania, Dialogus*. Loeb Classical Library 35. Edited and translated by William Peterson. Cambridge: Harvard University Press, 1970.
Tacitus, Cornelius. *The annales of Cornelius Tacitus. The description of Germanie*. Translated by Richard Grenewey. London: Arn. Hatfield for Bonham and Iohn Norton, 1598.
Tavares, Elizabeth E. 'Acts of Imagination: Curating the Early Elizabethan Repertories, 1582–1594'. Ph.D. Dissertation, University of Illinois at Urbana-Champaign, 2016.
Taylor, Gary. 'Shakespeare's Mediterranean *Measure for Measure*'. In *Shakespeare and the Mediterranean: The Selected Proceedings of the International Shakespeare Association World Congress Valencia, 2001*, edited by Tom Clayton, Susan Brock, and Vicente Forés, 243–69. Newark: University of Delaware Press, 2004.
The Riddles of Heraclitus and Democritus. London: Arn. Hatfield for Iohn Norton, 1598.
Thomas, Sidney. '"Enter a Sheriffe": Shakespeare's *King John* And *The Troublesome Raigne*'. *Shakespeare Quarterly* 37, no. 1 (1986): 98–100.
Thomas, Vivian. *Shakespeare's Roman Worlds*. London: Routledge, 1989.
Thomas, William. *The historie of Italie*. London: TB, 1549.
Thompson, Faith. *Magna Carta: Its Role in the Making of the English Constitution, 1300–1629*. Minneapolis: University of Minnesota Press, 1948.
Turner, Ralph. *Magna Carta*. London: Routledge, 2003.
University of Chicago MS 220, University of Chicago Library, Chicago.

van Metereen, Emmanuel. *A True Discourse Historicall, of the Succeeding Gouernours in the Netherlands, and the Ciuill Warres there Begun in the Yeere 1565*. Translated by Thomas Churchyard and Richard Robinson. London: Matthew Lownes, 1602.

Van De Water, Julia C. 'The Bastard in *King John*'. *Shakespeare Quarterly* 11, no. 2 (1960): 137–46.

Verweij, Sebastiaan. '"Booke, Go thy Ways": The Publication, Reading, and Reception of James VI / I's Early Poetic Works'. *Huntington Library Quarterly* 77, no. 2 (2014): 111–31.

Verweij, Sebastiaan. *The Literary Culture of Early Modern Scotland: Manuscript Production and Transmission, 1560–1625*. Oxford: Oxford University Press, 2016.

Waith, Eugene M. '*King John* and the Drama of History'. *Shakespeare Quarterly* 29, no. 2 (1978): 192–211.

Wall-Randell, Sarah. 'What Is a Staged Book? Books as "Actors" in the Early Modern English Theatre'. In *Rethinking Theatrical Documents in Shakespeare's England*, edited by Tiffany Stern, 128–52. London: Arden Shakespeare, 2020.

Wallerstedt, John F. *Returning to Prison*. Bureau of Justice Statistics Special Report, 1984.

Ward, Ian. 'Issues of Kingship and Governance in *Richard II, Richard III*, and *King John*'. *Shakespeare Yearbook* 8 (1997): 403–29.

Werner, Sarah. 'Two Hamlets: Wooster Group and Synetic Theater'. *Shakespeare Quarterly* 59, no. 3 (2008): 323–9.

Whitfield, Peter. 'Mapping Shakespeare's World'. In *The Cambridge Guide to the Worlds of Shakespeare*, edited by Bruce R. Smith, 1–13. Cambridge: Cambridge University Press, 2016.

Wilson, Richard. 'A Scribbled Form: Shakespeare's Missing Magna Carta'. *Shakespeare Quarterly* 67, no. 3 (2016): 344–70.

Wilson, Richard. 'As Mice by Lions. Political Theology and *Measure for Measure*'. *Shakespeare* 11, no. 2 (2015): 157–77.

Wilson, Theodore Halbert. 'The Third Murderer'. *The English Journal* 18, no. 5 (1929): 418–22.

Woolf, Daniel. 'From Hystories to the Historical: Five Transitions in Thinking about the Past, 1500–1700'. *Huntington Library Quarterly* 68, no. 1/2 (2005): 33–70.

Worden, Blair. 'Shakespeare and Politics'. In *Shakespeare and Politics*, edited by Catherine M.S. Alexander, 22–43. Cambridge: Cambridge University Press, 2004.

Yerli, Kenan. 'Understanding Shakespeare's King John and Magna Carta in the Light of New Historicism'. *Bilgi* 20, no. 1 (2018): 241–59.

Zurcher, Andrew. *Shakespeare and the Law*. London: Methuen, 2010.

INDEX

Anglicization 49–50, 62–4, 66–8

Bede 19–20
belonging, communities of 108–9
   Roman ancestry 108–9,
     120–22
   Roman culture and values
     112–15
   Roman political action 106–9,
     113–17, 116, 118, 122–3
   Venetian culture and values
     132, 159
   Volscian political action 109,
     119–20, 122–3
Boece, Hector
   Hystory 56, 62–3, 66, 68, 70–1
Botero, Giovanni
   Traveller's Breviat 59
Buchanan, George
   History of Scotland 51, 61–3,
     66, 71

Camden, William 51, 66
Cecil, William 23–4
censorship 10
'circumstantial' reading
   see Hutson, Lorna
common law
   and counsel 18–24, 27, 32, 47
   and inheritance 31
   and Magna Carta 18–22, 24
   as 'monarchical republic' 22
Contarini, Gasparo

*Commonwealth and
   Government of Venice*
   128–31, 148–9, 151
counsel
   in *Coriolanus*, 106
   in *King John* 18–20, 22–4, 29,
     32–3, 35–7, 39–40, 44–7
   in *Macbeth* 59, 60, 62
   monarch's right to reject 22
   nobles
     role in providing 19, 20, 22,
       35–7, 59, 60–2
     right to withhold 23, 40,
       43–4, 46
   obligatory 18–20, 22–4, 59
   unanimous 23–4, 26, 36–9, 45
Cowell, John 51, 66
Cox-Jenson, Freyja 80–1, 104
Craig, Sir Thomas
   Jus Feudale 52–4, 55–7, 61,
     66–7, 69
Cromartie, Alan 18–19

Dollimore, Jonathan 5, 166
ducal authority, Venice
   extra-legal, as rational
     investigation 147–59
   legal, as adjoined to courts
     129–30, 133–4, 137,
     143–4
   as restricted
     in governing the Venetian
       state 128–30, 132–3, 143

to protect Venetian
commercial and
geopolitical interests
130–2
to protect Venetian liberty
129–34
ducal authority, Vienna
absenteeism 164–6, 168
deputy, role of 165, 170–1, 174
as expanding, political and
religious 164–5, 168–9,
171–3
and James I, 166, 173

earldom
and Anglicization 62–3, 66
delivery of title 60
and masculinity 63–6
meanings of 58–9, 66–7
and political responsibility 63–6
and thanes 50, 53–4
Elizabeth I 21, 23, 30, 34–7, 52

factionalism
Brutus's view of 92–3
Caesar's view of 88–9
Cassius's view of 91–5
conspirators' view of 89
in early modern sources 78–81
early republic's factionless
politics 81, 92, 97
prehistory of, continual 78–83,
98–9
feudalism
development of, in *Macbeth* 50,
54–9, 65, 67–8, 70, 72–3
historiography of, early
modern 11, 50, 52–4, 67
Fortescue, Sir John 18–19, 22, 24,
128
friend and lover
in Brutus and Antony's
speeches 86–8

confusion of
Caesar's 88–9
Cassius and Brutus's 95–7
distinction between 83–8, 95, 98

Goodman Theatre 162–3, 170–1,
174–5

Henry III 20–2, 24, 47–8
historicism of setting 1–11, 13–14
in *Coriolanus* 101–2, 124
in *Julius Caesar* 78–81
in *King John* 17, 29–30
in *Macbeth* 50–4, 61–2, 67,
73–4
in *Measure for Measure* 161–4,
166–9, 173
in *Merchant of Venice* 130,
132, 138, 140
in *Othello* 147, 149, 158–60
and re-setting 9, 161–3, 170–1,
174–6
on stage 9, 10, 159
and topicality (early modern) 5,
10, 161–2, 166–8, 174
and transhistorical approach
5, 8, 14
Holderness, Graham 6, 130–2
Holinshed, Raphael
Chronicles 4, 11, 18, 20, 24,
53, 56, 62–3, 66–73
Holland, Philemon *see* Livy
Hutson, Lorna 6, 50, 61–2, 68

James I 3, 25, 52, 61, 67, 70, 166,
173

kingship
in *Julius Caesar* 89–94
in *King John*
absolutism 35–40, 44–5
coronation, second 35–7
effective kingship 27–35

224   INDEX

and legitimacy 27–30
and religious authority 25,
    33–4, 44
Knacke to Know an Honest Man
    134, 149
Knollys, Sir Francis 35–6

Lambarde, William 19, 51–2, 58,
    61, 66
Lewkenor, Lewis *see* Contarini,
    Gasparo
Livy
    Ab Urbe Condita 102–7, 119
Lloyd, Lodowick 79–80
lover *see* friend and lover
Lupton, Julia 6, 131–2

Magna Carta
    in chronicle histories 18–22, 24
    dating of 11, 20, 47
    in legal historiography 18–22,
        24, 27
    omission from *King John* 17,
        24, 26–7, 47, 73
masculinity 63–6, 71–3
Middleton, Thomas 1, 163, 168

North, Thomas *see* Plutarch

patricians 102, 105–6, 111, 114,
    116, 118, 123
Il Pecorone 134, 140
performance *see* repertory studies;
    setting, re-setting; setting,
    on stage
plebeians 81, 90–1, 102, 104, 107,
    111–17
Plutarch
    Lives 78–80, 90–1, 94, 98, 102,
        104–7, 112, 119
political structures, individual
    reactions to 4–5, 14. *See also*
    belonging, communities of

in *Coriolanus* 105 110, 116
in *King John* 24–5, 27, 39, 44,
    48
in *Merchant of Venice* 140,
    144–5

rebellion 26–7, 41–3, 45–7, 56–8
repertory studies 7–10
Richard I 31, 164–5
Richard II 29, 48

Selden, John 51–4, 56
Shakespeare, William
    Coriolanus 81, 102, 104–24,
        152, 176
    Henry V 99
    Julius Caesar 77–8, 81–99,
        124, 175
    King John 17–19, 21, 24–48,
        73–4, 84, 124, 174
    King Lear 39
    Macbeth 49–74, 84, 124, 148,
        176
    Measure for Measure 161–75
    Merchant of Venice 148, 150,
        174
    Othello 106, 127–8, 147,
        149–60
    Titus Andronicus 84
    Winter's Tale 69
Smith, Sir Thomas 22–3, 34, 44,
    52
Snagg, Robert 20–2, 32, 61
soft power *see* ducal authority,
    Venice, extra-legal
Steggle, Matthew 9, 159

Tavares, Elizabeth E. 7, 99
Taylor, Gary 13, 162–4, 166–8
thanedom
    Banquo's status 56
    delivery of 55–6
    and earls 50, 53–4

INDEX 225

and feudal model 52–7, 68,
  72–3
meanings of 50–4
transfer of 54–5
Thirty Years War 163, 167–8
Thomas, William
  History of Italy 129–32, 143,
    148–9
tribunes
  and Caius Martius Coriolanus
    102–4, 112–13, 117–18
  early modern English
    conception of 103, 110
  establishment of 102, 117–18
  and plebeians 110–11, 116–17
  and Roman Republic political
    structure 105, 110–12, 118
  as third party with political
    agenda 111–12, 116
Troublesome Raigne of King John
  26–7, 30–6, 38–9, 42–4, 46
tyranny 21, 38, 59–60, 62, 129,
  131–2, 148. *See also* counsel,
  nobles; ducal authority,
  Venice; ducal authority,
  Vienna; kingship, absolutism

Venice, legal-political system
  133–5, 137–8, 149–52. *See
  also* ducal authority, Venice

and Alien Statute 140–5
and bond 139–43
and commercial interests 130–2
council scene in *Othello*, as
  model of 149–52
court, functionality of 134–7
early modern English
  conception of 128–30,
  142–3, 149, 159–60
and English legal system 138–9
historical accuracy of 135
and mercy, exercise of 137–9
and monarchism 137–9
Shylock's case, as threat to
  131–3, 144–5
Vienna *see also* ducal authority,
  Vienna
and Austria 164–5, 167
and Bohemia 168
early modern English
  conception of 162–4,
  166–8, 172–4
and Hungary 166–8
liberties, political and religious
  164, 169–73
and London 166, 173
and Ottomans 163–4, 167–8,
  171
re-setting 161–3, 170–1, 174–6
setting 161–3

www.ingramcontent.com/pod-product-compliance
Lightning Source LLC
Chambersburg PA
CBHW062219300426
44115CB00012BA/2138